D1823918

BEHOLD THE MAN!
JESUS, MESSIAH, KING.

BEHOLD THE MAN!
JESUS, MESSIAH, KING.

A Biographical view
from a Biblical Perspective!

W.O. HARRIS

XULON PRESS

Xulon Press
2301 Lucien Way #415
Maitland, FL 32751
407.339.4217
www.xulonpress.com

© 2021 by W.O. Harris

All rights reserved solely by the author. The author guarantees all contents are original and do not infringe upon the legal rights of any other person or work. No part of this book may be reproduced in any form without the permission of the author. The views expressed in this book are not necessarily those of the publisher.

Due to the changing nature of the Internet, if there are any web addresses, links, or URLs included in this manuscript, these may have been altered and may no longer be accessible. The views and opinions shared in this book belong solely to the author and do not necessarily reflect those of the publisher. The publisher therefore disclaims responsibility for the views or opinions expressed within the work.

Unless otherwise indicated, Scripture quotations taken from the 21st Century King James Version®, copyright © 1994. Used by permission of Deuel Enterprises, Inc., Gary, SD 57237. All rights reserved.

Scripture quotations taken from the King James Version (KJV) – *public domain.*

Scripture quotations taken from the American Standard Version (ASV)) – *public domain.*

Scripture quotations taken from the Amplified Bible (AMP). Copyright © 1954, 1958, 1962, 1964, 1965, 1987 by The Lockman Foundation. Used by permission. All rights reserved.

Scripture quotations taken from the Christian Standard Bible. (CSB). Copyright © 2017 by Holman Bible Publishers. Used by permission. All rights reserved.

Scripture quotations taken from the Common English Bible® (CEB) Copyright © 2010, 2011 by Common English Bible.™ Used by permission. All rights reserved worldwide.

Scripture quotations taken from the Contemporary English Version (CEV). Copyright © 1995 American Bible Society. Used by permission. All rights reserved.

Scripture quotations taken from The Expanded Bible (EXB). Copyright ©2011 by Thomas Nelson. Used by permission. All rights reserved.

Scripture quotations taken from the English Standard Version (ESV). Copyright © 2001 by Crossway, a publishing ministry of Good News Publishers. Used by permission. All rights reserved.

Scripture quotations taken from the New English Translation (NET Bible). Copyright ©1996-2006 by Biblical Studies Press, L.L.C. Used by permission. All rights reserved.

Scripture quotations taken from the New King James Version (NKJV). Copyright © 1982 by Thomas Nelson, Inc. Used by permission. All rights reserved.

Scripture quotations taken from the Holy Bible, New Living Translation (NLT). Copyright ©1996, 2004, 2007 by Tyndale House Foundation. Used by permission of Tyndale House Publishers, Inc.

Paperback ISBN-13: 978-1-6628-3498-1
Ebook ISBN-13: 978-1-6628-3499-8

TABLE OF CONTENTS

INTRODUCTION

I commit this work to the Lord Jesus Christ, my Lord and Savior, and the Father, King of the universe. Thank you for the unprecedented journey from that tentative starting point.

And for finally allowing me to finish this; thank you, Abba. I praise you for the many dreams, visions, and inspirations as well.

In addition, I dedicated this effort in memory of my friend and Pastor, Winston.

My dearly beloved and life friend Rachel and my Mother Miriam, all three have now graduated to be with the Lord. (*I am confident they are observing with some delight from the mezzanine.*)

This has been a tremendous labor of love, great joy, and immense difficulties. Yet, I hope it will be of some help to someone! In some way or manner, and draws the reader closer to Jesus.

I have looked at, evaluated, and considered many things in compiling this book. Yet, I hope it is easy to see the emphasis is on keeping close to the biblical accounts as recorded for us in the gospels. Those accounts are rich with many nuggets of information that are too often overlooked.

The principal difficulty in compiling this biography; was in deciding what to exclude.

While considering how best to keep the narrative flowing effectively yet giving enough background information; so the reader can clearly understand the various relevant cultural contexts.

The temptation was always to include more facts and material, yet in so doing quickly shifts the account away from simplicity.

Also, some topics are controversial and would take a much deeper analysis and explanation. So with this in view, I invite the reader to do a deeper dive into many of the areas they may find of interest, where I may have merely introduced a topic or idea.

Hundreds of similitudes, parables, types, and figures of speech are used to tease out meanings and ideas throughout the biblical accounts.

In the following, we can observe four broad categories.

1. Peshat: *The literal direct meaning.*
2. Remez: *An allegorical, significant hint of something more profound.*
3. Derash: *The standard or practical application, hermeneutics (or general principles of biblical interpretation.)*
4. Sod: *The mystical or hidden meaning.*

Above are just summaries of their fuller meanings, but here is an example from the gospel.

We find an illustration of using one of these hints where I have written in the book, regarding 'the feeding of the multitude,' I said, 'they gave the leftovers collected by the disciples to the poor.'

The question is, how can I know that?

Well, for me to be confident in what I wrote, I have to ask several questions, and when I do, I find the Scriptures have pre-empted me and provided the answer in the text.

Let us look at the passage from Mark 8:14-16 (ESV) **Now they had forgotten to bring bread, and they had only one loaf with them in the boat. And he cautioned them, saying, "Watch out; beware of the leaven of the Pharisees and the leaven of Herod." And they began discussing with one another the fact that they had no bread.**

This happened immediately after the feeding of the second multitude. We are told the disciples' thought it was because they had no bread.'

Jesus pointed out that they had collected much leftover, twelve baskets with the first miracle and seven with the second.

This led me to ask two questions: whose baskets did they use, and what did they do with the bread?

Jesus instructed them to ensure nothing was wasted; therefore, my answer: They obviously gave the bread to the poor!

I have frequently found a type of blindness due to over-familiarity with some passages.

We have wrongly received and taught some ideas for so long that it has become hard to see the correct application or reading.

Here is an obvious example; it has been generally assumed and widely taught. The Magi or Wise Men visited Jesus and his parents at a stable sometime around the child's birth. Roughly the same time as the Shepherds sent by the Angel to witness the birth of their new Messiah. (Sadly, I have even seen this portrayed as such in a recent popular Television show, purported to be biblically accurate).

Yet, we see in Matthew 2:11 that they (The Magi) visited the family much later at a house.

We also see from Herod's cross-examination that Jesus was now just less than two years old. This myopia is not unique by any means. Once it has taken root, it is hard to overcome because of traditions.

I once gave a talk where I mentioned how Jesus, in his parable from Luke 15, did not say, 'there was the joy of the *Angels*' in heaven over one sinner repenting.' Instead, the joy was that of the Father.

Looking across at my audience, you would have been forgiven for thinking I had slapped them in the face and also insulted their dear old mother to boot.

In reality, this was much more shocking to Jesus' audience when he said it in first-century Israel.

We do not comprehend how very revolutionary it was for the people of that era to hear, 'when you pray, say Abba Father,'

The leaders had at various times picked up stones to throw at Jesus just for hinting that God was his Father. You can read one example in John 8.

To call God (Yahweh) Father was so far from their thinking or perception, in most cases, they would not even dare say the name but instead would use a substitute, Hashem (The Name). Pronouncing YHWH was regarded as too sinful, so Adonai (Lord) was employed instead.

Jesus told his audience about the Kingdom of Heaven using many examples and the nature and quality of the amazing love from the Father.

As he was speaking a parable in Luke 15, he made this statement in verse 10, 'I tell you, there is joy before the angels of God over one sinner who repents.'

Even today, among the Body of Christ, people still find it hard to believe Jesus is speaking of the Father's joy. So can you imagine the gasps that would have come from those listening and hearing this statement for the very first time? They would have been genuinely shaken and astounded.

Yet, Jesus went even further by following this statement with another parable, which has wrongly become known as 'the Prodigal Son.' This is unfortunate because it unduly emphasizes the son when it is actually about the amazing love and tenderness of the Father.

So just in case, they had missed the point when he had said, 'there is joy before the angels of God over the one sinner who repents.' Jesus strengthened the case by telling in the following parable of the Father's love and yearning for the restoration of the undeserving wayward son.

Obviously, the Angels spoken of are standing in front of the Father in Heaven. Therefore, if there is joy before the Angels, the Father is the one dancing and partying! No matter how much our religious upbringing stops us from seeing the obvious.

We find many examples such as these throughout the Gospels and beyond. Several I tackled head-on, some I touched on lightly. There are some I've just left alone, simply because it would take up too much space to delve deep into the explanations and reasoning.

I made sincere efforts to ensure that the flow of the narrative was not unduly interrupted.

There are constraints to what I have written; first, it is not a replacement for Scriptures, and it is NOT Scriptures.

I have taken many liberties in interpreting passages and words. My goal was to capture the essence of the thought or idea. This can be difficult, as some words and ideas do not lend themselves to clearly being described with English concepts.

An example of this is 'behold.' The original for this word means more than 'look,' which is often used.

(*In a vast crowd, if I was to shout, 'everything and everyone within the sound of my voice freeze, don't move, now pay close attention to what I'm going to say next, would hardly do justice to that one word.*)

Another would be when Jesus said. 'Any who believes in me,' the word we received simply as (believe), means much more than the English can convey; it includes faith, trust, confidence, hope, etc.

I have strived to write a biography of Jesus using the Gospels as the template; included or represented is every line in the gospels.

With the rich background of the culture of the day to draw from, it becomes valuable, complete, and I hope rounded, in so much as it should aide the reader to see some passages when you next read the bible, I anticipate that many obscure nuggets will become more prominent and complete for you when returning to the Scriptures.

W.O. HARRIS.

PROLOGUE

JESUS THE BEGINNING.

This story is the greatest of all stories ever told in all the Earth and throughout all times, and this is a story that could actually start any time in human history: for example, with the Exodus out of Egypt of God's people after over four hundred years. These children originated from Israel (Prince with God), who was formerly called Jacob.

These twelve extraordinary family groups that made up the Nation descended from Jacob could be the genesis of this remarkable story. After finding, they were in a seriously hopeless state, then ultimately freed from their crushing bondage; by the mighty hand of God through His servant Moses.

This account could begin with the setting up of the Royal Kingdom in Israel by Saul, under the guiding hand of Samuel the great Prophet of God: Afterward, Israel's most outstanding national leader, King David, united and further established this kingdom.

Or, with King David's very own relatives Ruth and Boaz, whose life told a great story of love, dedication, and sacrifice!

We could look back to the ark that saved Noah and his family, a significant time when God showed his sovereign divine hand, with grace, giving hope for a fresh start. Back even to the Garden of Eden; because here is the story of the Messiah, the anointed Saviour of the entire world. What's More, it was there in the very Garden of God the Creator; that He (the Messiah) was first mentioned as the coming Saviour of all humanity.

(This promised conqueror 'from the seed of the woman,' would crush the serpent's head! This remarkable promise was given by God, Genesis 3:15).

BEHOLD THE MAN! JESUS, (YESHUA).
ISRAEL'S MESSIAH AND KING!

(Psalms 40:7 NKJV **Then I said, "Behold, I come; In the scroll of the book it is written of me**).
(Jesus said, *"These are My words spoken while I was still with you: All the events concerning Me written in the Law of Moses, the Prophets, and in the Psalms must be fulfilled,"* Luke 24:44).

We can trace the outline of His story through the entirety of the biblical records as they altogether are His events.

It is also the story of God's vast love for humankind. Such intense love that he would even send a savior to rescue and restore lost humanity to our rightful place.

To do this, he showed various enactments through the people appointed to represent his ways, thoughts, love, and mercy.

So we see through the history of God's dealings with the Israelites, who were the descendants of Abraham, his chosen servant: to whom God had made a solemn promise. (Namely, many nations would receive favor through him).

Slowly and in increments, correct understanding of God continued to be shown through the many feasts and practices, later by creating and developing the Tabernacle and the Temple.

The many writings from the Prophets also steadily gave the people vast extents of revelations of what: He, the Lord, would do once he arrived.

They had all of this defined through living parables types and shadows, presented through the feasts and rituals of the people over generations.

As a result of this knowledge gained through these traditions, they could recognize their long-awaited Messiah, who is the Creator of all things — finally presented here on the Earth in the flesh as a man.

CHAPTER ONE

THE VERY EXCELLENT BEGINNING OF THE ACCOUNT OF THE MAN JESUS.

The commencement of the good news of god's gift and savior: the man Jesus. Who 'was' the Messiah ("Mashiach" the "Anointed One"), and the Son of God, first presented to us by those who were the eyewitnesses to his eminence and majesty.

Hence, you might know the certainty concerning the things reported and the story you have received.

The Word (The Logos) had already existed in the beginning. He was with God.

Besides, He was God. In the beginning, He was with God. He created everything; nothing subsists; that he did not make. The creative force of life itself was in him, and this life gives light to every person, as the light shines through the darkness, and the darkness can never grasp or extinguish it.

God sent his servant and Prophet John *(Yochanan),* Son of Zechariah and Forerunner, to tell everyone about the light. So that everyone might accept as accurate, trust in, with genuine faith the one to follow because of his testimony.

John was not the light; he was only a witness to the light, the one who is the true light and who gives that essential light to everyone coming into the world.

Yet, even though it was only because of him that the world was created! The world failed to recognize him when he arrived. Therefore did not accept him, not even within his land or among his people.

However, he gave to all who believed in him the right to become children of God. Who are then reborn through the Spirit! This birth is not physical or because of human passion, or by a personal plan.

This regeneration comes only from God. The Word, therefore, became human and lived here on Earth among us.

He was full of faithfulness and unfailing love. We were witnesses of his glory, the glory of the only Son of the Father. John pointed him out to the people.

He shouted to the crowds who went to hear him, "This is the one I was speaking about when I said, 'someone is coming who is far greater than I am because he existed long before I did.'" John stated, declaring this unwaveringly.

We have all benefited from the abundant blessings he had brought to us, gracious blessings one after another.

Although through Moses came the Law, yet the unfailing love and faithfulness of God, His grace and truth, came through Jesus the Messiah. No one has ever seen God. Except for his only Son, who is himself God and is near to the heart of the Father, he has enlightened us about him.

An event occurred that set in motion the revealing of the long-awaited arrival of the Messiah of Israel. It started with a Jewish priest named Zechariah (*Z'chariyahu*). He lived in Israel's history when King Herod the Great was ruling as King of Judea.

Zechariah was a Levite and a member of an order of all the priests. This order called Abijah was one of twenty-four used in service within the Temple in Jerusalem. The order of Abijah was the eighth division. (1 Chronicle 24:10, 'The seventh to Hakkoz division, the eighth to Abijah' division). Each division took a turn over the course of the year in the fixed service calendar.

So, the eighth course, Abijah, would serve its first regular week during the 'ninth' or 'tenth' week of the year's administration in the Temple, beginning on the second Sabbath of the third month (*Sivan*), May/June.

Nisan or 'spring' saw the beginning of the Jewish calendar, hence (Jehoiarib), the first of the priestly courses ensued.

Each group of priests would have served within the Temple twice a year as the cycle of courses repeats after the twenty-fourth course was completed. However, (Passover, Pentecost, and Tabernacles) are three major festivals where all the priests would serve in the Temple, bringing the total time of service to five times a year.

Zechariah was married to a woman, a descendant of the priestly Aaronic lineage, named Elisabeth, Elisheva (אֱלִישֶׁבַע). "My God is an oath"/"My God is abundance," from the Word אל ('el), God; plus the Word שבע (Shaba), oath/swear/vow.

Zechariah and Elisabeth were sincere in living within the things concerning God; they lived carefully, following all the Lord's commandments and regulations. The couple, now both advance in age, had no children. It was the assumption that this was because of a condition of barrenness with Elisabeth.

During the time that 'Abijah,' the order of priests to which Zechariah belonged was on duty.

(Zechariah had been elected from among them to serve God in the Temple during that week. The priests had a tradition of choosing through lots, the one who was to serve).

The chosen priest's duty was to enter the sanctuary and burn incense in the presence of the Lord.

During this time that the incense to God is burning, a great crowd would stand outside, waiting and praying.

Zechariah was at his duties in the sanctuary when an Angel of the Lord materialized into view, standing off to the right of the incense altar, causing Zechariah to be overwhelmed with fear. The Angel spoke, "do not be afraid, Zechariah!" He said, reassuring him.

"The prayers, from you and your wife Elisabeth, have been heard by God, and in answer, she will shortly produce a son by you!

This child, you will name John, (Yəhôḥānān, "Yahweh is gracious") from the roots יֹ (Yo,) referring to the true God and חָנַן (Chanan), "to be gracious." Yohanan (יֹוחָנָן), "Graced by Yah").

Great joy and gladness will be yours because of this, and many will celebrate with you over his birth because he will be great in the Lord's eyes.

He must touch no wine or hard liquor because he will be filled from the womb with the Holy Spirit.

Also, he will persuade many Israelites to turn to the Lord their God, a man like Elijah with the Spirit and power of that ancient Prophet.

He will go forward and prepare the people for the Lord's arrival. Returning the fathers' hearts to their children, changing once rebellious minds to accept godly wisdom," the Angel exclaimed, announcing the exciting news of this great miracle.

"I am now an old man; my wife is also well along in years, so how can I accept this and know it will happen?" Zechariah asked hesitantly. (*He is complaining that after praying so long about the matter. He had lost confidence that it could ever happen*).

"I am Gabriel!" The Angel said suddenly, to counter the uncertainly Zechariah was displaying.

(**Note: Angels rarely give their names. Gabriel saying who he was would instantly build faith in any Israelite. Because they would know that it was Gabriel who had visited and spoken with the Prophet Daniel on several occasions, giving him the details of the expected Messiah*).

"I always stand in the very presence of God. He sent me to bring you this good news!

Since then, you do not accept what I say as true; you will not be able to speak until after the birth of the child because my words will certainly come true at the exact time."

Gabriel affirmed to him.

While this was a mild reprimand, Gabriel gave Zechariah information and time through 'not been able to speak' to build his faith and confidence to its complete restoration.

(*'In the Presence of God,' is a way of saying, 'outside of time itself.' So as there is nothing impossible with God. A long wait is no barrier to fulfilling his purposes: Zechariah had made 'time' the issue in his grievance over losing faith.*

Likewise, the solution to the restoration of his faith would be via time, namely the period of his silence).

Meanwhile, the people outside the sanctuary waiting for Zechariah to come out eventually wondered why he took so long.

Finally, when Zechariah emerged, and it was apparent that he could not speak to them.

They understood from his gestures that he must have seen a vision while in the sanctuary.

Zechariah remained and completed his term of service at the Temple; he then returned home. Elisabeth, his wife, became pregnant shortly following his return home.

She wisely withdrew from local excitement and placed herself in quiet isolation for five months.

Elisabeth made this declaration of God's favor to her, "How kind is the Lord our God who erased and removed my humiliation and disgrace of bearing no children!" She exclaimed.

When her pregnancy reached its sixth month; God sent the Angel Gabriel to a village near Galilee, the town of Nazareth; the Angel visited a young virgin named Mary.

Mary was engaged in marriage to a descendant of King David, a man named Joseph.

Mary could palpably see Gabriel as this majestic Angel materialized. Having greeted her, he addressed her, "Do not be afraid, Mary, because you have found favor with God!" He said.

Confused and disturbed by the wonderful greeting, Mary tried to think what the Angel could mean.

"Do not continue to be anxious, Mary," The Angel told her, "Because I am sent here with a message for you, that God has decided that He will bless you!

Listen attentively; in a short period, you will become pregnant and then, in due course, give birth to a son. The name you are to give him is Jesus. (*Yeshua in Hebrew - to rescue, or deliver, means 'Yahweh [the Lord] is Salvation,' Greek Iesous, English via Latin, Jesus*).

He will be very great! The Son of the Most High will be his title.

Moreover, the Lord God will give him the throne of his ancestor King David. And his reign over Israel will be forever; his kingdom will never end!" Gabriel announced.

"How will it all occur that I will have a baby, considering I am a virgin and have not known any man?" Mary inquired modestly from the Angel.

"The Holy Spirit will descend to you, and the power of the Most High will soar above and eclipse you. Therefore, the baby born to you will be holy and will be called the Son of God.

Besides, your relative Elisabeth has become pregnant in her old age!

She was called barren, but she is now already in her sixth month because all things are possible with God." The Angel explained.

"As I am a servant of the Lord, I am willing to accept whatever he wants. May everything be accomplished just as you have said!" Mary responded, fully agreeing with the Divine messenger.

Satisfied upon hearing this, this mighty Angel promptly departed.

Just a few days later, Mary made a rushed visit to the hill country of Judea, to the town where Zechariah lived. She entered the house and greeted Elisabeth.

At the sound of the greeting of Mary, Elisabeth's child leaped within her, and Elisabeth was filled with the Holy Spirit.

Elisabeth then blesses Mary in a loud voice, "God blesses you above all other women, and your child is blessed. What a great honor this is that the mother of my Lord should visit me!

When you came in, and I heard your greeting, my baby jumped for joy in my womb the instant I listened to your voice!

Because you accepted as true, trusted with faith that the Lord would do what he said, you are blessed!" She exclaimed joyfully.

Mary Responded happily, "Oh, how I praise the Lord how I rejoice in God, my Saviour! Because He has taken notice of his lowly servant girl, and now generation after generation will call me blessed.

Since the Mighty One, He is holy and has done great things for me. His mercy carries on from one generation to another for all who revere him. The Lord's mighty arm has done tremendous things! See how he scatters the proud and haughty ones!

He shakes princes down from their thrones, exalting the lowly ones.

The Lord has satisfied the hungry with good things and sent the rich away with empty hands. Moreover, how much has he given help to Israel, his servant! The Lord promised to be merciful and has not forgotten, because He had guaranteed to be gracious to our ancestor Abraham and unto his children forever," She said happily, with sincere gratitude.

Mary stayed on with Elisabeth for about three months before she went back to her own home.

Elisabeth eventually went into labor and delivered a son; then, on hearing about it, her neighbors and relatives realized how very gracious and compassionate the Lord had been to her. They all rejoiced along with her.

(*Note: *Because Zechariah was from Abijah, the eighth division, whose fixed service began on the second Sabbath of the third month, (Sivan), May/June.*

This was about the time just after the Passover and the Feast of Unleavened Bread. Bringing the birth of the child to around the end of Iyar, into Sivan or the start of 'Tamuz.')

The local people of the area all came on the eighth day after the baby was born to attend the circumcision ceremony.

The people decided that the child's name should be Zechariah because that was his father's name. To this suggestion, Elisabeth very firmly replied, "No! His name is John!"

This surprised the people, who then said to her, "There is no John in your family line, and no one in all your family is by that name." They tried asking Zechariah what he wanted to name the baby; they needed to use signs and gestures for this.

Zechariah then gestured for them to bring him a writing tablet and then surprised everyone by writing, "His name is John."

As he did this, immediately Zechariah's speech returned, so he began praising God.

And there, in the middle of his praise and worship, Zechariah was filled with the Holy Spirit. He spoke this prophecy: "Blessed be the Lord, and God of Israel who has visited us to set his people free.

The Lord has sent us a mighty Saviour from his servant David's royal line and from the house of David, precisely as he had promised through the preaching of his holy prophets long ago.

So now, we will be rescued from the hands of our enemies and from all who hate us.

Our Lord has shown his mercy to our ancestors by remembering his sacred covenant, the covenant the Lord swore with an oath to our forefather Abraham. Therefore, because the Lord has rescued us from our enemies. We can now serve God without fear, for as long as we live, in holiness and righteousness.

"And my little son, you will be called the Prophet of the Most High God because you will Go ahead of the Master and get ready the way for the Lord. Presenting to his people the offer of salvation through the forgiveness of their sins.

And by this act of love and mercy from God! The morning light from Heaven like sunrise is about to dawn on us, to give a bright light to all those who sit in darkness and under the shadow of death; and to take us step by step onto the path of peace." Zechariah said, speaking by the power of the Holy Spirit to all the friends and local neighbors.

When Zechariah had finished speaking, a sense of wonder fell upon the crowd.

Then as the news of what had happened spread throughout all the Judean hill countrysides. Everyone hearing about these events asked, "What will this child turn out to be?"

It was plain that the hand of the Lord was undoubtedly upon him in an extraordinary way.

John grew up becoming strong in Spirit, living in the wilderness area until his public ministry to Israel began.

This is the account of events leading up to the birth of Jesus the Messiah.

When his mother, Mary, was engaged to be married to a man named Joseph. However, before the marriage took place, even though she was still a virgin, she came to be pregnant by the Divine power of the Holy Spirit.

Joseph, her fiancé, was a just man. (*A tsaddîyq, in Hebrew, was a man known for his unwavering obedience to keeping the Laws of the Torah, the writings of Moses*).

A man of good moral character, he did not want Mary to be publicly disgraced, so he decided to break the engagement as quietly as possible.

(*Proverbs 15:9 The Lord loves the one who pursues righteousness.*)

Then, as he was still considering this course of action, he had a visitation of an Angel of God in a dream.

"Joseph, son of David," the Angel told him, "do not be anxious to take Mary to be your wife because the power of the Holy Spirit conceived the child that is inside of her. Therefore, Mary will give birth to a son, and you must give him the name of Jesus because he is the one that will save his people from their sins."

The naming of the child would be an act of welcoming the child to be a part of his family line and would represent the adoption of Jesus, providing for him a recognizable name within a lineage and a place of honor in the social order. Jesus, by this, becomes qualified to be called in Jewish Law, the son of David through Joseph's line.

His mother, Mary, was already a descendant from the House of David. Therefore, he now wonderfully became the inheritor of both the line and the house of David.

All of this occurred to fulfill the message of the Lord. Which was spoken through his Prophet Isaiah: *'Therefore the Lord Himself will give you a sign: Listen carefully, the virgin will conceive and give birth to a son, and she will call his name Immanuel (God with us),'* Isaiah 7:14 (AMP).

Joseph, on wakening, was pleased to do just as the Angel of the Lord had instructed him. Then he took Mary and made her his wife! Even though he did not have any sexual union with her until after her son was born. Joseph, who was faithful to the Angel's instructions, did indeed give the child the name of wJesus, just a short time after his birth.

CHAPTER TWO

HERE IS THE BACKGROUND TO THIS STORY SURROUNDING THE PERIOD OF THE BIRTH.

The Romans had conquered and were ruling over most of the territories in the Middle East, including the land of Israel. Their territory extended as far to the East as Assyria and was blocked by further expansion east by The Parthian empire.

Augustus, the Roman Emperor of that time, made a declaration that a census of all people should be taken throughout the Roman Empire. (*This was to be the first census taken when Quirinius was of all of Syria.*)

This governor, 'Publius Sulpicius Quirinius,' was born near Lanuvium, a town close to Rome. He became influential in Roman politics through his success against tribes in the Sahara Desert, the Garamantes, based south of the Greek-founded Cyrene, which was populated by dispersed Jews and again against the 'Homonadensians,' while he was governor of Galatia and Pamphylia, central Turkey.

In 25 B.C, The Homonadensians had captured and killed Amyntas, a client king of the Roman. On Amyntas' death, his kingdom passed to Augustus becoming the new imperial province of Galatia.

Quirinius was appointed the capable guide and advisor to Augustus' grandson, Gailus Caesar, on his visit and administration of the eastern provinces.

Gaius met Phraataces, the new Parthian King, on an island in the Euphrates, where a peace treaty was agreed mainly over long-running conflicts regarding Armenia. This now puts Syria, including Israel, as the buffer zone.

Rome made an announcement through Herod of a small local inheritance tax on the land to pay the army's upkeep.

They issued the proclamation for all the people of the land of Israel to return to their ancestral towns and register for this census.

Joseph, who was a descendant from the line of King David, had to return to Bethlehem in Judea, as this was the ancient home of David. At this time, Joseph was living in the village of Nazareth in Galilee. From there, he made the journey to Bethlehem, taking with him Mary, his young wife, whose pregnancy was now quite noticeable.

At the time of their arrival, the little village was crowded, to the point where they could not find an adequate place in which to stay.

And during that period that they were staying there, the time eventually came for Mary to give birth; she gave birth to her first child, a son.

She used strips of cloth, wrapped him comfortably, and placed him in a small trough made for feeding cattle as a temporary cot.

During that same night, shepherds were staying with their flocks of sheep in the fields nearby. Abruptly and unexpectedly, they were startled by a brilliant and dazzling shining light that filled the entire area. An Angel of the Lord was suddenly there with them. This made them extremely frightened to the point of being distressed; surrounding them was this bright light which radiated the Angel also; the light was the glory of the Lord. The Angel comforted them with these words.

"Do not be afraid!" He said. "I bring you good news of such that will bring great joy to all people. The Saviour! Yes, even the Messiah, the Lord! Is born this very day in the nearby town of Bethlehem, the ancestral home of David the King! Here is a sign by which you will be able to recognize him: You will find a newborn baby wrapped snugly in strips of cloth, placed in a trough for the feeding of cattle."

Suddenly, that Angel was joined by a vast multitude of others! The magnificent armies 'from Heaven'! They were speaking praises to God, "Glory to God in highest heaven, and peace on the earth to all those with whom God is pleased."

After the Angels gave this excellent witness and then returned to Heaven. These shaken shepherds said to each other. "Let us go into the town of Bethlehem to see the occurrence of this great, amazing thing that the Lord has revealed to us!"

*Note: These Angels were soldiers in the Army of Host or Heavenly host. The Greek word *'stratia' is* host, referring to heavenly bodies, so we can compare a host to the stars in the sky. A 'multitude of hosts' is innumerable.

The Shepherd quickly went into the village, following the directions given. They found the parents' Joseph and Mary, along with the baby, resting on the makeshift cot.

And after seeing him, the shepherds went about and told everyone what had happened with the Angels' visit. And what they had been told about this child.

People were amazed when they heard all the details of the story from the shepherds!

They became the first of the witnesses to this spectacular event. The shepherds later went back to caring for their flock of sheep. While continually shouting praises and glorifying God for the wonders that they had heard and had seen, having been able to find everything that the Angel had told them about to be true.

[There was an explicit prohibition restricting the keeping of flocks everywhere in Israel, except in the wildernesses; the exception was those flocks kept for the Temple services.

The fields around Bethlehem were the very fields of Ruth and Boaz, the same fields King David used when he was a shepherd boy.

The shepherds were, in reality, performing Temple duties. Shepherds remained with their flocks all day and night during lambing season, living among the sheep or 'abided in the fields,' being there at the birth of a new lamb, spotting and marking the firstborn. This is vital as Ewes can have multiple lambs born at once.

All firstborn male lambs were to be offered to the Lord per the Law of Moses as a distinctive sacrifice.

Exodus 22:30 (NKJV) *Likewise, you shall do with your oxen and your sheep. It shall be with its mother seven days; you shall give it to Me on the eighth day.*

The firstborn lambs would need to be marked by the shepherds to distinguish them from the other newborn lambs.

Making sure the lambs were without blemish and entirely unharmed to be acceptable for the Temple use. Only the priests could perform these Temple duties. A priest usually remained in the Migdal Eder all throughout the night. (*Though this was likely very early in the lambing season, as yet still with little action*).

> Micah 4:8 (EXB) *And you, watchtower of the flocks [or Migdal-eder], hill [or strong hold] of Jerusalem [Daughter Zion], to you will come the kingdom [dominion will be restored] as in the past. Jerusalem [Daughter Jerusalem], the right to rule [kingship; sovereignty] will come again to you."*

Jerusalem, being only a few miles walk, the flocks under the shepherds' care near Bethlehem was destined as sacrifices in the Temple following the Jewish regulations.

These shepherds were the 'Levitical Shepherds' chosen and trained to attend to the flock of sheep destined to be used as sacrificial lambs in the Temple.

The mother ewe, when ready, was taken to the ritually purified nominated birthing cave. They immediately wrapped the newborn lamb in clean swaddling cloth to protect them and keep them from blemish and danger. Swaddling clothes comprised bandage-like strips of cloth.

They used a salt solution for cleansing. After drying, lambs were swaddled, restricting the limbs to prevent damage and keeping them clean, also spotless. For this, older priestly garments were cut into small pieces for use.

Lambs that were 'spotless and without blemish' as offerings; had to be male sheep marked and given to the Lord but kept outside until they were a year old.

Therefore, when the Angel tells the Shepherds, *'you will recognize him by this sign: You will find a baby wrapped in swaddling cloth lying in a manger.'*

They knew that the only place near Bethlehem that had a manger with swaddling clothes was at the watchtower of the Flock' *Migdal-eder.'*

It was a genuine, recognizable 'sign' that only the Levitical Shepherds would comprehend.]

After the birth, the small family would need a temporary shelter for a time, which they found by using *a Sukkah.*

Observed in autumn, Sukkot begins five days after Yom Kippur, from the fifteenth to the twenty-first day of the Hebrew month called Tishri (analogous to September).

Elisabeth, the cousin of Mary, had conceived six months before Mary, at the end of Zechariah's duties in the Temple, about Sivan 30, the eleventh week, bringing the birth of John, after the spring (Passover,) Iyar, Sivan or the beginning of 'Tamuz, and the birth of Jesus six months later, to the time around the Feast of Tabernacle, in the Autumn, Elul/Tishri].

(*A temporary shelter, A Sukkah, is built over seven days each year in the fall, with its association with the celebration of the Feast of Tabernacles.*
The fields during this harvest time would have been dotted with Sukkoth's since they are temporary shelters for people and animals.
The Word stable in Hebrew is called a Sukkoth).

Genesis 33:17 (KJ21) ***And Jacob journeyed to Succoth, and built him a house, and made booths for his cattle. Therefore the name of the place is called Succoth [that is, Booths].***

[*Sukkot or the Feast of Tabernacles, sometimes called 'the Feast of Booths.' It is a week-long festival used to commemorate the 40-year wilderness journey of the Israelites.*
This joyous celebration is a reminder of God's protection, provision, and faithfulness.
This is one of the three great pilgrimage feasts recorded in the scriptures. There was a requirement for all Jewish males to appear before the Lord in the Temple in Jerusalem. The Word Sukkot also came to mean booths.
Jews continue to observe this time throughout the holiday by building and dwelling in temporary shelters, just like the Hebrew people did while wandering in the desert.

The First Day of Sukkot was also when Solomon had finished the building of the Temple.
The dedication and with it the very first observance held there corresponded to the celebration of Sukkot.

2 Chronicles 7:8-11 (KJV) ***also at the same time Solomon kept the feast seven days and all Israel with him, a very great congregation, from the entering in of Hamath unto the river of Egypt.***

And in the eighth day, they made a solemn assembly: for they kept the dedication of the altar seven days and the feast seven days.
And on the three and twentieth day of the seventh month, he sent the people away into their tents, glad and merry in heart for the goodness that the Lord had shown unto David, and to Solomon, and Israel, his people.
Thus Solomon finished the house of the Lord, and the King's house: and all that came into Solomon's heart to make in the house of the Lord, and his own house, he prosperously effected.

*1 Kings 8:65 (KJV) **And at that time Solomon held a feast, and all Israel with him, a great congregation, from the entering in of Hamath unto the river of Egypt, before the Lord our God, seven days and seven days, even fourteen days.***

After the seven days of the feast, God's presence dwelt in the Temple on the Eighth Day (Shemini Atzeret).

1 Kings 8:10-11 (KJV) ***And it came to pass when the priests were come out of the holy place, that the cloud filled the house of the Lord so that the priests could not stand to minister because of the cloud: for the glory of the Lord had filled the house of the Lord.]***

On the other hand, Mary kept all the events and happenings to herself and within her heart, where she reflected on them often.

When it came to the eight days after the birth, the 'Eighth Day of Assembly' (Shemini Atzeret), the baby was circumcised at this time. Joseph named the child Jesus; this was the name chosen before he was conceived and was told to them by the Angel.

Just about thirty days later, the time came for the new parents to fulfill their purification offering, which is a mandatory requirement of the Law of Moses after the birth of a child.

This is the requirement of the Law of the Lord, "When a woman's first child is male, the child must be dedicated unto God."

Exodus 13:2 Dedicate to me all firstborn males: that is, each one that first opens the womb among the children of Israel.

Hence they offered the sacrifice required in the Law of the Lord! "This is either a pair of turtledoves or two young pigeons." (*Leviticus 12:4, 8*)

Joseph took Mary and the baby Jesus to Jerusalem so that they could present him to the Lord. This was done when the child was 40 days old.

In Jerusalem, at that time, there was a man named Simeon (*Shimone*) who was honorable and lived a spiritually devoted life.

Keenly waiting for the Messiah whom he knew was to come, he hoped his arrival would mean Israel's rescue from all oppressors. Shimone is from the Hebrew root word 'shemah,' which means in part to Hear or listen intelligently and attentively.

The Holy Spirit was resting upon Simeon and had made it known to him that he would not die before he had personally seen the appearance of the Lord's Messiah.

That day he was led by the Spirit into the Temple, the very same time as Joseph and Mary, who had arrived to present the baby Jesus to the Lord, as the Law required.

When Simeon saw the family, he took the child in his arms and praised God, and made this speech, "Oh Sovereign Lord, Now let your servant die in peace as you have promised.

I have now seen your salvation with my own eyes, which you have prepared for all people.

He is the light to reveal you to all the nations, Almighty God; he is also the glory for your people Israel!" He exclaimed.

Then Simeon blessed the child's parent and then turned to Mary, "This child is selected to cause the ascending and the falling of many in Israel. A figure misunderstood and contradicted, yet he will be a joy to so many others.

He has been sent as a great sign from God, but many will oppose him.

As a result, the deepest thoughts and intents of many hearts will be forced to be revealed. And the pain of a sword will pierce your heart." He stated. Simeon was the first witness in the Temple to the identity of Jesus.

The parents of Jesus were astonished at the things that were being said about the child.

Then also, at the same time, in the Temple, was a woman who was the daughter of Phanuel (*of the tribe of Asher*), a Prophetess. Her name was Anna (Hannah), this remarkable woman was a widow.

Hannah is Channah in Hebrew and means favored. 'Phanuel' means, 'I have seen the face of, the Mighty One.' Asher is located in the area of Galilee.

Then eventually, after getting married, Anna, who was now an older woman, had remained unmarried a significant amount of time past the usual marriageable age. Her husband had died after just seven years of their marriage. Following his death, Anna continued to live as a widow. She dedicated her life to God, so she never left the Temple but stayed there day and night, worshiping God with fasting and prayer. She had now reached the age of eighty-four.

Anna came along at the time Simeon was talking with Mary and Joseph; she immediately started praising God.

Anna went about talking about the child to everyone who had been expectantly waiting for God to rescue Israel and free Jerusalem (*the center of temple worship for the Nation*).

Anna became the second of the two witnesses, which in the Law establishes the truth of a matter.

After Joseph and Mary had fulfilled all the requirements of the Law of the Lord, there in Jerusalem, they returned home to Bethlehem with the child Jesus. Then later, they eventually settled in Nazareth in Galilee. Where the child grew up healthy and strong, he was filled with wisdom, and the favor of God was on him.

Magi Arrive, Journeying From The East To Find And Worship The Messiah.

Now going back to the time before the family moved away from Bethlehem and finally settled in Nazareth. After the dramatic events that occurred when Jesus was born in the town of Bethlehem. Joseph and Mary continued to live for well over a year without any further incidents. Their home was in a house in that small town situated in the territory of Judah. (*Both Joseph and Mary had much-extended families and relatives in the region, as this town held the kinfolks and descendants of King David.*)

This period was during the kingship of Herod the Great (*Named for his many building projects.*)

There came a time when a delegation of Priestly Scholars called Magi's, arrived in Jerusalem from eastern lands.

East of the land of Israel was the Parthian empire, where all the tribes of Israel had been taken captive during the time of Daniel the Prophet.

The Babylonian Kingdom had been captured and subdued by King Cyrus two generations later, which was the catalyst for the ending of the captivity of the Israelites.

The vast majority of the captives had remained behind after the release of the people by King Cyrus.

When by Royal Proclamation, they were allowed to return to Israel and rebuild and rededicate the Temple, including rebuilding the walls of Jerusalem.

[The ancient Magi's was a hereditary priesthood of the Medes, 'Later became known as the Kurds.' The Magi's who were called 'Wise Men' because of their use of Oneiromancy! (Being the practice of predicting the future through interpreting dreams) and was recognized as having insightful and extraordinary religious knowledge.

There was a period when they became recognized by Darius the Great and were acknowledged as superior over the old state religion of Persia. This came about because of some extraordinary episodes. Where some Magi attached to the court of the Median King established themselves as experts in the interpretation of dreams, becoming the supreme priestly caste of the Persian Empire.

They then held and consolidated power in the civil and the political arena and through their religious authority. The prominence and influence of these Magi's had, continued, and strengthened through succeeding periods.

These Magi's were influential members of one of the two branch assemblies, entrusted with the selection of Parthian monarchs.

One branch was composed of royal family members (The Arsacids), and the other consisted of the priests (The Magi). And also influential Parthians of non-royal blood (The Wise Men). The Magi and Wise Men were jointly known as the Megistanes. The agreeing vote of both councils was necessary for the appointment of a new king.

Much of this influence of these scholars was due to the rise of the Israelite Daniel.

Among many titles that Daniel was given was the title of Rab-mag, the Chief of the Magi! (Daniel 5:11, the King made him Master of the magicians, astrologers, Chaldeans, and soothsayers). Later on, king Darius appointed this Israelite outsider to be Chief over the previously hereditary Median priesthood. Which then prompted a failed plot in retaliation involving the ordeal of throwing him into the lion's den.

(*The abysmal failure of that episode only served to clinch Daniel's ascendancy. See the book of Daniel: Chapter six*).

After this, a separate branch of the Magi, who were the resurgence of the old Median priesthood, became the wider known Zoroaster. These Zoroasters took on an exclusive and independent spiritual course. (*Note: Jethro, Moses' father-in-law, was a Median Priest. See Exodus 18:1).

Daniel had apparently entrusted a Messianic vision (to be announced in due time by a "star") to a select sect of the Magi's for its eventual fulfillment.

> Numbers 24:17, *I will see him, but not now: I will behold him, but not soon: there will come a Star out of Jacob, and a Sceptre shall rise out of Israel, and will slash the corners of Moab, and destroy all the children of Sheth (The crown of their head the sons of tumult* [or boasters], (as in Jeremiah 48:45... *heads of 'arrogant Moabites' those in tumult*).

Living roughly six centuries before the birth of Jesus, Daniel had indeed received an incredible number of Messianic prophecies.

Two hundred years after the Prophet Micah identified Bethlehem as the birthplace of the Messiah, the Lord told Daniel the time of his (Messiah's) death. It would be exactly 483 years after issuing the decree to rebuild and restore Jerusalem and its walls, following the end of the Babylonian captivity, and before it (*the Temple*) was destroyed again by the arrival of an enemy army. (Daniel 9:24-27).

The Babylonian Empire issued three separate decrees, Cyrus in 538 B.C., found in Ezra 1:1-2. Then by Darius in 520 B.C., specified in Ezra 6:8. Artaxerxes' decreed the third edict, issued Tishri 458 through Elul 457 BC, which enabled the restoration and rebuilding, Daniel 9:25 is concerned with (*starting the 'prophetic clock' for precisely 483 years*).

In addition to several summaries and detailed outlines of the entire world's history; regarding the Gentile Nations that Daniel had revealed to him. The Angel Gabriel also told him the precise day that Jesus would present Himself as King to the Nation of Israel in Jerusalem.

Descending from these priests, Magi's who became a very influential political force in Parthia as Persia came to be known, remained faithful to the commission tasked to them by Daniel.

And as a result, after witnessing the long-awaited star, set out west towards Israel and particularly to Jerusalem, its capital].

They arrived in Jerusalem in their usual grand tradition and pageantry when traveling. They began asking around, "Where can we find and pay homage to the newborn King of the Jews?" They questioned the residents.

"We had observed a star in the sky while we were in the east; this star signaled his birth. So we have come on pilgrimage to worship him." They exclaimed as an explanation.

(This Star was most likely a sighting of the moment the same Angel had appeared to the shepherds in the fields, delivering the message announcing the Savior.

The Magi would have also witnessed *'whilst stargazing'* the exceedingly bright light *'descending and ascending,'* as those innumerable Angels appeared to the Shepherds on the night of the birth). Job 38:7 (EXB) *while the morning stars sang together and all the angels [sons of God] shouted with joy?*

When eventually the news about their inquiry got to Herod, it terrified him! And not just Herod alone, but the rest of Jerusalem as well (*in Political language, Herod could assume that they had come intending to pay tribute money to the true Jewish King. Of which Herod was not, as he was not even a descendant of the children of Israel, but an Edomite*).
*Note: These men traveled in vast caravans, with a large entourage of troops, yet even the Romans stationed in Jerusalem did not interfere with them.

When Herod arranged a meeting with the visitors, he lost no time in trying to impress them. He summoned together all the High Priests and religious scholars in the city. He ordered them to inform him of the facts about any predictions.

"Where is the Messiah expected to be born?" He demanded.

"In the town of Bethlehem in Judea," the religious Priests and scholars promptly answered after checking.

"The Prophet Micah wrote it plainly, (Micah 5:2). The following is what the Prophet wrote. *'And you, O Bethlehem of the land in Judah, are not the least from among the ruling cities of Judah, because a ruler will emerge out of you, who will be the shepherd, for my people Israel.'"* They assured the King.

Herod then arranged a secret meeting between him and the scholars from the east.

While he also pretended to have the same interest and was as equally devout as they were. He persuaded them to tell him exactly when the star that signaled the birth had appeared. When Herod had obtained the information that he needed, he told the prophecy about Bethlehem to the Eastern Scholars. "Go find this child.

Investigate in detail and do all that you can. Send Word back to me as soon as you do find him, and I will come and join you at once in your worship." Herod said, trying to appear sincere to these learned men.

These sages knew the expected time of the Messiah from the writings of the Prophet Daniel. And now they also confirmed the place, as was written by the Prophet Micah.

After having this interview with Herod the King, the Eastern Scholars went on their way to re-join their main camp outside the city.

Then as they set off again resuming their travel in the early evening, the star once again appeared the same star they had seen in the eastern skies. It was ahead of them and led them on until it was directly overhead, hovering over an area with a house. They could soon establish that this was the house with the young child. Now, these travelers were so filled with joy! Since they knew they had found the right house, having also arrived there after such a long trip at precisely the right time! That they could hardly contain themselves.

They entered the house and saw the young child Jesus at last, and with him his mother Mary, after greetings and introductions, they bowed down and worshipped him. They had gifts with which to honor the new King, and they presented those gifts to him. The lists of presents that they gave him were gifts of Gold, Frankincense, and myrrh.

We can link this episode to the writings in Isaiah 60 and Psalm 72, which report Gold and Frankincense as the actual gifts given by kings. (These gifts represented, Gold for a king, Frankincense is a priestly gift offered to God, and myrrh, which could be burned as a type of incense, and for embalming during preparation for burial).

Myrrh is a resin, a natural gum (an aromatic oleoresin, a natural blend of oil and resin, also used as a perfume and medicine) extracted from various trees native to Africa, Arabia, and India. Both Frankincense and Myrrh were more valuable than Gold.

From Exodus, we see that myrrh was essential for marking and setting apart significant persons for service. (Exodus 30:23, the LORD told Moses, *'Go find the finest spices. Gain twelve pounds of liquid myrrh'*).

Here God is setting out the plans for the Tabernacle and the Temple to come later.

Flowing myrrh was primary among the ingredient in the oil prepared for the anointing of elements of the Tabernacle and members of the priesthood.

The use of oil of myrrh was prohibited for laymen or any other non-related Tabernacle uses.

It was time for the Priestly Scholars to leave, having stayed some time to worship the young King.

As they were making preparations to start their journey the next day, they received warnings about what Herod was planning in a dream by God and was told not to report back to the King.

These men immediately obeyed what God had told them, showing that they were not only worshippers of the true God but obedient servants. They quickly worked out another route. That would allow them to leave the territory without being seen.

And so they could return to their own country with no further contact with the people of the city of Jerusalem.

After the Scholars left out for their land, the Angel of the Lord gave Joseph some instructions in a dream. "Get yourself up now! Swiftly escape with the child and his mother out of this land and go to Egypt." The Angel said, "Remain there until I tell you when it is safe for you to return because Herod will try to hunt for the child to kill him."

That very night Joseph left for Egypt with Mary and the child. He was living there in that country until after the death of King Herod. This became the fulfillment. Of what the Lord had spoken, through Hosea the Prophet: "*I have called my Son out of Egypt.*" (Hosea 11:1).

Hosea wrote how God had first called His son Israel out of Egypt. They, the children of Israel, had failed. As they went on to sacrifice to 'Baalim,' burning incense to idols.

Jesus is the true also perfect Son of God, sinless and faultless in obedience towards God.

News eventually got to Herod that the Eastern Scholars, called 'Magi's,' had left the territory. And when he realized that his plan to use the Magi's for his purposes had come to nothing. The news kindled his fury. Herod showed his true intentions; by sending soldiers to kill all the boy children in and around Bethlehem, that was any, aged two years old and under. This is the age that he concluded the child would be because of the Magi's information about the star's first appearance.

This brutal action of King Herod in the murdering of the innocents fulfilled what God had spoken through the Prophet Jeremiah:

> "In Ramah, a cry of weeping and great mourning was heard: Rachel refuses to be comforted as she weeps for her children because they are dead." (Jeremiah 31:15).
> [Rachel, while journeying with Jacob to Ephrath (Bethlehem), had died in childbirth and was buried there.
> (Genesis 35:19-20 NKJV Jacob set a pillar on her grave, which is the pillar of Rachel's grave).

She has become the symbol of all Jewish mothers who suffer on account of their children].

Eventually, when Herod died, Joseph, still in Egypt, was told of it through a dream. The Lord's Angel said to him. "Joseph, Get yourself up and return to the land of Israel. It is now safe to take the child and his mother because the ones who were seeking to kill the child are now dead."

So Joseph made preparations, then took his young family and re-entered the country, traveling again into the land of Israel, he and the child Jesus along with Mary, his wife.

Joseph became concerned upon receiving news that Archelaus, the son of Herodas, was now ruling over the Judean region. All his fears were soon resolved, as once again he was directed, in a dream. He decided against settling back in the same area of Galilee. Still, instead, the family went to live in a small and inconsequential town called Nazareth.

Fulfilling what the Prophets (Isaiah, Jeremiah, and Zechariah) had said about him as 'The Branch' - the hidden shoot: saying, "He will be called a Nazarene."

Isaiah 4:2: *In that day, the branch of the LORD will be beautiful even glorious. With the fruit of the Earth excellent also attractive for them that are escaped of Israel.*

Jeremiah 23:5, 6, *a righteous Branch... Called, THE LORD OUR RIGHTEOUSNESS.*

Zechariah 6:9-13, *the man whose name is The BRANCH; and he will grow up out of his place, and he will build the Temple of the LORD: Even he will build the Temple of the LORD!*

Archelaus (Meaning: *The Prince of the people*) was the son of King Herod the Great of Judea. By Malthace, one of Herod's several wives, who were from Samaria.

After the death of his father, Herod Archelaus was appointed the King. Although the Roman emperor Augustus wrote to him that he had to content himself with the title of Ethnarch (*'National leader'*) of Samaria, Judaea, and Idumea (*except for the cities of Gaza, Gadara, and Hipo*).

CHAPTER THREE

JESUS VISITS JERUSALEM AS A CHILD.

A significant incident happened about the time of the early adulthood of the life of Jesus.

Every year when the time of the Passover festival was held, it was customary for Joseph and his family to attend, and when Jesus was twelve years old, the whole family journeyed to Jerusalem for the celebration as usual.

After his twelfth year, and between thirteen to fourteen years of age, a boy child of the sons of Israel was obliged to apply himself to the Law of Moses. It was at that age a Jewish boy could become a Bar Mitzvah, a 'son of the covenant or law,' a full member of the synagogue, assuming all the responsibilities implicit in his circumcision.

To be prepared, they should take a boy to the observance a year or two years before he turned thirteen.

This year when it was all completed, the family and pilgrims from Nazareth set out to return to their hometown. However, the child Jesus did not leave to return with them; he instead remained there in the city of Jerusalem.

Then it was some considerable time before his mother and father became aware that he was not in the group of travelers. Unknowingly they had journeyed for a whole day without the boy since they assumed he was among the friends and relatives who made up the company.

They became anxious when he did not show up. The parents returned a day's journey to Jerusalem, searching for him—eventually finding him in the Temple.

When they saw Jesus, he was sitting with the religious teachers—listening to them and asking them questions. From the answers he gave them, the people hearing this was stunned and astounded at the clarity of his discernment.

When his parents saw Jesus, they were amazed; Mary, his mother, questioned him about this, "Child, why have you done this to your father and me?" She asked him.

"We have been suffering the ordeal of worrying and have been searching for you anxiously." She informed him, with the deep concern of an anxious parent.

The young Jesus tried to reassure them he could never be lost, "Why were you searching for me?" Jesus asks her, "Did you not know that I had to be in my father's house about his business?" He said, establishing his dedication to the will of his heavenly father, even over earthly relationships.

His parents, however, did not realize what he meant by this.

After this, Jesus returned to Nazareth with his parents, continuing as before, remaining obedient to them. Mary, his mother, kept all these things as significant memories in her heart.

Jesus grew and matured, continuing to increase both in wisdom and stature; he plainly had the favor of God and all the people.

THE PREACHING IN THE WILDERNESS OF JOHN THE BAPTIZER.

While Jesus lived and grew in the hills of Galilee, John called 'The Baptizer' was out in the Judean desert preaching a sober and straight-forward message of repentance.

This was now somewhere in the fifteenth year of the reign of Tiberius, the Roman emperor. Pontius Pilate was the appointed governor over Judea. And after Herod the great's death, Israel was divided into three separate regions. Rome gave these to Herod's three sons; Herod Antipas became ruler over Galilee; his brother Philip ruler over Iturea and Traconitis; with Lysanias ruler over Abilene.

The High Priests in Jerusalem during this period were Annas and then Caiaphas.

At this precise moment in time, A message from God came to John, the son of Zechariah the Levite Priest. Who was living in the wilderness! So John went preaching on both sides of the Jordan River, telling the people they should be baptized. To show they have repented of their sins and wanted to be forgiven. Then turn back to God.

The Prophet Isaiah had spoken of John when he had said, "*He is a voice of one in the wilderness crying out, 'Prepare the way for the coming of the Lord! Clear the road for him!*" (Isaiah 40:3.)

The clothes of John were basic and austere, woven from coarse camel hair; he also wore a leather belt around his waist.

And the diet of John had been just as simple; for food, he ate locusts and wild honey.

The Carob (Ceratonia-siliqua), also called locust bean (*Locust tree*), is a green dioecious type tree with young brown-reddish stems.

The seed is called 'gerah' found in (Exodus 30:13), from where the Word carat comes, used as a unit of weight, equalling (*one-fifth of a gram*).

The seed pod contains a sweet juice called carob honey.

People from Jerusalem and all Judea and all over the Jordan countryside went out to see and hear John's message that he preached, and as they massed right there at the Jordan River, those who confessed their sins, he baptized in the river.

"What should we do?" The people who constantly came to John asked.

John told them how they should show each other mercy and justice, "If you have two shirts, give one to the poor. If you have food, share it with those who are hungry." He expounded in a loud, clear message to them.

Even the corrupt tax collectors came to John to be baptized, "Teacher, what should we do?" They asked.

"Collect only the taxes that the government requires and be sure that you never add any more," John replied to them.

"And what about us, what should we do?" asked some soldiers.

"Do not use your position to extort money or make any false accusations. Just be satisfied with your pay." John instructed them.

Time after time, John cried out in ringing, echoing tones, "Repent of your sins and turn your life to God, change your life, because God's Kingdom, the Kingdom of Heaven, is near."

John the Baptizer had chosen the place in the Jordan River, which means 'flowing downward' or 'the descender.'

At a point directly opposite Jericho at a ford in the river and is known as 'Bethabara,' or Beit' Abara ('the House of Passage' or 'House of the Crossing'). In this place, Israel had passed over the river.

Baptism (*mikveh*) was not new or unique; mikveh was a ritual that has been regularly practiced in Israel since Moses. We see in Exodus 30:17-21 the likely kernel of the practice as part of the requirement to serve at the Tabernacle; the priests needed to be ritually clean (*tahor*). Before that, (tevilah, *to completely immerse*) was experienced in the crossing of the Red Sea.

Mikveh, or baptism as the outward symbol just for repentance (*not cleansing*), was for proselytes (*converts to the children of Israel*), as far as the Jews, particularly the Pharisees, saw it.

New Gentile believers, if the person were male, would be circumcised then immersed as a symbol of being placed under the Old Testament Law.

Joshua 24:27. (CEB) *Joshua said to all the people, "This stone will serve here as a witness against us, because it has heard all the Lord's words that he spoke to us. It will serve as a witness against you in case you aren't true to your God."*

At the Jordan, a splendid lesson of resurrection was taught to Israel, who faced a flooded Jordan River, which they could not cross to fully enter the Promised Land.

The wonderful truth is; that by God's mighty hand, the redeemed of God at the Jordan River had passage through death and resurrection, and then enacted for the twelve tribes of Israel the fact, by the figure of the twelve stones, placed in the Jordan, and the twelve stones taken out of it.

John's message at the Jordan called those who would prepare for the coming King and Messiah to be baptized and re-enter the Promised Land and to remember the original promise of Israel made at that very spot, where the stones were the permanent witness.

However, when he saw many of the religious leaders, including the Pharisees and Sadducees, coming all the way out to the desert to watch him baptize, he criticized them. "You brood of snakes!" He shouted. "Who warned you to depart from God's coming wrath? Show true repentance of your sins by the way you live your lives, proving that you have indeed turned to God. Do not think to say to each other, 'We are safe because we are the descendants of Abraham.' That means nothing because I tell you this; God can produce children of Abraham from these very stones.

Even now, the judgment of God is poised like an ax, ready to sever the roots of the trees. And yes, every single tree that does not produce good fruit will be chopped down and thrown into the fire." John said, fearlessly delivering his message with passion and power.

> *Psalm 95:6, 8-10 (KJV)* ***O come, let us worship and bow down: let us kneel before the LORD our maker...***
> ***Harden, not your heart, as in the provocation, and as in the day of temptation in the wilderness: When your fathers tempted me, proved me, and saw my work.***
> ***Forty years long was I grieved with this generation, and said, it is a people that do go astray in their heart, and they have not known my ways***.

There was great excitement among the people. Since everyone had an enormous expectancy of the promised Messiah of Israel, they were eager to know whether John might be the Messiah.

Yet whenever they asked him if he was the Messiah, John would tell them, "I baptize with water, those of you who repent of their sins and turn to God. Approaching soon is someone much greater than I, so much more significant, that I would not be worthy even to be his slave and untie or carry his sandals. With the Holy Spirit and with fire, he will baptize you.

He is ready to separate using his winnowing fork the chaff from the wheat; as a result, he will cleanse his threshing floor.

He will then gather the wheat into his barn, but burning the chaff with fire that never ends." He said, vigorously preaching his meaningful message.

John's words gave strength to the ordinary people; his mighty cry for God's righteousness put within them hope and a renewed heart.

He continually preached the Good News of God's Kingdom to the people.

THE BAPTISM OF JESUS IN THE JORDAN.

Then one day, Jesus traveled from Nazareth in Galilee over to the Jordan River to be baptized by John.

Although when Jesus arrived, John, upon seeing him, did not want to perform the ritual. Instead, attempted to talk him out of it, "I am the one who truly needs to be baptized by you," he told Jesus, "As you know this is so why are you coming to me?" John asked, being amazed.

"It should be done because we must carry out fulfilling all that God requires completing righteousness," Jesus replied.

(*Note: *Righteousness is the right way of doing things according to the principles of the Kingdom of God.*

Here, earthly authority, which John carried, and Jesus agreed with and submitted to).

As a result, John then agreed to and baptized him.

After his baptism, Jesus came up out of the water and was praying. And as he prayed, the heavens above him were opened. And John could see the Spirit of God, in a bodily form descending and settling on Jesus. The Spirit came down softly and gently in the manner that a dove would descend when it came to land on a branch.

At that moment, there was a voice from Heaven, and the voice said, "Here is my dearly beloved Son. He brings me great joy."

Psalm 42:7: *Deep calls unto deep at the noise of your waterspouts: all your waves and your billows are gone over me.*

Jonah 2:3: *Because you have thrown me into the deep, in the middle of the seas; and the floods surrounded about me: all your billows and your waves passed over me.*

(*Note: There is a significant difference between 'the heavens' and 'heaven,' HEAVEN is God's abode, the heavens include the things, Stars, etc. That can be seen, as well as the things that we cannot see yet are not the realm of God's abode).

Here are a few examples.

Job 15:15 says, "consider; he puts no trust in his saints; yea, the heavens are not clean in his sight.

*Note: The First recorded Christian Martyr as found in Acts 7:55-56.

Stephen, gazing into Heaven, being full of the Holy Spirit, saw God in his Glory and Jesus standing at his right hand. "*Look, I see (the heavens) opened, with the Son of Man standing at the right hand of God!*" He proclaimed.

> 2 Peter 3:10. **Conversely, the Day of the Lord will come "like a thief." On that day, the 'heavens' will disappear with a roar, as the elements melt and disintegrate, with the Earth and everything in it burnt up.**

> Ephesians 4:10 **He that descended is the same also that ascended far above all heavens, that he might fill all things.**

> Matthew 24:29 (KJV) **Immediately after the tribulation of those days shall the sun be darkened, and the moon shall not give her light, and the stars shall fall from Heaven, and the powers of the heavens shall be shaken.**

> Ezekiel 1:1 (KJV) **Now it came to pass in the thirtieth year, in the fourth month, on the fifth day of the month, as I was among the captives by the river of Chebar, that the heavens were opened and I saw visions of God.**

JESUS IS TEMPTED IN THE DESERT.

Then Jesus returned from the Jordan River, and he was full of the Holy Spirit. During that time, the Spirit led Jesus, and he directed him to go into the wilderness.

While he was there, Satan tempted him for a total of forty days. Throughout the entire period of his temptation, Jesus ate nothing at all; he continued fasting and grew very hungry.

During that time of his most immense hunger, the Devil came and tried to test him, seeking to destroy him, "If you, in reality, are the Son of God, tell these stones to become loaves of bread." He said to Jesus, who summarily replied, "No! The Scriptures says, "Man does not live only by bread. However, true life is by every Word that comes from God's mouth!" This rebuke from Jesus was via a quote from (Deuteronomy 8 *Yes, God did provide manna to the children of Israel, but he had humbled them*).

Then the Devil took Jesus to the Holy City Jerusalem, to the highest point of the Temple, "Since then you are the Son of God, jump off! Seeing as in the Scriptures, it says, "He will order his Angels to guard, protect and hold you up with their hands then you can never even hurt your foot on a stone." The Devil said, countering with Scripture, using the powerful Messianic Psalm 91. Although he placed within a blatant misquote to tempt Jesus in using and showing the people his power.

Even if its use initially looks right and is by his trust in God's ability to fulfill explicit promises in the Word.

The temptation is still via him using his will to fulfill his desires rather than God's. It is always a slippery slope and was the very thing that got this high-ranking fallen Angel in trouble in the first place.

[This shows the power Satan uses of shrewdly misquoting or removing Scriptures; as he had cleverly omitted the all-important, 'To keep you in all your ways,' Verse 11, from his altered rendering.

> Ezekiel 28:15 tells this about him, **"You were perfect in your ways from the day you were created, until iniquity was found in you."**

The scriptures make it clear 'regarding all our ways' matching all of God's ways.

> Proverbs 3:6 *Confess and reveal Him in all your ways, and He shall direct your paths.*

> Proverbs 4:26 *Consider the path of your feet and let all your ways be established.*

> Psalm 25:4 *Show me your ways, O LORD; teach me your paths.*

> Psalm 119:15, *I will meditate in your teachings and have respect for your ways.*

> Revelation 15:3 (KJV) **And they sing the song of Moses the servant of God, and the song of the Lamb, saying, Great and marvelous are your works, Lord God Almighty; just and true are your ways, O Sovereign of the ages, King of the saints**].

"The Scriptures also says," responded Jesus, "you should not test the Lord your God."

(He used Deuteronomy 6:16, *which speaks of Massah. Back in the Wilderness Period in Massah and Meribah, the children of Israel tempted the LORD in demanding a miracle instead of trusting God to meet their requirements*).

The Devil, after that, took him to the peak of a very high mountain, from where he was able to show Jesus the kingdoms of the entire world, all in a brief moment, along with all their glory and splendor.

"I will give you all the glory and total authority over these kingdoms," The Devil said, "since they are all mine, I can give them to anyone I please. I will give them all to you if you will bow down to me and worship me." He boasted proudly, soliciting Jesus to take the shortcut to glory, avoiding the path and outworking of God's plan.

"Get yourself out of here, Satan," Jesus demanded immediately. "For the Scriptures say, 'you must worship the Lord your God and serve only him.'" Jesus rebuked him using Deuteronomy 6:4, proclaiming the greatest commandment of God and affirming the total authority of the Word.

After seeing that he couldn't test Jesus being resisted at all points, the Devil was constrained and compelled to finish tempting him. So he went on his way; however, he only left him until the next convenient time came.

Jesus was out in the desert among the wild animals; after this, the Angels came and helped him, ministering and taking care of him.

[*Note: Jesus did not contend with the Devil over his claim to have possession over the kingdoms of the world. These are not just in the natural realm. We see the domains in Ephesians 6:12 Ruling powers over the darkness of this world and spiritual wickedness in high places. Spiritual powers of evil operating in the heavenly world (*realm*), also, we see in Ephesians 2:2. He is the prince of the power of the air.

In John 14:30, Jesus stated, "After this, I will not talk much with you: as the prince of this world is arriving, yet he has nothing in me."

> 2 Corinthians 4:4, *In their case, Satan, who is the 'god' of this world has blinded the unbelievers' minds 'that they should not recognize the truth,' preventing them from receiving the*

illuminating light from the Gospel of the Glory of Christ (the Messiah), Who is the Image and Likeness of God.

As the prince (*or God little 'g's*) of this world, he utilized the three key areas of temptations, namely the lust of the flesh, the lust of the eyes, the pride of life. All of which failed, defeated by Jesus' use of the Word of God.

> 1st John 2:16. *Since all that is in the world, the lust of the flesh, 'yearning for physical gratification.' And the lusting of the eyes, 'greedy longings of the mind' and the pride of life, 'our assurance in our own possessions or in the stability of earthly things.' Are not coming from the Father, but are from the world*].

THE JERUSALEM LEADERS CHALLENGES JOHN.

From Jerusalem, where the Jewish leaders held their power base, they often sent priests and Temple assistants to go and question and investigate John out in the wilderness. This was the testimony of John when they arrived with questions of his identity and authority, "who are you?" They asked John.

"I am not the Messiah," John told them point-blank, knowing what they were driving at.

"Well then, who are you?" They demanded. "Are you Elijah?"

"No," He replied, refusing to engage with them.

"Are you the Prophet we are expecting?" They continued to ask.

"No." He again told them.

"Then, who are you? We need to return to those who sent us with an answer. What do you claim about yourself and who you are?" They insisted half mockingly.

John would only reply in the words of the Prophet Isaiah, "I am a voice in the wilderness; exclaiming, prepare the way for the Lord's arrival!' He said without compromise.

The officials who had been sent to investigate John then showed their disdain. "If you are not the Messiah, Elijah or 'the prophet we are expecting,' then what right do you have to baptize?" they asked him, finally getting to the point.

"I can only baptize with water; however, right here in the crowd is someone you do not recognize. And though his ministry follows mine, I am not even worthy of being his slave or untying the straps of his sandal." John warned them.

This encounter took place over at Bethany east of the Jordan River, where John performed baptisms.

Then on the following day, John looking up, saw Jesus walking toward him, "Pay attention! There is the Lamb of God, the one who takes away the sins of the world! He is the one that I was talking about when I said, 'A man who is arriving after me is far greater than I am because he existed long before me.' I did not recognize it was he who was the Messiah; however, I have been baptizing with water so it would reveal him to Israel." He announced to the people.

(*Note: This was the fulfillment of the prophecy from Abraham, 'Whom God had declared a prophet' in Gen; 20:7 when He said of him, "He's a prophet; he will pray for you so you may live."

This Prophet Abraham was the first one to see in prophecy the day of the Lord Jesus when he declared in Genesis 22:8, "God will provide himself a lamb."

God had called Abraham to offer up his son as a test. However, 'a lamb' was not provided; a ram was discovered instead 'caught in a thicket by his horns.' (*Abraham would have needed a lamb as a substitute instead of his son for the offering*).

*The "Akedah" in Hebrew, binding (*of Isaac*).

> Genesis 22:10-13 (NLT) **And Abraham picked up the knife to kill his son as a sacrifice. At that moment, the Angel of the Lord called to him from Heaven, "Abraham! Abraham!"**
> **"Yes," Abraham replied. "Here I am!"**
> **"Don't lay a hand on the boy!" the Angel said. "Do not hurt him in any way; for now, I know that you truly fear God. You have not withheld from me even your son, your only son."**

Then Abraham looked up and saw a ram caught by its horns in a thicket. So he took the ram and sacrificed it as a burnt offering in place of his son.

Now here was the Prophet John, who was the son of Zechariah, who himself was (*a true Levite priest*) because he was a member of the descendant of that order. He had the authority to declare the fulfillment of Abraham's statement. Saying here then is 'that lamb' that God has provided—proclaiming Jesus as the perfect 'Lamb Of God,' the one who can take away the world's sins.

John announced to everyone, with pure delight, full of joy, the following, "I saw the Holy Spirit descending from heaven just how a dove comes down and resting upon him."

He continued, "I did not know that it was him. Yet when God sent me to baptize with water, he told me, 'The one on whom you will see the Spirit descend and then rest on. He is the one who will baptize with the Holy Spirit.'

I witnessed this happened to Jesus, so I testify that he is the Chosen One of God."

THE FIRST DISCIPLES OF JESUS.

The following day after John's testimony, he stood with only two others; these were two of his disciples. As John saw Jesus walking by, he observed him, "Take note! There is the Lamb of God!" John declared, signifying that Jesus was superior.

So after the two disciples of John heard this, both left John and started following Jesus.

Then after some time, Jesus looked around and saw them following him; he turned and addressed them, "What is it that you want?" He asked.

"Rabbi" (Teacher), "where is it you are staying?" They ask, a gentle way of requesting to be a disciple.

"Come, and you will see for yourselves," Jesus invited, granting their request.

When this took place, it was about four o'clock in the afternoon; they went with Jesus to the house where he was staying, remaining with him for the rest of the day until sunset.

Andrew was Simon Peter's brother and was one of the men who had heard what John had said about Jesus, then they had followed him.

Andrew went off and found his brother, Simon, and told him, "We have found the one who is the Messiah" (*Christ, in the Greek, the Anointed One*), "the one about whom Moses and all the Prophets wrote."

The tangible, even particular excitement of this extraordinary event, would extinguish all the anguish from centuries of longing, even yearning, of all who had waited in hope for this moment to arrive; the realizing of Israel's Messiah, the King.

Then Andrew went to get Simon and brought him to meet Jesus.

Staring intently at Simon, "Your name is Simon," (*He Who Hears to 'hear; listen.'*)

"Son of John (*Yôḥānān, Jehovah has been gracious*), Still your name will be Cephas," (*Peter*). Jesus told him.

The day following John's declaration, Jesus decided to go to Galilee. Then having found Philip there, he invited him also, "Come, and follow me." Jesus told Philip.

Philip's hometown is called Bethsaida; this is the same town from which Andrew and Peter came. (The name Bethsaida is of Aramaic origin, meaning the "fishing house" or "the house of fishing." The town's location was on the north shore of the Sea of Galilee east of the Jordan River).

Philip went off to look for a close friend Nathanael (*God has given*), and having found him, he told him the thrilling news, "We have found the very person, the Messiah of Israel, the one that Moses and the Prophets wrote about! He is called Jesus, who is the son of Joseph from Nazareth," said Philip excitedly, using language that would appeal to his friend.

"Nazareth!" exclaimed Nathanael. "Can anything good come out of Nazareth?" He asked although he was adamant yet showing a depth of knowledge of the Scriptures.

"Well, just come and see for yourself," Philip replied, echoing the invitation that Jesus had given, knowing that this is the real need of this man who is true to himself.

As the two of them approached Jesus, he spoke about Nathanael, "Now here is a genuine son of Israel! A man without guile and one of complete integrity," said Jesus to the others as a way of greeting his arrival, carrying significant meanings for Nathaniel, the seeker of the Messiah.

Jacob (*whose name had meant deceiver before being changed to Israel*), was the father of the Israelites, often (*full of guile*), yet Nathaniel would know (Psalm 32 CEB which starts, **'Blessed is the man against whom the Lord counts no iniquity, and in whose spirit there is no deceit**.')

So this surprising greeting reminded the seeker Nathanael; of the prophecy in Zephaniah, chapter 3: 'The restoration of Israel,' which responded with a well-known song.

First, it says as prophecy, *'The remnant of Israel shall not do iniquity, nor speak lies; neither will they will find a deceitful tongue in their mouth,'*

And is responded to with the singing of, *'The King of Israel, even Jehovah, is in the midst of thee; you will not fear evil any more.'*

"How do you know about me?" Nathaniel asked with surprise.

"Before Philip came and found you, I could see you under the fig tree," Jesus replied. (*The fig tree was the symbol for God's salvation in Israel, and being under it was often a place of deep reflection on the nature of that salvation.*)

"Rabbi, you truly are the Son of God! The King of Israel," Nathanael exclaimed.

"Do you now accept this as true because I told you I had seen you under the fig tree?" Jesus asked him, "You will see greater things than this."

"I tell you the solemn truth. You will all see the heavens open and the Angels of God going up to Heaven and returning down to the Son of Man, the one who is the stairway between Heaven and Earth," said Jesus, taking his mind back to the great dream of Jacob.

CHAPTER FOUR

JESUS AND SOME DISCIPLES RECEIVE AN INVITATION TO A WEDDING.

The following day there was a wedding celebration in the village of Cana in Galilee.

Mary, the mother of Jesus, was one of the guests at the celebrations; also, Jesus and his disciples were among the guests invited to the festivities.

At some time during the feast, the wine supply ran out, so Mary found her son, "They have no more wine; it is just about all finished." She told him.

"Dear woman is that any of our business," Jesus replied, "My time has not arrived as yet."

However, his mother went to speak to the servants about her son, "Do whatever it is that he instructs you to do." She told them.

Nearby within the house's compound were positioned six stone water jars, used to hold the water supply for Jewish ceremonial washing. Each could hold twenty to thirty gallons.

Jesus instructed the servants, "Fill up all the jars with water." He directed them.

The servants did this, and they filled them to the brim.

When the jars had been filled, "Now fill your pitchers and take them to the host." Jesus instructed.

Accordingly, the servants followed his instructions.

When the master of ceremonies had a taste, he found he was tasting wine. He did not know where they had gotten the wine. (*Though, of course, the servants knew*), he beckoned for the bridegroom. "Every host always begins by serving their finest and best wine first," he exclaimed with wonderment. "Then, and only after the guests have had a lot to drink, he brings out the less expensive wine, while you instead have kept the best until last!"

This miraculous sign done at Cana in Galilee marked the first time Jesus revealed the first glimpse of his glory. And after his disciples had seen this, they knew he was the Messiah trusting and had faith in Jesus.

After the wedding, he stayed in Capernaum for a few days with his mother, brothers, and disciples (*Capernaum, meaning 'consolation' from 'Kefar Nahum'*).

JESUS DEMONSTRATES HIS AUTHORITY IN THE JERUSALEM TEMPLE.

It was nearly time for Israel's Passover celebration, so Jesus went to Jerusalem. As he entered the Temple area, he saw merchants selling animals for sacrifices, including cattle, sheep, and doves. Also, he noted at tables, dealers exchanging foreign money for local coins.

Jesus went and found some ropes, then made a whip, and with the whip, he chased them all out of the Temple, driving out the sheep and cattle, scattering the coins of the moneychangers as he overturned their tables.

Then, going around to those who sold doves, he shouted, "Remove these things and get them out of here. Stop destroying my Father's house by making it into a marketplace!"

When his disciples saw this, they remembered a prophecy from the Scriptures written in the Psalms: "*The Passion for the house of God will consume me.*" (Psalm 69:9).

Psalm 119:139 (NKJV) ***My zeal has consumed me because my enemies have forgotten your words.***

However, the Jewish leaders arrived demanding of him, "What are you doing? If God gave you the authority to do this, show us a miraculous sign to prove it!"

"You shall destroy this Temple, and in three days, I will (*raise it up*) again!" was the only reply Jesus would give them. Turning, he walked away from them.

"What!" They exclaimed, calling after him. "It has already taken forty-six years to build this Temple, and you can rebuild it in three days?"

However, when he said, "This Temple," he spoke here of his own body, and it was only later after he was raised from the dead that his disciples remembered he had said this, and then they believed both the Scriptures and what Jesus had said.

During this time that he was at the Passover Feast in Jerusalem, many people spoke well of Jesus. They approved of him after they noticed the miracles he was performing and recognized that those miracles demonstrated the power of God.

However, Jesus did not place any confidence in them. He was aware of their human nature and knew how untrustworthy they were. He did not need their testimony or any help in seeing the truth about them.

THE PHARISEE NICODEMUS MEETS WITH JESUS AT NIGHT.

One of the Pharisee sects was Nicodemus, a prominent ruler among The Chief Priests and Leaders!

One evening after dark, he came to speak with Jesus, "Rabbi," he greeted Jesus, "all of us know you are a teacher straight from God. Your miraculous signs are the evidence that God is with you."

"In truth, I tell you, unless you are born again, you cannot see the Kingdom of God," Jesus told him, with no preamble or hesitation.

"What do you mean by born again?" Nicodemus asked genuinely, grasping to understand. "How would it be possible for an old man to go back into the womb of his mother and be born again?"

"You are completely right." Jesus replied, seeing Nicodemus's confusion, "I tell you the solemn truth." He continued. "Unless a person is born from above, it is not possible to understand what I am telling you about the Kingdom of God.

I assure you beyond doubt; Where the Kingdom of God is concerned, no person can enter unless born first of water and then of Spirit.

Humans are only capable of reproducing human life, but the Holy Spirit gives birth to spiritual life.

So do not be amazed when I say, 'You must be born again.' See how the wind blows wherever it wants. And just as you can hear the wind, but you cannot tell from where it is coming or where it is going, in the same way, you cannot explain how people are born of the Spirit." Jesus explained patiently.

"What do you mean? How can these things be possible?" Nicodemus asked, his faith shaken, being completely surprised at what he heard.

"You are a leader in Israel, a respected teacher, and yet you do not understand these things?" Jesus asked him with surprise, expecting him to have known this from the scriptures.

(*Note that Jesus expected Nicodemus to know about this from the scriptures; there are several places where the Word of God dealt with this. There are both implied and explicit references.

We see in Ezekiel 36: (NKJV), from verse twenty-five, five salient points.
- *Then I will sprinkle clean water on you, and you shall be clean; I will cleanse you from all your filthiness and from all your idols.*
- *I will give you a new heart and put a new spirit within you;*
- *I will take the heart of stone out of your flesh and give you a heart of flesh.*
- *I will put My Spirit within you and cause you to walk in My statutes,*
- *And you will keep My judgments and do them.*

As a prominent teacher of the people, Nicodemus would have intimate knowledge of these writing in scriptures but would have only ever appended them to the Nation of Israel, not to personal internal rebirth.

We see in Psalm 51 (NKJV) corresponding five points from verse two.
- *Wash me thoroughly from my iniquity and cleanse me from my sin.*
- *Purge me with hyssop, and I shall be clean; wash me, and I shall be whiter than snow.*
- *Create in me a clean heart, O God.*
- *And renew a steadfast spirit within me.*
- *Restore to me the joy of your salvation, and uphold me by your generous Spirit).*

We can find implied examples in the scriptures, such as in the book of Genesis; note in the life of Judah his astonishing conversion; from being a rogue to a reformed repentant man of God. Who would even offer his own life to save the life of his brother Benjamin Genesis 44:33, a far cry from being the one who wanted to make a profit, from selling his brother Joseph into slavery! (Genesis 37:26.)

Right in the middle of this incredible transformation, we see Judah's speech that convinced his reluctant father to release Benjamin into his charge.

> Genesis 43:8-9. (NKJV) **Then Judah said to Israel, his father, 'Send the lad with me, and we will arise and go, that we may live and not die, both we and you and also our little ones. I myself will be surety for him; from my hand, you shall require him. If I do not bring him back to you and set him before you, then let me bear the blame forever.'**

Is it any wonder then it's said of the glorified Jesus ("...*Behold, the Lion of the tribe of Judah, the Root of David*... Revelation 5:5, NKJV).

"I tell you truthfully, our testimony is about what we know and has seen, and yet you will not believe. However, if you do not accept it as true, when I tell you about earthly things, how will you possibly trust and have faith in me if I tell you about heavenly things?" Jesus asked him resolutely to reinforce his faith.

"No person has ever gone up to Heaven and returned. Yet the Son of Man has come down from Heaven." He continued.

"As a bronze snake was (lifted up), on a pole by Moses in the wilderness (Number 21:4-9), so similarly, the Son of Man must be 'lifted up,' by this everyone who receives as true, trusting with faith in him will have eternal life.

Because God has loved the world so much that he gave his only begotten Son, so everyone believing as true, trust and have faith in him will not perish but will have eternal life.

The Son of God was sent into the world by God, not for him to judge the world; instead, the world will be ransomed through him.

No judgment is made against anyone who believes the truth, trusting with faith in the Son. However, anyone not taking as true or trusting in him is already judged, having not accepted the only Son of God.

The judgment is based on this. God's true light came into the world, yet people loved the darkness more than the light; because they knew their actions to be evil.

Those who perform evil hate the light and refuse to go near it for fear their sins will be exposed. While those who do what is right. Advance to the light. So others can see they are doing the things God wants." Jesus explained authoritatively.

Nicodemus went away with the deepest, most profound truths he had ever heard to ponder and digest.

Along with his disciples, Jesus left Jerusalem, traveled over into the Judean countryside, and spent time baptizing many people.

John, the son of Zachariah, was also baptizing at Aenon; this is near Salim, a region with plenty of water needed for the volume of people coming for his baptism. (*This, of course, was during the time before Herod Antipas threw John into prison*).

Aenon is situated on the west side of the Jordan, located close to Salim. Gen 14:17-24 Melchizedek was the King of Salem (Gen 14:18), the City of Sikima, which is Shechem.

A debate had broken out between John's disciples and some Pharisees; the issue was over ceremonial cleansing.

[The Pharisees, meaning (*pure or separated*), was a fitting name for this fanatical group, who restricted themselves from any person they considered being unrighteous. While establishing many irrelevant commandments associated with their pursuit of holiness. They viewed even treating a sick person on the Sabbath (official rest day) to be working.

Made up of two factions, the largest group following the teachings of a rabbi named Shammai. Developed to become religious fundamentalists, shunning and prohibited eating with, purchasing food from, or even entering the house of a Gentile; otherwise, they would consider themselves to have become defiled.

A smaller group was followers of a rabbi named Hillel. Who placed people and the need for justice as their core interpretation of the Torah and accepted Gentile converts. Hillel died about the time Jesus was still in his early teens, and in due course, was succeeded by his grandson Gamaliel, who had a famous pupil by the name of Saul of Tarsus].

The disciples of John approached him to inform him about the Pharisee's dispute. Saying, "Teacher, we saw the man you identified as the Messiah that you met on the other side of the Jordan River. He is here baptizing people as well. And everyone is going over to him instead of coming to us," they reported, a little woeful.

"No one can receive anything unless God from heaven gives it to him," John replied, squashing any ideas of rivalry.

"You know how I told you plainly, that, 'I am not the Messiah. I am only here to prepare his way.' The bridegroom is the one who marries the bride. The best man is just glad to stand with him and hear his vows. As a result, I am filled with joy at his success. He must now become greater and higher, and I must become less and less." He spoke, making his situation unambiguous to them.

> Hosea 2:19-20 (CEV) *I will accept you as my wife forever, and instead of a bride price I will give you justice, fairness, love, kindness, and faithfulness. Then you will truly know who I am. I will even betroth you to me in faithfulness: and you will know the LORD.*

> Isaiah 62:4 (NKJV) *You will be called 'Hephzibah (my delight is in her), and your land Beulah (Married),' for the LORD delights in you, and your land will be married.*

"He has come from above, and therefore, he is greater than anyone else." John continued, "We speak of earthly things because we are of the Earth. However, he has come from Heaven and is greater than anyone who is of the Earth.

His testimony is about what he has seen and heard, yet how few accept as real the things that he tells them!

By accepting his testimony, that person will affirm that God is true since God has sent him. He speaks the words of God; the reason is that God has given him the Spirit without limit.

The Father who loves his Son has put all things into his hands.

Likewise, anyone who believes in the Son of God has eternal life. Anyone who does not obey the Son will never experience eternal life. Still, that person remains under the angry judgment of God." John explained plainly and firmly so that his audience had no misunderstanding of the situation or whom they needed to look to or hope in.

Jesus then realized that some were busy keeping count of the number of baptisms he and John performed (*even though his disciples, not Jesus, did the actual baptizing*).

The Pharisees were making an issue by announcing the score that Jesus was ahead—intending to turn him and John into rivals in the people's eyes.

From this point in time, Jesus left the Judean countryside going back to Galilee.

MEETING WITH A SAMARITAN WOMAN.

News and reports about him spread quickly throughout the countryside and over the entire region. Jesus was returning to Galilee, filled with the power of the Holy Spirit.

He taught in all the local meeting places in each town, to the acclaim and the delight of everyone.

On the route traveling back into Galilee, Jesus had to walk through the region of Samaria. He eventually came to the Samaritan village of Sychar, near the field that Jacob gave to Joseph, his son. This place was where Jacob's well was situated. After being tired from the long walk, Jesus sat beside the well to rest; the time was about noon.

Before long, a Samaritan woman approached from the town to draw water; Jesus addressed her as she arrived at the well, "Please give me a drink of water?" was his simple request.

Jesus had sent his disciples ahead into the village to buy food and provisions, so he sat alone by the well when he met the woman.

It shocked the woman that he had spoken to her, "You are a Jew, and I am a Samaritan woman. Then why are you asking me for a drink?" She asked him, showing great surprise. Her amazement was that the Jews habitually refused to do anything to do with the Samaritans, seeing them as non-Jews and inferior.

"If only you knew who it is that you are speaking to and the gift God has for you, instead you would ask from me, and I would give to you, not ordinary water, but living water," Jesus replied.

"But sir," She said quickly, "you do not have a rope or a bucket, and this is an especially deep well. Therefore, from where would you get this living water?

Our ancestor Jacob gave this well to us and is where he and his sons drank, and even his animals.

How can you offer better water? Are you greater than our forefather who gave the well to us?" She asked him stridently as if that would settle the matter.

> Joshua 24:32 (NKJV) **The bones of Joseph, which the children of Israel had brought up out of Egypt, they buried at Shechem, in the plot of ground which Jacob had bought from the sons of Hamor the father of Shechem for one hundred pieces of silver, and which had become an inheritance of the children of Joseph. And it became the inheritance of the children of Joseph.'** (Genesis 33:19).

"I assure you; those who drink of this water will before long, become thirsty again. Yet, those who drink the water that I give will never become thirsty again. It develops into a fresh bubbling spring within, giving eternal life," replied Jesus, confirming that he was indeed greater than Jacob.

"Sir," Said the woman, her tone softened, "Please give me this water! After that, I will never be thirsty again, and I will not have to come here anymore to get water."

"Go get your husband and then return," Jesus instructed her.

"I do not have a husband," The woman replied.

"Yes, you are right to say that you do not have a husband! Indeed, for you have had five husbands, and you are not married to the man you are living with now. Therefore, you certainly spoke the truth!" Jesus told her.

"Sir, I can see now that you are a Prophet," Said the woman, finally thinking spiritually.

"Well, can you tell me this, how is it you Jews maintain Jerusalem is the only place of worship? Whereas we Samaritans say, it is here at Mount Gerizim, where our ancestors worshipped?" She asked, now seeking spiritual truth.

"Dear woman, believe me, the time is coming, and indeed it is here now when it will no longer matter whether the Father is worshipped on this mountain or in Jerusalem.

You Samaritans discern very little knowledge about the one you worship. In contrast, we Jews know the truth about him since salvation comes through the Jews. However, I tell you the time is coming; in reality, it is here now, for all who worship the Father will do so in spiritual worship as well as in the truth.

The Father is seeking those who will worship him in that way. Since God is Spirit, therefore, those who worship him must worship in Spirit and truth." Jesus explained.

"I know that the Messiah called The Anointed One that we have been waiting for! After He arrives, He will explain everything to us." The woman exclaimed; her faith and her discernment were increasing.

"I, who is speaking to you, am the Messiah!" Jesus told her bluntly.

At that moment, his disciples arrive back. Though they were surprised to find him talking to a Samaritan woman, yet none of them dared pose the question, "What do you seek with this woman?" Or "Why are you conversing with her?"

(*The surprise by the disciples is because the leaders taught that Rabbis did not speak with any women in public, even family members.*)

Leaving the water jar beside the well, the woman hurried back to the village, "Come and see a man who told me about everything I ever did! Could he possibly be the Messiah?" She said eagerly, telling everyone she met with excitement and joy.

On the strength of this statement, the people came streaming from the village to see Jesus.

Meanwhile, his disciples were concerned about Jesus, "Teacher, please eat something." They urged him.

"I have food, a kind of food about which you know nothing," Jesus replied.

This statement confused the disciples; they asked each other. "Where did he get food? Did someone bring it to him while we were away?"

"My sustenance," Jesus interrupted their misperception, "is from doing the will of God, who sent me; and from completing the work of my Father.

You know the saying, 'there are up to four months to harvest, after the planting.' However, I tell you, wake up and look around you. The fields are already ripe for harvest."

He said, trying to get their minds away from food to more profound spiritual matters. As they stood observing the approaching people streaming out from the village.

"Harvesters receive good wages, and the fruit they harvest is people brought to eternal life. So what joy is equally awaiting, the planter and the harvester!

Yes, you know the saying, 'there is one who plants and then other harvests.' Yes, it is true. I send you harvesting where you did not plant; others had already done that work, but now you gain the opportunity to gather in the harvest." Jesus told them, conveying to them his enthusiasm.

Many Samaritans from the village came to believe who Jesus was, because of the woman's testimony, when she informed them, "He told me about everything that I ever did!"

After they had turned out to see him, they begged him to stay in their village. So he stayed with them there for two days, long enough for many more to hear his message and believe he was the Messiah of Israel.

The people from the village spoke about Jesus to the woman, "Now we do believe," They declared with conviction, "not only because of what you have told us, but because we have now heard him for ourselves. We know he is, without a doubt, the Saviour of the world."

MEETING THE OFFICIAL WITH A SICK SON.

Jesus continually preached this message during this time, "Repent of your sins and turn to God, observe how near the Kingdom of Heaven is to you.

After the end of the two days, Jesus continued his journey onwards to Galilee. Jesus himself had said before that his own does not exalt a Prophet either in his hometown; as a result, even though the Galileans initially welcomed him when he arrived in Galilee, it was only because it had impressed them through what he had done in Jerusalem during the Passover Feast.

As Jesus traveled through the region of Galilee, he came to Cana, 'where he had turned the water into wine.' In this region, there was a government official in the nearby town of Capernaum whose son was very sick.

When he heard that Jesus had come back to Galilee from Judea, he went and pleaded with Jesus to go with him to Capernaum to heal his son, whom he said was about to die. (*This government official was of the Royal household, possibly a relative of the Herods.*)

"Will you never accept me as true, having trust and faith, unless you see miraculous signs and wonders?" Jesus asked, addressing the people in general, about their level of belief or lack thereof.

The Official asks all the more, "Lord, please come now before my little boy dies." He said with deep reverence.

"Go on back home. Your son will live!" Jesus told him this would now be a matter of faith in his word.

The Official believed what Jesus said, whom he had just proclaimed 'Lord,' and so started back home.

Some of the official servants met him with the good news of his son's recovery while he was on his way and announced that his son was alive and well.

He inquired of the servants, the precise time that the boy had begun to get better, "Yesterday afternoon at one o'clock, the fever suddenly disappeared!" They replied.

The child's father realized it was the very time Jesus had told him. "Your son will live."

So he and his entire household came to believe the good news about Jesus as the Saviour. This made the second miraculous sign that Jesus performed in the Galilee region.

*(Note, the issue here is that the people of Cana had arrived with the Official, looking to see a miracle. His need was real and desperate; theirs was just one of curiosity.

Jesus had left Jerusalem going through Samaria proceeding north, and word had spread about all the things he did whilst in the city, but he knew it was too soon to have a great outpouring of Messianic fever and was always careful not to stir it up.

Had he gone with the Official to his home, the crowds would have followed for the wrong reasons. Jesus did miracles so people would believe God is a loving father; here, the people were unbelieving, even dismissive and skeptical about him. He was local to them, and there was no belief or faith; they just wanted to know what he could do. People were sure that nothing great could come from the region of Galilee as wrongly taught by the experts in the law. The Prophets Nahum, Jonah, and others had come from Galilee. But National prejudice against the Galileans persisted even from the locals. The Official left quietly with faith in Jesus' word, so the people who wanted to see proof had no excitement that day).

PREACHING IN THE SYNAGOGUE AT NAZARETH.

On his arrival back in his hometown where he grew up, the village of Nazareth, he went as it was his usual practice to the synagogue on the Sabbath.

Jesus stood up to read the Scriptures. An attendant handed a scroll to him; it was by Isaiah the Prophet. After unrolling the scroll, Jesus found and read these verses, "The Spirit from the Lord rest on me since he has anointed me to announce the good news to the poor. He has sent me to proclaim freedom (deliverance) for the captives, the recovery of sight to the blind and setting free the oppressed; to proclaim also the year of the favor of the Lord" *(Jubilee).

This Scripture from Isaiah 61 spoke of the Messiah and the five areas of his mission. Yet, he halted before the part of the verse, which reads, "And the day of vengeance of our God." That portion will have its fulfillment during the kingdom era, which could begin immediately.

(The Kingdom, which was announced 'at hand,' he would soon offer officially).

But it may not apply to this, which could be his first and his only advent, subject to the Nation's choice.

Then after rolling up the scroll and then handing it back to the attendant, he sat down.

All the eyes of the people in the synagogue scrutinized him.

Then he addressed them, "The Scripture that you have just heard, has now, being this very day comprehensively completed!" Jesus affirmed, stating it with authority.

The people were voicing many praises, as they spoke well of him, they were astonished about the very gracious words he was saying. "How can this be?" They asked. "Is this not the son of Joseph?" Some questioned.

"You will surely quote me this proverb, 'Physician, heal yourself,' meaning, 'Do for us here in your hometown, the miracles, like the ones that you did over in Capernaum.' However, I tell you the solemn truth; People accept everywhere a Prophet save in his hometown.

"Without doubt, there were many needy widows in Israel in the time of Elijah, when for three and a half years the heavens had been closed up, and a relentless famine devastated the land. Nevertheless, not even to a single one of them was the Prophet Elijah sent.

He was sent instead to a foreigner, a widow of Zarephath in the land of Sidon. There were many lepers in Israel also in the time of the Prophet Elisha, but the only one healed was Naaman, a Syrian," said Jesus, shocking his audience by pointing out that just being an Israelite was not enough to routinely get God's favor.

The people of the synagogue, when they heard this, became enraged and furious. They jumped up, mobbing him, and bodily forced him to the edge of the hill.

Nazareth's location was above a valley on a hill; they fully intended to throw him over the cliff situated there. However, with no effort, Jesus calmly passed right through the entire crowd and went on his way.

*Note: They conducted synagogue meetings over a lengthy period, with much debating and reasoning back and forth, and as this exchange developed.

Jesus is perhaps too familiar to his locals. They cannot identify who he really is, and as his speech is worrying and challenging; thus, they reject him. Yet, they advocate that he can gain their approval; if he performs some of the miracles they had heard about from others.

It alarmed the Nazareth locals in the synagogue when Jesus pointed out; in Israel, God would show through Grace his favor to Gentiles and not just Jews.

For them, God must show favor to Jews much more than Gentiles. It dismayed them since they had placed their security in their Jewish heritage, looking back to promises obtained by the Patriarchs.

Yet God received and is gracious to those who had accepted him.

The widow of Zarephath readily went to bring Elijah a drink of water on being asked; she willingly gave him the last of the food she had.

This was not very palatable to the hearers, not only because she was a Gentile. But their low opinion of women's status and acceptance was a severe stumbling block. With a long and steadily growing list of reasons, they would advance for not including women in many things, from being untouchable as unclean to lack of credibility.

Naaman is the perfect antidote to their lack of faith and stubborn behavior. On hearing, he could be healed, responded in faith with action by traveling to Israel.

Though initially incensed, Naaman repented from his fury, going as Elisha told him to bathe in the Jordan.

Naaman obeyed the Word of God from the Prophet to wash in the Jordan seven times, yielding his pride; he obeyed in humility after his original irritation.

Then he went back down to the Galilean town called Capernaum. This was a walk of about 20 miles, and he stayed there and taught in the synagogue every Sabbath day.

So because he had first gone to Nazareth and then after leaving there had settled in Capernaum, by the Sea of Galilee, in the region of Zebulun and Naphtali. It became the fulfillment of what God said through Isaiah the Prophet,

> "In the land of Zebulun and Naphtali on the side of the sea, over past the Jordan River, in Galilee, where so many Gentiles live. The people who had sat in darkness have now seen a glorious light. And for those who lived in the land where death casts its shadow, a light has now shined." (Isaiah 9:2).

> Hosea 1:10-11, however, the number of the children of Israel will be as the sand of the sea, which cannot be measured or numbered. It will take place, that in the place where it was told to them, 'You are not my people,' yet there they will be told, 'You are the sons of the living God.'
> Then the children of Judah and the children of Israel will be gathered together, appointing themselves one head and will come up out of the land: because great will be the day of Jezreel.

> [The region called Galilee was part of the portion of land distribution given to the tribes of Zebulun and Naphtali.
> Also, what was termed 'Galilee of the Gentiles' was where Israel and the Gentile world came together. The western shore along the Sea of Galilee, or the Jezreel Valley, had a long history of a mixture of people, populated first with the Canaanites and Hittites, then with Hebrews, later Arameans, and conquered people from Mesopotamia.
> The expression 'the way of the sea' referred to the Roman road that ran from the Sea of Chinnereth, the ancient city of Damascus, going to the Mediterranean northern Seaports.

The northern Kingdom, collectively known by the two largest tribes, the land of Zebulun and the land of Naphtali, had been subdued over seven hundred years before the time of Jesus (Kings 15:29).

The Assyrian King Tiglath-Pileser 3rd; ruler over the Assyria empire (744-727 BC), was used by God to conquer Israel's Northern Kingdom, as he said he would because of their sin in the land.

There was also a second wave of invasion by Shalmaneser, King of Assyria.

Later the Assyrians repopulated the land with various foreign groups they had taken in Conquest.

Samaria was one of the areas taken over.

(2 Kings 17:24, the King of Assyria brought men from Babylon, and Cuthah, and Ava, and from Hamath, and Sepharvaim, and placed them in the cities of Samaria instead of the children of Israel: and they possessed Samaria, and dwelt in the cities).

He will give up Israel due to the sins Jeroboam has committed, causing the Israelites to sin by leading them into idolatry. 1 Kings 14:16

However, Isaiah named two of the ten northern tribes Zebulun and Naphtali. He said that God would in the future give great honor to Galilee of the Gentiles. Yes, indeed, there was a time coming when a glorious light would shine in Galilee, removing all the darkness and gloom resulting from the invasion and the spoiling of the land by the Assyrians].

Beside the Sea of Galilee, one day, two brothers were busy fishing! Throwing a net into the water because fishing was what they did for a living. These two men were Simon, who Jesus had earlier said would be called Peter, and Andrew, his brother.

Jesus saw them at their work as he walked along by the shore and shouted to them, "Come and follow me. I will teach you how you will fish for people from now on!"

Straight away, they left all their nets there and followed Jesus.

Note; Fishes as living creatures died after being caught; the Ekklesia (called out: assembly) of Jesus catches people that are spiritually dead for life to be given to them.

As he walked a little farther up the shore, he saw two other brothers, James and John; they sat in a boat repairing their nets with Zebedee, their father.

Jesus also called them, "come follow me." He told them.

Without delay, they left the boat and their father and the business behind and followed Jesus; the time had come, and the master was calling them to something new.

This selection was now the official call to discipleship. In that era, it was an immense honor for any Israelite to be one of those selected as a disciple of any great Rabbi.

A day came when Jesus was preaching near the lake, by the shore of the Sea of Galilee, great crowds had gathered to listen to the Word of God, and as the crowd swelled, they pressed in on him. Jesus noticed two empty boats at the edge of the water; the fisherman who owned the vessels had cleared them out and was on the beach washing and cleaning the fishing nets.

Of one of the empty boats that was moored there, Jesus stepped in and asked Simon, its owner, to push out into the water. From this position on the water, he taught the crowds while sitting in the boat.

After he had finished teaching the people, Jesus spoke to Simon, "Now, push the boat far out to deeper water; then let down your nets for a catch of some fishes." He clearly instructed him to let down the nets, including the ones they had been washing, being the newer and stronger nets.

"Master," Simon replied, "We worked hard all through last night and did not catch a thing. Though if you say so, I am going to let down again one of the nets," He explained.

Simon did this reluctantly. Because of this, he did not return for the nets that they were washing before setting out. Jesus had directly told him to let down all of his fishing nets.

When he let the net down into the water, he found this time that the single fishing net was so full of fish; it began to tear! Simon had to shout to his partners in the other boat for some help. Soon, both ships were so full of fish caught; that they were on the verge of sinking.

Simon, when he had finally grasped what happened. He fell to his knees with sorrow for his behavior, "Oh, Lord, please leave me! Because I am too much of a sinner to be around you," He said, pleading with Jesus.

As they work to pull in the catch of fish, all the fishermen helping Simon, including James and John, the sons of Zebedee, were amazed at the number of fishes they had caught.

"There is nothing to fear!" Jesus replied to Simon, "From this time on, I will instruct you to be the fishers for people!" He reassured him.

As soon as they navigated the boat to the shore, they left everything there with relatives and hired hands so that they could follow Jesus.

Jesus set off with his disciples back to the town called Capernaum. As usual, when it was the Sabbath day, he went to the synagogue, stood up, and was teaching the people.

His teaching amazed all; because quite unlike the teachers of religious law. Who taught by quoting how Rabbi said such, and Rabbi taught this or that thing. Jesus taught directly and distinctly from his unique, authentic authority and with power.

Abruptly, right there in the synagogue, a possessed man who was tormented with an evil spirit began shouting out, "Why are you here interfering with us, Jesus of Nazareth? Have you come to put us in distress? He screamed. "I know who you are," He spoke challengingly. "The Holy One sent from God!"

Jesus told the demon to be silent. "Be quiet! Come out of the man," He ordered. At that, the evil spirit screamed, and after throwing the man into a convulsion, it then came out of him.

Astonishment gripped all the people, and they started asking each other just what had happened. "What sort of new teaching is this?" They exclaimed excitedly. "It has such power and authority! Even the evil spirits obey his commands!"

After this, news about Jesus' teachings, power over sickness, and the authority he commanded quickly spread over the entire region of Galilee.

Upon leaving the synagogue, Jesus went with James and John to the home of the brothers Simon and Andrew. The mother-in-law of Simon was in bed sick with a high fever. Right away, they notified Jesus about her condition.

As a result, he went to her bedside; he took her hand and helped her sit up. Straight away, the fever left her, and she could go off and prepare a meal for them.

That evening after sunset, the people of the region bought many sick and demon-possessed people to the house for Jesus to heal.

The entire town had gathered at the door and about the house to watch. Then, Jesus healed the people who were ill with various diseases, and he cast out all the demons out of many of them.

Demons possessed many people, and the demons had to come out at his command. They did so, shouting, "You are the Son of God!" Since they knew he was the Messiah.

Jesus rebuked them and refused to let them speak or give any of their unwanted testimony about him.

By the end of that day, he had healed all the sick that they bought to him, bringing to completion the Word of God spoken through the Prophet Isaiah, who said, "He took all our sicknesses and removed our diseases."

Jesus left early the following day and went off to pray in an isolated place. Simon and the others went out to search to find him. When they eventually found him, they asked him to return, "Everyone is out looking for you." They informed him.

The crowds had been searching everywhere for him, and when they finally saw him return, they urged him to stay with them and not to leave them.

"I must also go preach the Good News of the Kingdom of God in other towns as well; that is the reason I was sent," Jesus explained to them.

Jesus and the disciples then left the area as Jesus continued to travel around, preaching near Galilee and throughout Judea, teaching in the synagogues, healing, and casting out demons.

CHAPTER FIVE

TEACHING THE BENEFITS AND PROTOCOLS OF THE KINGDOM.

Jesus traveled out to the lake with his disciples, and a large crowd followed him. The crowd was made up of people from all over Galilee, Judea, Jerusalem, Idumea, and east of the Jordan River. Some came even from as far north as Tyre and Sidon. The good news about Jesus and the miracles that he did had spread throughout these regions. This caused large numbers of people to come to see him.

Jesus gave instructions to his disciples for them to have a boat ready, so the size of the crowd would not mob him.

He had healed many of the people that day, and because of that reason, the sick people eagerly pushed forward to touch him. So whenever those people who were possessed or tormented by evil Spirits would see him. The Spirits would immediately throw them to the ground before him, shrieking, "You are the Son of God!"

Each time, he would sternly command the spirits to not reveal who he was, not wanting any verification from them.

Not long after that, Jesus went up on a mountain where he prayed; he remained in prayer to God right the way through the night. Then at dawn, he called all of his disciples together, and from them, he chose twelve of them he later named apostles. They were selected to be with him; as a result, he would be able to send them out to preach and to give them the authority to heal sicknesses and to cast out demons:

These are the names of those disciples chosen.

The first was Simon, also named Peter by Jesus, and his brother Andrew. James, and his brother John the sons of Zebedee, he surnamed them Boanerges (meaning, Sons of Thunder). Philip and Bartholomew (or Nathanael), Bar-tholomew (son of Tolmai). Matthew, the tax collector, (Who is Levi). Thomas, James, the son of Alphaeus, Simon the (Canaanite), the Zealot as he was known, Judas or Lebbaeus, whose surname was Thaddaeus, the son of James. Judas Iscariot, who became a traitor and also who it was that betrayed him.

On his arrival back down from the mountain, Jesus could see a great multitude of people waiting all over the hillside for him. He went a little way back up the side of the hill and found a level place where they rested with several disciples. The disciples got the crowds seated and settled comfortably on the grass.

Presently he was seated, and his disciples came close and assembled around him.

Jesus embarked on teaching all the multitude of people, including the disciples, the correct means of happiness in the Kingdom, through inner conversion.

The beautiful lake below them saw the sun glistening as the light shimmered across it; the water sparkling with life and the warmth of the day: as it reflected the surrounding blue-green hills and a sky dotted here and there with drifting white clouds.

Tall, elegant fir trees swayed genteelly at the edge of the lake; from its edge, a mound was richly dotted with these and other vegetation, all competing for closeness to the edge of the water. The birds and other creatures made a constant rich symphony as a backdrop to the day.

Out from among the trees and up the hill proper, beautiful long grass was everywhere; people sat in groups, some comprising families, grouped there also were arrays of friends and traveling companions.

All listened intently as the Lord's voice was carried on the soft breeze; the words came crisp and clear, with his voice firm and rich.

He informed them, "Bless *(Happy, set apart, exalted, complete), are you, those that are poor in Spirit! *(Humbly accepting that they are empty and have a desperate need for the Spirit of God), the reason is that they will have the Kingdom of Heaven.

Bless are you, those who mourn, *(a sincere and deep sorrow for all sin, ours, and others); the reason is that they will be reassured, *(total freedom from the weight of guilt and oppression).

Bless are those of you, the humble, *(to view, carrying through God's standards with patience and humility, in his power, rather than our own). They are the people who inherit the land.

Bless are you, those who hunger and thirst for righteousness, *(seeing God's just way of living as the only essential for life). The reason is that there is a fullness that they will receive.

Bless are you, those of you who weep now, *(we mourn because we are slaves to sin, a 'filthy garment'). The reason is that you will be full of joy.

Bless are you, those that are merciful, *(knowing God's Law of the Kingdom and his Grace, and how much forgiveness we have received, so be ready to extend that Grace through love). The reason is that they will acquire mercy.

Bless are you, the ones that are pure in heart, *(the truth within the heart, where God is always first). The reason is that they will see God.

Bless are you, those that are the peacemakers, *(only the ones justified by faith in God can carry true peace, which is his Spirit). The reason is that they will be called the children of God.

Bless are you, those of you who had been mistreated. Since you are committed to living for God's righteousness,' *(you are sure to be falsely accused, but you will be in the company of the honorable). The reason is that yours is the Kingdom of Heaven.

"Bless are you, when people accuse you, mistreat you, and say all kinds of evil against you falsely because you carry my name.

Bless are you, when men will hate you, and when they will exclude and ridicule you, putting your name out as evil because of the Son of Man.

In that day, celebrate and be especially joyful, leaping with delight; because great is your reward in Heaven. |Since their fathers did the same to the Prophets, as it is how the prophets who were here before you were persecuted.

"However, watch out to you who are rich since you have already received your comfort.

Watch out to those of you who are full now because you will be hungry. Watch out, to you, who laugh now, because you will mourn and weep.

It would be best for you to be aware when men speak well of you since their fathers were doing the same to the false Prophets.

"You are akin to salt, the salt of the Earth, but when the salt has lost its flavor, then how can it be re-salted?

It is then not good for anything except to be cast out and trampled under the feet of men.

You then are the great light, giving that light to this world. Just as no city can be concealed or obscured while its location is the top of a hill.

People will not place a lamp under a measuring basket after lighting it, but on a stand, and it shines, giving light to the occupants of the entire house.

Likewise, your light should also shine before men; that way, they can see your good works, and after they see it, they will glorify your Father, who is in Heaven.

Do not imagine that I came to destroy the writings in the law or the works of the Prophets. I did not come to destroy, but in fact, to fulfill.

Most certainly, I will tell you this from now until Heaven and Earth pass away. Not even one of the writing's smallest letters or even one of the tiny pen strokes having been established in the Word of God and Scriptures will in any way disappear because they will complete all the things written in them.

For that reason, the one who will break one of the least of the commandments and teach others to do the same, that person will be called least in the Kingdom of Heaven. However, any person who will do what they say and explain them to others will be called great in the Kingdom of Heaven.

I tell you unless your ways and standards towards God surpass those of these Pharisees and Scribes, no way can you enter the Kingdom of Heaven."

(*Note: Breaking one of the least of the commandments here is not referring primarily to the laws of Moses. But the new standards of the Kingdom surpassing those of the Scribes and Pharisees, which presumes all Moses' laws, are already kept and exceed).

"It was told to your forefathers as you no doubt heard, 'You shall do no murder,' and also, 'Anyone who commits murder will be in danger of the judgment.'

However, hear what I am saying to you; everyone who is even angry at his brother with no just cause will be in danger of facing the judgment.

Also, anyone who will say to his brother, 'idiot!' shall be in danger of the council, and the one who will say, 'You fool!' will be at risk of the fire of Gehenna."

*('I am saying to you,' and 'I am telling you.' Means Jesus is placing his commandments; on a higher level than the laws given to Moses. The Pharisees were very zealous about keeping the laws of the Torah. Yet, Jesus is declaring; 'the kingdom standards' surpass their efforts, even as those Pharisees were also standing there among the crowds.

Nine of the ten main commandments given to Moses dealt with our outwards posture, attitude, and behavior. Which meant those that were super religious could put on an outward show, with the appearance that they kept and satisfied the requirements even if they did not.

All of Jesus' commandments go further and require a change in the inner man to keep them. (*Pretence is still possible but harder*).

An eye for an eye now becomes; love, and pray for those who wrong you!

Do not commit murder becomes, do not hate your fellow man.

No human can keep all of Moses' law, not even Moses, who sinned.

And no human can by themselves without God's Spirit keep the much harder Commandments of Jesus).

"Suppose you should go to the altar with a gift. To make an offering, and you remember when there, anything that your brother has against you. Leaving your gift there before the altar, go resolve the issue with your brother, then return and make the offering of your gift.

Quickly make efforts to find agreements with any of your enemies. Correct things with him while you are still with him in the street; it is better than waiting for him to make peace. He may only want to prosecute you, and by letting it end up in front of a court and judge, it may get you locked in prison, where you would be required to pay a high price.

Some say you no doubt heard, 'You must not commit adultery.' Still, I tell you, everyone, staring at a woman lusting after her has already committed adultery in his heart.

So with this in mind, if you find that your right eye is the cause of you stumbling, pluck it out and throw it away from you. As it is much better for you to have one of your body parts cease its function than for you to end up thrown into Gehenna with your whole body.

Should you find the cause of your stumbling to be your right hand, then cut it off, throwing it away from you, as a lost body part is more profitable to you than for your whole body to end up cast into Gehenna.

Remember how in the Scripture it said. 'Anyone who divorces his wife let him give her legal writings of divorcement.'

However, I am telling you, if you divorce your wife in favor of any reason except the cause of sexual immorality: You make her an adulteress.

Then the one who marries her when she is divorced also commits adultery.

Remember how the Scripture said to them of ancient times. 'You will not make any false vows but will always perform your vows to the Lord.' Still, I am saying to you, do not swear by anything at all: never by Heaven, it's God's throne; nor by the Earth, being the footstool of his feet.

Swear not by Jerusalem either, as the city of the great King. Neither by your head, since you cannot make one hair on your head white or black.

Instead, be sure all your 'Yes' are 'Yes,' and your 'No's, are 'No,' everything further than those is from the evil one.

You will have heard it said, 'An eye for an eye, and a tooth for a tooth.'

However, I am telling you, do not resist the evil person; instead, if a person were to strike you on your right cheek, then turn to him the left cheek as well."

(*Note: This spoke more to Jewish legal customs than to an act of aggression or violence. There were clearly defined legal penalties and remedies' for someone to receive satisfaction and compensation via the law of the day. To say turn the other cheek was not only an act of forgiveness but stating. 'I wave that right to the fixed legal solution').

"If a person prosecutes you to take away your shirt, let him have your coat as well."

Deuteronomy 24: 12-13 (NLT) *If your neighbor is poor and gives you his cloak as security for a loan, do not keep the cloak overnight. Return the cloak to its owner by sunset so he can stay warm through the night and bless you, and the Lord, your God, will count you as righteous.*

Deuteronomy 24:17 (NLT) *True justice must be given to foreigners living among you and to orphans, and you must never accept a widow's garment as security for her debt*.

*Note: Because a cloak (*himation*) could not be taken as security against a loan (because a cloak could be used as a blanket at night), the inner garment (*chiton*) or tunic was often demanded as surety.

If a person insists you must go with him one mile, then go with him two. *(Roman soldiers had a rule (*but not a formal law*) concerning occupied Nations, allowing them to order (*compel*) a person they considered capable of carrying the soldier's belongings (*this pack could be heavy*), doing so for up to a distance of a thousand paces or a Roman mile (*mille passus*). As expected, the practice was generally a detested and contentious issue in Israel).

"Give kindly to the one who asks you; do not turn away anyone who desires to borrow from you.

You no doubt have heard the saying, 'You should love your neighbor, and many have indirectly used it to hate your enemy.'

However, I am telling those who hear, love not only your neighbor but your enemies as well. Those who curse you, bless them, those who hate you do them good, and pray for those who mistreat you and discriminate against you.

Give generously to everyone who asks you and those who would take away your goods. Let it go without asking for it to be returned.

You know how you like others to treat you, precisely the same way you should also be doing for them.

This way, you will be your Heavenly Father's children since he always makes his sun rise on the evil as the good, sending rain on the just and unjust alike.

By only loving those who love you, what kind of tribute is that to you? What reward do you have for that? Even the tax collectors do the same, right? Yes, even the sinners also love those who love them.

If you only ever greet those that are your friends, what have you done that is more than others? Do not even the tax collectors do just the same?

If you only do good things to those who do good to you, what compliment is that to you? For even sinners do the same.

When you lend only to those you hope to collect from, what compliment is that to you? Given that the sinners lend to sinners, to get back as much, do they not?

Instead, you must love your enemies and do good, and when you lend, expect nothing back. And then your reward will be great, because of this you will be the children of the Most High; since he is kind toward the ones showing no gratitude and the evil ones.

For that reason, you should be sure to be perfect and merciful, just as your Father in Heaven is perfect and gracious toward you.

Be cautious not to do your charitable giving, just so that others can see. You doing this will have no reward from your Heavenly Father.

For that reason, when you do kindly actions, do not sound a trumpet before yourself as the play-actors do in the synagogues and the streets, to receive credit and fame from men. I tell you truly, that is all the reward they will receive.

Instead, when you do kindly actions, do not allow your left hand to know what your right hand does, so that your kindly actions may be in secret, your Father who sees in secret will then reward you openly.

In your prayer time, you should be sure that you are not like the specialist play-actors. Because they love standing to pray in the synagogues and the corners of the streets so others will see them. I tell you honestly, they have received all the rewards they are going to get.

Instead, whenever you pray to your Father, go into your secret place, shut in, and pray. Your Father, who sees all secrets, will openly reward you.

While praying, do not as the Gentiles use vain repetitions; they think they will be heard for their much speaking.

For that reason, do not be like them, since your Father knows of the things that you need, even before you ask him.

Your prayer should be like this:

Our Abba, Father in Heaven, may your name always be kept holy.
Permit your Kingdom to come.
So may 'your own will' be done, as it is in Heaven, may it be also here on the Earth.
Give unto us today our daily bread, *(Needs).

Forgive us all our failures and weakness, as we also forgive others the same.

Bring us not into a time of testing, but deliver us from the evil one.

For yours, Father is the Kingdom, the power, and the Glory forever. Amen.'

Because if you forgive men of their failures and faults, you're Heavenly Father will also forgive you for your mistakes. However, if you do not forgive men for their transgressions, neither will your Father forgive you, your faults.

Furthermore, whenever you fast, do not be like the hypocrites showing sad faces because they disfigure their faces so that others may see that they are fasting. I am telling you the solemn truth; they have received all the rewards they will get.

Instead, when you fast, this is what you do, anoint your head and wash your face; so that others do not see you fasting, you are doing it unto your Father. Then you will be rewarded by your Father, who sees all secrets.

Do not build up treasures for yourselves on the Earth, where moth and rust can consume it and where thieves can break through and steal it. But stock up for yourselves treasures in Heaven; there is no moth, any rust, or thieves to rob since your heart will always be in the place where you have placed your treasure.

The eye is the body's lamp. As a result, if your eye is sound, your entire body will be full of light.

On the other hand, if your eye is evil, your entire body will be full of darkness. If, therefore, the light that is within you is just darkness, how great is that darkness!

A servant cannot serve two masters because he will either hate the one and love the other or be loyal and dedicated to one and despise the other. In the same way, you cannot possibly serve both God and Mammon *(Money).

So, I tell you, don't concern yourself for your life: or for what you will eat, or drink, not even for your body, and what you will wear. Is your life not worth so much more than food and the body more than just clothing?

Observe then that the birds of the sky do not sow, and they do not reap nor gather into barns. Yet our Father in Heaven feeds them. Then how much more value are you than they?

By being worried, are you able to add one moment to your lifespan?

Why are you concerned about clothing? Study the lilies of the field; think how they grow; they do no labor, neither do they weave cloth, yet I tell you, Solomon, in the entirety of his splendor, even his clothes could not match one of these.

Therefore, God who clothes the grass of the field, existing today only to be thrown into the oven the next day! Oh, you of little faith! He will much more clothe you, will he not?

For that reason, don't concern yourself or say anxiously, 'What will we eat?' 'What will we drink?' or even, 'what clothed will we have?'

Because the Gentiles seek after these things, yet your heavenly Father knows your needs.

I tell you, first seek God's Kingdom and his righteousness; then He will also give you all these things. So do not be fearful for tomorrow because tomorrow will be anxious about itself. The evil of each day is sufficient of its own.

Do not judge if you want to ensure that you will not be judged.

Since with whatever judgment you used to judge others, you will also be judged; with whatever measure you used to measure, it will be applied as a measure to you. Set free, and you will also be set free.

Give generously, and to you will good be given: good measure, pressed down, shaken together and running over, will be given to you since with the same standard that you measure it will be measured back to you." Jesus announced, setting out the way to live according to the Kingdom

Jesus then continued by telling a parable to the people. "How can the one who is blind guide another that is blind also? Surely both would fall into a ditch?

How can you notice the speck of sawdust that's in your brother's eye yet cannot think about the beam in your own eye?

Alternatively, how will you tell your brother, 'Brother, 'Let me get rid of the speck of chaff from your eye,' but do not regard the beam that is in your own eye?

Do not be a phony pretender! Remove the massive beam out of your own eye first, and then you will see clearly to remove the speck out of the eye of your brothers.

Be sure not to give that which is holy to the dogs, neither throw your pearls before the pigs, in case they trample them under their feet, and turn and rip you into pieces.

You will be given the things you ask for; by seeking, you will find what you requested; knock, and doors will open to you. Because every person asking receives and those seeking will find, and to the one who knocks, the door will be opened.

Otherwise, which one of you, who, if your son asks you for bread, will give him a stone, alternatively, if he was asking for a fish, who would give him a serpent?

So then, if you that are evil know how to give good gifts to your children, how much more then will good things' be provided' by your Heavenly Father, to those who ask him!

So for that reason, anything you desire, others should do for you. You also do it for them because this is the meaning behind the Law and the Prophets.

Enter into the Kingdom by the narrow gate, since the road that leads to destruction is broad and its gateway is wide, and those who enter in through it are many.

The way that leads to life is restricted! Very narrow is the gate, and those that find it are few.

Be aware that false Prophets will approach you, dressed up in clothing looking like sheep, yet inwardly are ravening wolves.

You will know them by their fruits. Have you ever gathered grapes from thorns or figs from thistles?

Similarly, good fruit is produced from every good tree, but the corrupt tree produces evil fruit.

A good tree cannot produce evil fruit; neither can a corrupt tree produce good fruit.

As a result, every tree that does not grow good fruit is cut down then cast into the fire.

You will subsequently know them by their fruits.

The good man will bring out that which is good, out of the good treasure of his heart. The evil man will bring what is evil out of the evil treasure of his heart since from the abundance of the heart, his mouth speaks.

It is not everyone saying to me, 'Lord, Lord,' that will enter into the Kingdom of Heaven; instead, it will be the one who does the will of my

Heavenly Father. If you make a significant effort to call me, 'Lord, Lord,' why not go all the way and do the things I say?

On that great day, there will be many people who will say to me, 'Lord, Lord, we have prophesied in your name, and by your name casts out demons, and through your name did many mighty works. Did we not, Lord?'

I will then reply, 'I have never known you! Get yourself away from me, you who work iniquity.'

Each person hearing my words and performs them, I will compare to a wise man, who, when building his house, built the foundation on solid rock.

The heavy torrential rainfall and flooding came, and strong gale force winds blew and battered that house, yet it did not fall due to its foundation being on the rock.

After hearing my words, each person who does not perform them will be like a foolish man, who, when building his house, placed its foundation on the sand. The heavy torrential rainfall and flooding came, and strong gale force winds blew and battered that house. Immediately it fell, and the wreck of that house was great as it collapsed with a mighty crash."

After he had completed saying all these things, the depth and quality of his teaching amazed the people in the audience. Jesus' teachings were unique and with such authority being unlike any instructions from the Scribes.

*Note: Scribes: Were the religious lawyers, their job expanded from a basic clerk who copied the Scriptures. (In Nehemiah 8:1-8, it describes Ezra as a scribe.)

Their focus shifted to the details or the letter of the law. Then later grew from simple copying duties to teachers of the Scriptures.

The Scribes and Pharisees insisted that the purity of the individuals and the Nation came through strict observance of the Torah. And, along with the Rabbis, taught the people to obey oral traditions that they had developed since the time of Ezra. (*They thought God would never free the Nation from foreign yoke until every person kept the commandments exactly as they interpreted or presented it, regardless of how Draconian they needed to become*).

Then after he had finished speaking in the hearing of all the people, Jesus descended the mountain, as vast crowds of people followed him.

At the end of his address to the crowd, Jesus underlined that genuine faith is not merely a matter of words but actions, and it is not only those who hear that are saved. But those who heed the words with correct corresponding actions.

The authority and power of Jesus thrilled the crowds following from the sermon.

[Jesus was setting the agenda as Israel's Messiah, and underpinning this, he referred to himself as 'Lord.' This is remarkable news since the Lord is Adonai. And only God or The Messiah is called Adonai].

As they neared a town, there was a man who had been following along from the hillside caves; this man was an outcast because he had an advanced case of Leprosy.

The leper approached with courage after hearing Jesus speak. The law strictly forbade lepers to come nearer than ten feet of anyone. Bowing his face to the ground, he begged to be healed, "Lord, if you are willing, I know you are able to heal me and make me clean." He said, calling Jesus Lord (*Adonai*) unashamedly in the public's hearing, this was an act of incredible faith in Jesus' words and courage on his part.

Jesus reached out and touched him. "I am willing," he said. "Be healed!" So instantly, his Leprosy disappeared.

Jesus then instructed him not to stop to tell anyone what had happened. "Go directly to the priest so that he can examine you. Take with you the offering required in the Law of Moses for those who have been healed of Leprosy. This will be a testimony to the Priests that you have been cleansed." Jesus gave explicit instructions to him.

*(In Leviticus 14, *if a person was cured of Leprosy, they were to bring two sparrows to the priest. One was to be cut open and killed.*

Running water was to be poured over the first sparrow, and the water and blood mingled together would run over the living bird.

The living bird could then go free. The blood of the sparrow was put on the cleansed leper's thumbs and his big toe, and the person could then go free).

[All the people of Israel were keenly waiting for the arrival of the Messiah. Moreover, it had been so since the times of the Maccabees and up to the formation of the Pharisees.

Also, the authorities had a compiled list of requirements. By which they were to determine if the Messiah had indeed arrived.

They had often preached and taught about it in the synagogues. The Messiah would speak things never before heard and will, in effect, issue a new Torah, and he will possess divine healing powers.

There were detailed and specific things that only the Messiah could do.

The casting out of demons was possible by the Priests. It was done by asking the demon what its name was, and once told the name, they would then command the demon to come out, using the learned name of the demon.

Although it could not be done if the person was a deft mute, only the Messiah could heal a deft mute.

They also knew that only God could restore a person with Leprosy. Furthermore, no person born an Israelite, who had contracted the disease, had ever been healed in the land of Israel since after the time of Moses.

They taught that none but the Messiah could give sight to any person that was born blind, as that would be a creative miracle.

They knew that only the Messiah could raise the dead, and this act was one of the many things that 'had to be observed.'

The person who died had to be well known by everyone and attested to be evidently and patently dead. (This was due to a prevalent belief that the Spirit could re-enter the body within a short period, thought to be up to three days).

They taught that the Prophet Isaiah would arrive and blow 'a mighty trumpet,' to herald the coming of Messiah. He would then do 'this act of resurrection' as a final testament to his validity.

The Great Council immediately on the confirmed witness of any one of these great miracles. They had to spring into action if or when any of these miracles were to be reported. First, they had to verify that the miracle had taken place.

Then they were to assemble a delegation, specifically to go and observe the one who had performed the miracle.

This would be the start of a seven-day investigation and observation period. The investigators followed the person in question, observing all that he said and did yet could neither speak nor ask questions during the period.

Another phase followed when they could put forward questions, the conclusions would then ensue.

Positive findings of Israel's Messiah would prompt the official announcement of his arrival, jubilantly made to the Nation by The Great Council].

This man cleansed of the Leprosy went spreading the word to everyone, making known what had happened. Although his only choice was to go to the priest and the Temple, making the relevant offering was the only way to re-enter society as a community member.

He failed to follow the direction in his joy. Even after calling Jesus Lord, despite Jesus' instructions 'to go directly to the priest.'

Reports of his power spread faster; soon, vast crowds came to hear him preach, bringing the sick to be healed from diseases.

Jesus, as a result, had to work mainly in the more secluded places, yet people came from everywhere to find him.

Large groups soon surrounded Jesus, and he could not publicly enter a town anywhere.

As often as possible, Jesus withdrew to remote, even wilderness places for prayer.

CHAPTER SIX

ROMAN SOLDIER WITH UNUSUAL FAITH.

Jesus climbed into a boat going back across the lake to his hometown for a short while.

Later he returned to Capernaum. In the city, a Roman officer had a servant, who was as dear to him as a son; the servant had become sick and was at the point of death.

The Roman officer heard about Jesus; then asked some elders of the Jews to ask for him to come and save his servant.

The elders arrived pleading intently, "He is worthy for you to do this for him; he loves our nation; he even built our synagogue for us." They said.

The officer also sent a message to Jesus, informing him, 'Lord, my servant is lying paralyzed in the house, suffering critically.' The statement said using the Messianic title, showing the officer's perception and faith.

"I will follow you to where he is and heal him," Jesus replied.

Jesus set off with them towards the house. Long before he came close to the home, the officer came to meet him and said, "Lord, do not trouble yourself; since I am not worthy for you to come under my roof.

As a result, I did not even think myself worthy to come personally to ask you; still, you only need to say the word, which will be enough to heal my servant, for I also am a man in a position of authority, having under myself soldiers. I give a command to one, 'Go!' and he obeys and goes; to another, I command, 'Come!' He obeys and comes; and to my servant, 'Do this,' and he does it."

When Jesus heard these things, he wondered at him, so he turned and said to the sizeable crowd who followed him, "I tell you honestly, I have not found such great faith any place in Israel.

Many will arrive from the east and west in the Kingdom of Heaven, sitting down with Abraham, Isaac, and Jacob, while they will expel the children belonging to the Kingdom, to the outer darkness, a place of great anguish with weeping and gnashing of teeth."

*(Purposely when speaking, Jesus used established common Jewish ideas, idioms, and adages.

His audience knew about the Day of the Lord, about the Messianic reign in its relation to the Feast of Sukkot, called Tabernacles, from the writings of the Prophet Zechariah.

> **"Watch, because The LORD Comes and Reigns, A day of the LORD is coming a special Day of Judgment, Jerusalem...,"** Zechariah 14:1-21.

In speaking, Jesus referred to the Festival and its traditional guests of honor called the Ushpizin, or seven shepherds who were the exalted guests, invited into every Succah *(tabernacle), at the Feast of Sukkot in the Hebrew head of the year. Traditionally one of seven Ushpizin, illustrious spiritual guests visiting the Sukkah is exalted each night of the holiday.

The seven shepherds in descending order are Abraham, certified on the first night of Sukkot. The second night honors Abraham's son, Isaac, with Jacob on the third night, Moses on the fourth night, Aaron, Moses' brother, on the fifth night. Joseph portrayed as a dreamer in the Bible on the sixth night. The final exalted guest is David the King.

Through specifying the feast and three of the seven shepherds, Jesus' audience immediately understood the reference to the Messianic age, or little-understood 'Millennium' or 'Day of the Lord.'

Mentioned also as 'the kingdom of heaven,' that is the Kingdom we are told to, 'pray for to come on earth as it is in heaven.' This is separate and different from 'the kingdom of God,' which, although rules now, is in Heaven; this Jesus told to Nicodemus when he said, 'you must be born again.' We enter by faith and trust in Jesus, even if we have to seize it by force.

The Kingdom of Heaven, or more correctly, the Kingdom from Heaven, Is the political Kingdom, the extension of David's throne, ruling from the Earth by Jesus. Yet, its start or delay was subject to the acceptance or rejection by Israel).

"Go on back home," Jesus proclaimed to the officer, "as you have believed, then let it be do As he walked ne so for you."

The messenger, sent out first before the officer came to Jesus, returned to the house, finding the servant who had been sick, now recovered. The servant's healing and recovery were in that same hour that the officer came to Jesus.

*Note: This officer would have heard of the royal official's incredible experience with Jesus, kindling his faith.

THE RELIGIOUS LEADERS SEND REPRESENTATIVES TO INVESTIGATE.

Within the next few days after Jesus had arrived in the Capernaum region, the news quickly spread that he was back. He was teaching the people from the area one day, Pharisees and other religious teachers who had arrived from Jerusalem and were sitting around observing him. *(This was the commencement of the seven-day official observation period, sent by the Great Counsel selected from various factions in the leadership. Within this period, they could not speak or question Jesus. This resulted from the healing of the leper).

The crowds of people had come from nearly every village throughout Galilee and Judea. Some people there had even journeyed from as far away as the city of Jerusalem. This was because all saw that Jesus had the healing power of God resting on him.

It was not long before the house where he was staying was so packed with visitors that there was no more room; the people filled even the door entrances and outside.

As Jesus was preaching the word of God to the crowd of people, four men arrived carrying a paraplegic man on a mat. Since they saw they could not bring the man to Jesus because of the size of the crowd.

The four men surprised everyone by going up onto the flat roof, after that digging through, making a hole above the people's heads, next lowering the mat with the man on it in front of Jesus. Jesus saw just how much faith they had in him, so he said to the paraplegic man, "My child, your sins are forgiven."

However, some teachers of religious law sitting there within their official role as observers: Thought to themselves. 'What is this man saying? This is blasphemy! Only God can forgive sins!'

Jesus immediately knew what they were thinking. "Why question this in your hearts?" Jesus asked them, exposing their thoughts.

"Which one would be easier," He asked rhetorically, "to tell this paralyzed man, 'your sins are all forgiven,' or to say, 'stand up, pick up your mat, and walk'?

Therefore, I will reveal to you that the Son of Man has the authority on Earth to forgive sins." He told them forcefully. Then Jesus turned to the paraplegic man, "Stand up, pick up your mat, and go on home!" He commanded.

At that, the man jumped up, picked up his mat, and walked out through the stunned onlookers, who were all astounded and praised God. "We have witnessed nothing quite like this before!" They exclaimed.

A short while later, he went out to the Lakeshore again and taught the crowds coming to him. During this time, as he was walking along near the Lakeshore. He saw Levi, who was the son of Alphaeus, sitting at his booth. This man, Levi, was a tax collector. "Get up and follow me and be my disciple," Jesus summon him.

As a result of this direct invitation, Levi got up and followed him, leaving his booth and everything behind.
Later Levi made a feast; Jesus, the disciples, included various friends, were the invited guests to his home. These comprised many tax collectors and others, people whom the establishment thought of as disreputable sinners. *(By this time, these were many of the types of people welcomed among the followers of Jesus).

*Note: Tax collecting was a huge franchise business. A set amount went to the Romans, and any extra collected was profit.

The Romans used this to ensure the right people with influence were always favorable towards the Roman occupation.

The Romans were clever in awarding any tax contracts for Judea to the Temple High Priest and the other chief rulers. All ruled over the people with a tight grip. They allocated the responsibility mainly to those in the priestly orders. Hence, Matthew, who was a Levite (priest), was also a tax collector.

Though the Pharisees teachers of religious law, observing him eating with these tax collectors and others they identified sinners, approached his disciples asking, "Why does he spend time with and eat in the company of such riff-raff?""
*(The Leaders had now entered the period of intense questioning before they arrived at their conclusion).

On hearing this, Jesus countered with, "Healthy people do not need a doctor, but sick people.

I have not arrived to call those who consider themselves to be righteous, but those who know they are indeed sinners." Jesus informed them.

Another time as the disciples of John the Baptizer and the disciples of the Pharisees were observing a religious fast. People sent by the leaders arrived and questioned Jesus about this. "Your disciples do not seem to fast in the way that the disciples of John and those of the Pharisees do. Why is this?" They asked.

"The disciples of John are renowned for keeping fasts and saying prayers. However, you seem to spend most of your time at parties." They stated disapprovingly.

"Do wedding guests mourn as they are celebrating with the groom?" Jesus asked, "Of course not. However, someday the groom will be taken away from them, and then they will fast. Plus, who would think of patching old clothing with new cloth?

The new patch would shrink, ripping away from the old fabric, leaving an even more severe tear than before.

Besides, no one would put new wine into old wineskins. As the former, inflexible skins would burst from the force, spilling and ruining the wine and the skins. No, new wine should be placed in new wineskins preserving both the skin and the wine."

> Luke 5:39 (EXB) *no one after drinking old wine wants new wine, because he says, 'The old wine is ·better [fine; good].' [The religious leaders are content with the old ways of Judaism and not interested in the "new wine" (salvation blessings) of the Kingdom.]*

Next, Jesus traveled a great distance to Nain, a village about 25 miles southeast of the Sea of Galilee, two miles below Mount Tabor.

Many of his disciples traveled with him, together with a large crowd. Requiring that the Pharisees, the lawyers, and the other observers (still within their fact-finding phase), also accompanied and were part of the group.

*(Nain facing west toward the Jezreel Valley, at the North base of the hill called Little Hermon. Mount Tabor encloses the north-western slope of Jebel Ed-Duhy on the east. Mount Carmel on the west, the Plain of Esdraelon to the north, to the south is the Plain of Sharon, leading to the northern slope of the Hill of Moreh.

Nain in Hebrews means green pastures, or lovely, lying Southeast of Nazareth and southwest of the Sea of Galilee).

As the entire entourage approached the village, there, at the entrance by the town's gate, was a commotion. A dead person was being carried on a litter, a boy who was the only son of a woman, she herself a widow.

A good deal of townspeople accompanied the woman in a vast, crowded procession.

As he approached the scene, Jesus saw the widow seeing that she was grieving; he was full of sympathy for her, "Do not cry." Jesus told her tenderly with great compassion.

He went over to the mat and having touched it, the bearers stood still.

"Young man, I tell you to rise up!" Jesus commanded.

Immediately the child who had been dead sat up, and as he did, he was speaking. Jesus presented him back to his mother.

Great fear and astonishment filled all the people, who then loudly praised God, "A great Prophet has arrived among us!"

"God has certainly visited his people!" They were shouting.

This account of what Jesus did, spread widely throughout the entire region of Judea and the surrounding areas.

*(Located just over the hill from Nain was the ancient town of Zarephath, a short distance from Shunem, where Elijah had once performed a similar miracle, which would have been famous with the people of Nain, who were now proclaiming that Jesus is a great Prophet that God has sent to them).

JOHN SENDS SOME DISCIPLES TO JESUS.

The disciples of John the Baptizer reported to John, who was imprisoned by Herod, informing him about all these things.

John selected two of his disciples, sending them to ask Jesus, "Are you the promised one who is expected, or should we be looking for another?"

The men arrived and delivered John's message, spending some time in the company of Jesus and his disciples. During that time, Jesus healed many people of diseases and infections, cast out evil spirits, and restored sight to many who were blind.

Jesus then instructed the disciples of John, "Go to John and tell him the things that you saw and heard: how the blind regain their sight, the lame walk, the lepers are cleansed, the deaf hears, the dead are raised, and the poor have good news preached to them, besides the one who is not offended by me, he will be blessed." He told them.

The two disciples took their leave from the other's, returning to John with the good news of Jesus' work and ministry.

As they were going, Jesus addressed the crowds concerning John, "What was it you went out into the wilderness to see, a reed the wind had shaken?

What, in fact, was it you went out to see, a man in beautiful soft clothing?" He asks.

"Consider this; people stunningly dressed in soft clothing who live delicately are in the courts of kings.

Yet, why indeed did you go out? Was it to see a Prophet? Yes, truly I tell you, and much more than a Prophet.

Because the Scripture says, 'See, I will send my messenger, and he will make ready the path before me,' they wrote this about John.

Without a doubt, I tell you, there is not a greater Prophet than John the Baptizer among all who are born of women, yet the one who is the least in the Kingdom of God is greater than John." Jesus declared.

He continued, "Thinking that they are honoring the Law and the Prophets, men of violence have been attempting to take the Kingdom of Heaven by force.

Yet it was prophesied during the Law and all the Prophets until John. Yes, from the days of John the Baptizer until now. The Kingdom has allowed (*suffered*) violence.

However, since then, the good news about the Kingdom of God has been proclaimed, even as everyone entering it encounters hostility.

If you are willing to receive and to understand, then this is Elijah, the one who is to come.

Everyone who has ears to hear let him hear," Concluded Jesus with force and authority.

When all the ordinary people, including the tax collectors, heard this, they rejoiced and declared God to be just; because they had been baptized with the baptism of John.

On the other hand, the Pharisees and lawyers all rejected the counsel of God; John had not baptized them. *(they only went to John to observe him but would not receive his message or offer of repentance).

Therefore, this is what Jesus expressed.

"This generation to what will I compare its people? What are they like?

They are similar to children who sit in the marketplace calling one another, saying, 'we played for you the flute, but you did not dance.

And when we mourned, you did not weep.'

Because John the Baptizer did not come eating bread or drinking wine when he arrived, you, as a result, said of him, 'he has a demon.'

The Son of Man has appeared eating and drinking, and you say, 'Take a look, a greedy and excessive man, who is a drunkard; the friend of tax collectors and sinners!'

Yet wisdom is always justified by all her children."

*(*This example that Jesus gave was a well know and popular game played by children. The children would divide into two groups. One group pretends to play instruments or weep. The other would fitly respond either by dancing or weeping and mourning.*

Those demanding proofs Jesus compared to the children squabbling over the wrong response of the game. Usually, after the first group had made all the correct responses, the game would break down when the second party failed to do likewise.

Jesus likened it to these peoples' demand for a performance to suit their character, fads, and ideas of what a Prophet of God or even the Messiah should be).

Jesus then spoke about and criticized the cities where he did most of his mighty miracles because they did not repent.

"Watch out! To you, Chorazin! Watch out! To you, Bethsaida! Wretched desolation and misery are yours.

Because of all the incredible miracles, had I done them in Tyre and Sidon, those cities long ago would have repented in sackcloth and ashes.

Yet I tell you, for Tyre and Sidon on the Day of Judgment, it will be easier than it will be for you.

You, Capernaum, exalted to Heaven. You will go down to Hades, since the mighty miracles you have witnessed, had I done them in Sodom, it would have remained until this day.

Yet I tell you, for the land of Sodom on the Day of Judgment, it will be more tolerable than for you." Jesus proclaimed.

"Abba, Lord over the Heaven and Earth, I thank you, Father, you have hidden all these things from those that are wise and educated, yet revealed them to the infants.

Yes, Father, since this was all so well-pleasing in your sight." He prayed, giving thanks.

Jesus exclaimed resolutely, "Father has given all things to me. Except for the Father, no one knows the son."

Jesus cried out. "All of you who labor and your burdens are heavy, come to me, and I will give you rest.

Take up my yoke, as you learn from me, as I am gentle and humble in heart; then your souls will find the rest you need.

As my yoke is very easy, and my burden is very light." He said, giving a warm invitation to all the ordinary people.

*(A physical 'Yoke' is a crossbar harness of burden linking two animals, binding them together for work. The idea was that the stronger, more experienced animal in the team would pull the other, bearing most of the burden until the weaker got used to the task and the path. At which time they would do the work in unison and with ease).

[The Rabbis encourage people to learn to keep the Torah. They called this taking the yoke of Torah, or sometimes the yoke of the Kingdom of Heaven.

Rabbi's who had been 'authorized' with s'mikhah *(usually refers to the rabbi ordination) would have a new interpretation or 'yoke.'

Torah teachers would instruct the accepted explanation or yoke of their community.

To all listening to the many alternative teachers and interpretations heard in the vigorous religious debates, yet remained unsure of the many conflicting definitions, Jesus' invitation would present a sincere clarification, light to grasp and remember.

For Jesus to have a rabbinical yoke, he would have to send out his disciples on their own to complete their learning. They would have to commit his teachings to memory and follow them.

They would have to stay with him so that they could follow his example].

The Pharisees Still Remain Undecided.

A man named Simon, a member of the Pharisees sect, invited him to have dinner at his home.

*(The Pharisees, 'pure' or 'separated,' were a society of scholars and known for their piety. Principally shown by the things along with people they separated themselves from and through much ritual purification.

They believed in the principle of the ongoing progression of the law, comprising the Written Law added to the oral traditions of the Jewish people. Making the Law that God gave to Moses of dual importance allowing men to use their reason in interpreting the Torah and applying it to any current problems).

Accepting the invitation, he went to dine in Simon's house even though the Pharisees were the foremost critics and the most hostile to Jesus. This was a Sabbath meal, the most important meal of the week, and carefully prepared from the day before. Simon was a wealthy Pharisee but somehow forgot to provide all the exact things needed for an important guest. This would include water and a towel for washing as shoes and sandals were not worn inside the house.

Many from the liberal wing among the Pharisees remained undecided about Jesus as the Messiah and would use such private circumstances in various settings to arrive at a formal conclusion on the matter.

During the occasion, when Jesus was seated at the table in the correct reclining position for an exalted guest, a woman hurried into the house. She was a woman who was known in the city. And given a poor reputation that had stuck: She had been labeled by all the people! *(*Note: They were still in or near the city of Nain).*

She had heard that Jesus was dining there in the house of Simon. She entered the room with an alabaster jar of ointment.

She stood behind at his feet and wept, so her tears were wetting his feet. She then quickly wiped them away with the hair of her head. Then, after kissing his feet to show honor and respect, she anointed them with the costly and precious ointment.

Then when Simon the Pharisee who had invited Jesus saw all of this, he said to himself critically. "This man had he really been a prophet; he would have recognized this woman and know that she is a sinner, this woman who touches him."

"Simon," Jesus said to him, "I have something to say to you."

"Teacher, speak freely," Simon replied.

"A particular lender had two people who owed him money. The first one owed five hundred coins, and the other fifty.

When he realized they could not pay the debt, he forgave them both. As a result, which of them will love him the most?" Jesus asked.

"I suppose," said Simon, "that it would be the one that had been forgiven the most."

"You have judged correctly," said Jesus.

Turning and facing the woman, he spoke to Simon, "Do you see this woman? I entered your house, and you gave no water to me for me to wash my feet, yet she has wet my feet with her tears and wiped them with the hair of her head.

And even though you also failed to greet me with a kiss, she has continued kissing my feet since the time I entered your house.

She has anointed my feet with ointment, though you failed to anoint my head with oil.

So I will tell you, her many sins are forgiven because of her great love.

The one who only has a little to be forgiven of, that same person will only love in a small way." He said chidingly.

"Your sins are forgiven," Jesus told the woman direct.

The other people that were also seated at the table questioned this, "Who is this man? He can even forgive sins?" They murmured.

Jesus raised his voice so they could hear, "Go in peace; you have been saved because of your faith." He notified the woman.

There were also many other women. Who faithfully followed and were regular supporters of the work of Jesus. And who would quietly and steadily assist the disciples! They included Mary, who was called Magdalene. She was the woman healed of illness and had seven demon spirits cast out of her. There was also Joanna, the wife of Chuzas, the steward of Herod and Susanna, and many others. These women gave some of their resources for support.

Shortly after this, Jesus the disciples and the many followers traveled through the many towns and small villages, preaching and bringing the people the good news about the Kingdom of God.

They arrived at a house, the news of this was soon known, and the crowds quickly gathered from everywhere, so many people the disciples could not even find the space and time to eat.

Some people came to find Jesus, and they bought a Demon-Possessed man; the man was suffering from blindness and was also a mute. Jesus healed the man casting out the demon, giving him back his sight and his speech. This so much amazed the people who were crowded in and around the house that they excitedly asked each other. "Can this man indeed be the son of David?" (*The Kingly title for the Messiah*).

This infuriated the Pharisees who were plotting to find something against Jesus.

Then because of their intentions, they made sure that some of their representatives always mingled in wherever the people gathered to see him. They accordingly could make reports to the leaders and Chief Priests.

On hearing the crowds exclaiming many praises regarding him, these agents voiced their own opinion. "This man is casting out demons, except it is by Beelzebub, the prince of the demons." They were declaring to the people.

*(By this time, the Pharisees had formed their opinion of the situation. And this was the conclusion they had resolved to use—a decision to hide what they had found to be the truth and plot against Jesus.

To confuse the people by telling them how Jesus' incredible powers were only Earthly, not from Heaven, and were via forces counterfeited by Baal, the false god of Israel's previous enemies.

After all, he was a northerner with a rough northern dialect. Not a refined city scholar, he did not attend the schools approved by the Pharisees).*

Because of the leader's failure in correctly inaugurating the first part of the two-pronged investigation (After the witness of any of the listed Messianic miracles), then make the appropriate official announcement of their true findings at the end of the second period involving questioning.

They initially initiated parts of this procedure. Yet, they refused to make the appropriate announcement, being bogged down with what they saw as the important details, such as their own traditions and customs.

(*What the Pharisees were speaking was the very opposite of the very rules that the leaders were meant to be following*).

They drew the lists of Messianic miracles from the scriptures, including prophecies from Isaiah, the Psalms, and many other writings, from Moses to Malachi.

Isaiah 29:18 (NKJV) *in that day, the deaf shall hear the words of the book, and the eyes of the blind shall see out of obscurity and out of the darkness*.

Isaiah 32:3-4 (NKJV) *the eyes of those who see will not be blind, and the ears of those who hear will listen.*
Also, the heart of the rash will understand knowledge, and the tongue of the stammerers will be ready to speak plainly.

Isaiah 35:5 (NKJV) *Then the eyes of the blind shall be opened, and the ears of the deaf unstopped;*

Psalm 146:8 (NKJV) *The Lord opens the eyes of the blind; The Lord lifts up those who are bowed down;*
The Lord loves the righteous.

Jesus would need to operate in a low profile manner until the next six days had expired; often, he would altogether leave the area. (*He did this to grant Grace and mercy instead of judgment*).

JESUS'S FAMILY ATTEMPTS A RESCUE MISSION.

When his relations heard these comments, they were concerned with the things that the Pharisees were spreading among the people. They went intending to take him away from there. The family tried to make excuses for him. So they countered by telling the people, "He is only out of control (*overwhelmed with emotions*)." They declared.

Although some of the people there were not convinced by any of these things said by the Pharisees or even by the family, instead, they were asking Jesus to give them a sign from heaven so that they could form an opinion of him.

Jesus was aware of all of their thoughts and the things in their hearts, so he called everyone together and spoke to them in these parables, "How can Satan cast out Satan?

Any kingdom, if it is divided against itself, that kingdom cannot stand and is sure to be ruined.

Any house that would be divided against itself, that house cannot stand, and it will fall.

If Satan has rebelled, defying himself, and so casts out Satan, how will his kingdom stand? He is divided; he cannot endure but is finished.

If it is by Beelzebub that I am casting out demons, in that case, by whom do your children cast them out, Jesus asked them.

Then he said, "They then, for this reason, will be the ones who will judge you.

If I force out demons by the Spirit of God and the finger of God, then the Kingdom of God is here with you.

The goods and valuables belonging to a strong man remain safe while he is fully armed and is guarding his home, so then, how can anyone enter into the house of the strong man and raid his goods unless he has first bound that strong man? Then he will raid his home.

As long as the strong man, fully armed, guards his own home, his possessions are safe.

However, when someone stronger attacks him and overcomes him, the stronger strips him of his whole armor, which he trusted, and then ransacks his valuables.

Every person who is not with me stands against me, and those who are not gathering with me are scattering.

For that reason, I tell you that men will receive forgiveness for every sin and every blasphemy they speak. However, the blasphemous remarks that are made against the Holy Spirit will never be forgiven. The person, who speaks a word against the Son of Man, will be forgiven; however, the person who speaks against the Holy Spirit and blasphemies against the Holy Spirit never has forgiveness neither in this present world or in the age to come but is guilty of an eternal sin, *(Having eternal damnation).

[Without the Holy Spirit, there is no chance of being saved because He is the truth. And it is by the truth that He convicts the heart of sin, and after repentance, the heart is regenerated. This is the 'New Birth.

The Pharisees knew that Jesus, without a doubt, was the Messiah. Yet had decided to oppose Him and spread false teachings to misdirect the people. In doing so, they were rejecting the very thing that could save them.

They purposely rejected the Holy Spirit, who brought truth and light to their hearts, which was not done by error. They knew the truth and were standing against the Holy Spirit, without whom no power in the whole of creation can save them].

"The tree is either good, and the fruit of it is good, or the tree corrupt, producing corrupt fruit. Trees are only known by their fruit, Jesus continued.

*(Have it either one way or the other but make up your mind; you can't have it both ways).

How can you a generation of vipers, being evil, speak good things?

Because out of the storehouse of the heart comes the words of the mouth.

Every good person brings good things out of their good treasures, and the evil person brings evil things out of their evil treasures.

I tell you, truthfully! That every idle word that is spoken, you will give an account of it in the Day of Judgment.

I assure you! By your words, you will be justified, as, by your words, you will be condemned.

A lamp is to give light, and when it is lit. No one puts it in a cellar or under a basket, no! It is placed on a lampstand to give its light to all.

The body also has its lamp, which is the eye, and a good eye fills the whole body with light, but when it is evil, then your body is also filled with darkness. Therefore, be sure that you have pure light in you and is not, in fact, darkness.

If, as a result, you find that your whole body is full of pure light, and no part, no corner is dark, it will be like a lamp that fills everywhere with its bright shining light; you will be that light, Jesus told all the people, silencing the Pharisees.

As Jesus was sitting and teaching the crowds that had come to hear him, when some of the Scribes and Pharisees that always mingled in the crowds, spoke up, "Teacher, we very much need to see a sign from you, They said waveringly, knowing that they were not able to get the better of him.

"This generation is evil and faithless; that is why you ask for a sign, but the sign of Jonah the Prophet, is the only sign that will be given.

This generation will have the same sign that Jonah was to the Ninevites.

Jonah, who had been within the belly of the whale for three days and nights, so the Son of Man, will likewise be three days and nights in the heart of the Earth.

This generation will be condemned when they stand up along with the men of Nineveh in the judgment because through the preaching of Jonah, they repented! And think about this, someone greater than Jonah is now present.

Also, the queen of the south, who traveled to meet Solomon and hear his wisdom, will condemn this generation in the judgment. Journeying from the ends of the Earth, yet you now have someone greater than Solomon with you.

The evil actions of this generation are those of an unclean spirit in a man who having been forced out. Set off through dry places, seeking rest, and seeing that he cannot find any.

He decides I will return to my old home, and on arrival, finds it clean, tidy, and set in order. In that case, that spirit goes and finds seven other more evil spirits than he is, to enter with him into the house and reside there.

Making the end condition of that man so much worse than it was at first, Jesus again told them with uncompromising directness.

The crowds of people swelled in and around the house, where Jesus was speaking and teaching. Meanwhile, outside, his mother Mary and his brothers arrived because they wanted to talk to him.

They had arrived with the idea of rescuing Jesus, from what the Pharisees were openly spreading among the people with the hope and intention of putting him to death.

The size of the crowd prevented the family from approaching close to the place.

The news was relayed through the crowd and given to Jesus. "Your mother and brothers are outside waiting, wanting to speak with you," the message said.

"Who then is my mother? And who are my brothers," Jesus asks the man.

Jesus looked around at all of those who sat there around him. He gestured towards his disciples and said, "Take a look at my mother and my brothers, since those who will hear the word of God, and also does the will of my Heavenly Father. That person is my brother, my sister, and my mother."

Later as he was still speaking, a woman in the crowd interrupted, calling out, "the womb that delivered you and the breasts that nursed you is truly blessed, she said with great enthusiasm, *(She said this as Jesus' mother Mary was possibly still outside and in earshot).

"On the contrary," He replied, "it is those who hear the word of God and keep it that is bless."

CHAPTER SEVEN

CONTINUING TO TEACH ON THE KINGDOM.

Later on that day, Jesus left the house and went and sat by the seaside. From there, he continued to teach the people from the edge of the sea.

More and more people arrived. Some even via the sea, as the people from various cities came to hear him.

Then because of the vast numbers, Jesus entered a boat, where he sat, the people all stood along the beach.

Jesus used illustrations and stories as the perfect method of teaching the people many memorable things; this is what he told them.

"Hear this! And think about it. A farmer went out sowing some seeds by hand for his Crop.

As he sowed, some of the seeds he scattered fell on the path by the roadside. These seeds were trampled under the feet of the passers-by, and soon the birds came consuming them.

Some other seeds fell on hard, rocky types of ground; they had little soil in that spot. Resulting in them immediately sprouted up as the Earth had no depths.

Later they became scorched after the sun rose. Due to their lack of roots, they received no moisture from the Earth, so they quickly withered away.

Then there were some seeds falling in among the thorns. Which sprang up, choking and overwhelming them; those seeds could not yield any fruit.

Some seeds were landing on good soil; these grew up and increased healthily, growing plenty of fruit: some, one hundred, some sixty and some thirty times as much," he told his audience, who listened eagerly to the teachings.

After he finished telling this story, Jesus raised his voice, "He who has ears to hear, let him hear, He announced.

Then he continued by explaining the principles of God's Kingdom. "A comparison to The Kingdom of God could be thought of like this. If a farmer wanted to grow fruit and then placed the correct seed in prepared Earth, even if he started watching it night and day, by sleeping and rising and waiting, when the seed eventually springs up and grows, he still will not know-how.

This is because it is natural for the Earth to bear fruit: even though it starts with just the blade, then the ear, then the full grain in the ear.

All the farmer has to do is wait until the fruit has ripened. Then right away, he uses the sickle to gather in the harvest.

And in another of the illustrations, Jesus said to his audience. "The Kingdom of Heaven can be thought of like a man who sowed good seed in his field, but while people slept, his enemy came and also planted some darnel weeds among the wheat and went away.

But when the blade grew to maturity and produced its fruit, the darnel weeds also emerged alongside.

The man's hired workers came to him and said, 'Sir, you only sowed good seeds in the field? So, where did all these darnel weeds appear from?

'This is the work of an enemy, He replied to them.

The workers asked, 'Do you want us to go and gather them up?

'No,' he replied to the workers, 'because possibly while you are collecting all the darnel weeds, you could disturb the wheat along with them.

For that reason, until the harvest, allow them both to grow together, then at the time of the harvest, I will summon the reapers and instruct them," The ruler stated. "Gather all the darnel weeds first, bind them in bundles for burning, as you do separate the wheat into my barn," *(The reapers always represent the angels).

JESUS GAVE HIS KEEN LISTENERS ANOTHER ILLUSTRATION.

"How will we compare the Kingdom of God? Or with what comparison will we illustrate it?

The Kingdom of Heaven could be compared to a grain of mustard seed, which a man took and sowed in his field; it certainly is smaller than all seeds. However, after it is planted, it grows up and becomes more significant than all the herbs, growing great branches becoming a tree so that the birds of the air come and stay in its branches.

He continued with this other illustration. "We could compare the Kingdom of Heaven to yeast, which a woman took, working it into three portions of Flour, awaiting the rising of the whole thing!"

With many similar stories, Jesus presented his message of the kingdom to the people, matching the stories to their level of understanding. He always spoke with a story to illustrate his meaning.

His telling of stories fulfilled the prophecy of David in the Psalms, which declared.

I will open my mouth in a parable (in instruction by numerous examples); I will utter dark sayings of old [that hide important truth] *(Psalm 78:2 AMPC). Psalm 44:1.

(Tehillim is the Hebrew for Psalms, meaning 'songs of praise,' some Psalms are Tephillot, 'prayers, individual Psalms are referred to as Mizmorim).

When he and his disciples were away from the crowds, he recounted the stories and explained everything to them.

Jesus' disciples and close followers were fascinated with his methods. They asked him. "Why do you only use illustration with the crowds?"

"The mysteries of the Kingdom are for you to know, given as a gift," He replied.

"And to the others outside, it is not given to them. So, all things are done in parables.

This is so that the one who seeks will be given, and they will have large quantities, but he who will not seek will lose his small amount. That is why I speak to them only in parables, because seeing they do not see or perceive, and hearing, they do not hear or understand but fulfill the prophecy from Isaiah, which says, 'By hearing you will hear, and in no way understand; seeing you will see, and in no way perceive: in case they should turn, and have their sins forgiven.

'Since the heart of these people's has grown insensitive, and their ears are dull of hearing. They have also closed their eyes. If not, they might observe with their eyes, hear with their ears, understand with their heart, then they would change and turn to me, and I would heal them, *(Isaiah 6:10.)

Your eyes, however, are blessed because they see; also your ears, because they hear.

I tell you many prophets and righteous men wanted to see the things that you see, and did not see them, or to hear the things that you hear, and could not hear them." He patiently explained to them.

[Because of what the Pharisees had done. In working to convince the people that Jesus was not their Messiah and because the people had received the truth, starting with John's preaching in the desert, they now had to decide which kingdom they wanted. The Kingdom of God was offered and is Spiritual and is only entered through the New Birth.

Alternatively, the Kingdom of Heaven awaits and is Jesus' Kingdom in which was promised to Israel where their Messiah would rule on David's throne, here on the Earth.

Nothing further would be offered from this point forward, which is why Jesus from then on would only speak in parables to the people].

The disciples then ask what the explanation of the story of the farmer was.

"If you cannot know what this represents, how will you be able to see the comparisons of all the other stories? Jesus asked.

"So take note — the explanation of the farmer and planting of the seed parable. Here is what it means: The seed represents the word of God. The farmer plants that grain by taking the word of God to others.

The seed that had fallen on the footpath represents those hearing and not understanding the message about the kingdom.

Then the evil one comes at once and snatches out of their hearts the planted seed.

The seed falling on the rocky soil symbolizes those instantly and with delight receiving the message they had heard.

Though, since they do not have deep roots, they do not last long, falling away quickly over problems or persecution for believing the word of God.

The seed falling among the thorns represents those who hear the word of God; however, the message is crowded out all too quickly by the worries of this life and the lure of wealth, so they produced no fruit; these never grow into maturity.

The seed falling on good soil represents honest, good-hearted people who hear the word of God, adhere to it, and steadily produce a huge harvest.

Those who truly hear and understand the word of God produces a harvest that is thirty, sixty, even a hundred times more than had been planted," Jesus explained.

"Pay close attention to what you hear," He added. "The closer you listen, the more knowledge you will be given! And you will receive even more. Anyone who listens to my teachings will gain knowledge. But for those who do not listen. From them will be taken even the little they imagined they understood.

The farmer planting the good seed is the Son of Man. The field represents the entire world, the good seed of the kingdom and its people!

The weeds represent people belonging to the evil one. Then the devil is the enemy who planted the weeds among the wheat. The harvest represents the end of the world, with the harvesters being the angels.

As they separate natural weeds, sort, and then burn in a fire, so will it be the same at the end of the age!

The Son of Man will instruct his angels to remove everything causing sin and all who do evil out of his kingdom. Hurling them into the fiery furnace, where weeping and gnashing of teeth will be.

Then in their Father's Kingdom, the righteous will be shining like the sun. All those having ears to hear should listen and understand," He said.

"Would anyone, after lighting a lamp, then put it under a basket or a bed, Jesus asked them?

Of course not! No person having lit a lamp then covers it with a bowl or hides it under a bed.

No, they placed lamps on a stand, where all who enter the house can see by its light because it will eventually bring all things secret into the open, just as everything covered will be exposed to the light, as it is made known to all.

All those with ears to hear should listen and understand," He told them categorically.

EXPLAINING THE KINGDOM THROUGH PARABLES.

"The Kingdom of Heaven, it could be considered as a hidden treasure a man had discovered in a field. In his excitement, he hid it again, then sold everything he owned to give him enough money to purchase that field!

We can also think of the Kingdom of Heaven as a merchant on the lookout for choice pearls. Then having discovered a pearl of great value, he sold everything he owned and bought it!

The Kingdom of Heaven is again like a large fishing net that was thrown into the water, catching fish of every kind. That net, when it was full, was dragged up onto the shore. The fishermen sat down to sort the good fish, which went into holding crates. But the bad ones hurled aside.

At the end of the world, it will be similar! When the angels arrive to separate the wicked from righteous people, the wicked are to be heaved into the fiery furnace.

They will be there weeping and gnashing their teeth. Do you understand all these things?" He asked his disciples pointedly in finishing.

"Yes," they declared, "we do."

Jesus then added, "Every teacher of religious law having become a witness in the Kingdom of Heaven is like a homeowner bringing from his storeroom new gems of truth as well as old."

(*Note: Here, Jesus gives a total of seven Kingdom parables. They are significant because through them, a plan of God's Kingdom, Spiritual. And Jesus' Kingdom, 'On earth, a literal Kingdom' is unveiled).

- The Parable of the Sower: = Jesus, who sows the word into the entire world, but not everyone receives it or produces fruit.
- Parables of the Tares: = Is the work of the enemy; the plan is to disrupt God's work.
- Parable of the Mustard Seed: = God uses small things over a very long period or time to achieve the right results. At the same time, the birds of the air, 'the evil ones,' are working against God's plans, as in Genesis 15:11, where 'Abraham had to chase them away.
- Parable of the Leaven: = Women in Scripture represent either false religion or God's people; this one corrupts God's work and is a continuation of the Tares right up until the end of the age.
- Parable of the Hidden Treasure: = God's people, and the lengths that He will go to so that he can rescue them, first the people of Israel, and then the ones called out of the world.

- Parable of the Pearl of Great Price: = Even down to an individual, a single person, Jesus gave all He had to rescue what is precious to God; a Pearl is a living stone because of the way it's made. It is initially formed from something that was considered unclean.
- Parable of the Dragnet: = The very end of the age, where there is a final separation of God's people from the Tares.

When it was near time for one of the Jewish holy days, Jesus and his disciples returned to Jerusalem to attend the celebrations held there!

As Jesus continued inside the city, near the Sheep Gate was the pool of Bethesda (*House of Mercy*), with elegant columns and five covered porches. Where there were crowds of sick people waiting day by day.

Some there were blind, or lame, even paralyzed, lying on the porches.

(*People waited there for the moving of the water in the pool, the belief was that an Angel would go down into the pond from time to time and stir up the water. Then the first one who got into the water after the stirring would thus recover from whatever sickness they had*).

This belief was widespread among the people there, even though the pool was within sight of the Temple of God, where they should have been looking for their help!

Among all of them was a man lying there. This man had been sick for thirty-eight years.

Jesus went there and observed that the man had been ill for a very long time.

Jesus addressed him with a question, "Would you like to be well?" He asked.

"I cannot, sir," he said, "since I have no one to help me and who could place me in the pool whenever the water bubbles up.

Then, even as I am attempting to get in, someone else always gets there ahead of me." The man explained his dilemma, though he did not directly answer the question.

"Stand up," Jesus instructed him, "pick up your mat, and walk!" He commanded.

Instantly, the man became restored! He then stood up, rolled up his sleeping mat, and began walking!

(This man had a disability for thirty-eight years. Deuteronomy 2:14, (ESV) *And the time from our leaving Kadesh-Barnea until we crossed the brook Zered was thirty-eight years, until the entire generation,*

***that is, the men of war, had perished from the camp, as the Lord had
sworn to them.'***

Describing here the length of time the Israelites had spent in the wilderness, the place where they had received the law.

To fulfill the need for Israel's salvation, they could not keep the necessary Laws.

Israel's dilemma was in its inability to keep the law. Because their sins always intervened yet, they would not have needed saving if they could have kept the law.

Like the infirm man at Bethesda (House of Mercy), Israel needed someone to show them mercy in their impossible situation. They desperately needed a savior to liberate them from their condition. The Lord revealed the mercy of God to a man in his infirmity, and through this 'living visible parable,' was offering to do the same for lost Israel).

*Note: *Though the man had nearly two decades to reflect on, the only one who could heal him. When the time came, and he received his total recovery, he failed to praise God or give him the Glory; and his confession was that he did not know who had made him well.*

This miracle had taken place on a day that was the Sabbath. When the Jewish leaders saw him carrying his mat, they objected vehemently.

"You cannot work on the Sabbath! You are breaking the law by carrying around that sleeping mat!" The leaders told the man who had received the healing.

"I was told by the man who healed me, 'stand up, pick up your mat, and walk.' "He replied.

"Who was it that told you to do that?" The leaders demanded.

The man did not know who the Lord was; Jesus, by this time, had left and joined the vast crowds.

Sometime later, for the second time that day, Jesus once again sought out and found the same man in the Temple and spoke to him, "Now that you have received this healing, stop sinning, if you do not. Something may happen to you that will be even worse." Jesus told the man.

Afterward, the man went to the Jewish leaders and told them the truth that it was Jesus who had healed him.

As a result, the Jewish leaders began to harass Jesus over his apparent breaking of the Sabbath rules.

"As my Father is always working, and so am I," Jesus told them.

This seriously offended the Jewish leaders. In their view, he had not only broken their interpretation of the Sabbath law, but Jesus also called God his Father.

He, in so doing, was making himself equal to God. (Then they tried to find some way to kill him).

Jesus, as a result, took the time to make it unequivocal to them, "I am telling you the solemn truth, the Son cannot do anything by himself. He only presents those things that he sees the Father doing. So whatever the Father does, that is also what the Son does.

The Father loves the Son, so he shows him everything he is doing.

The Father will show him how to do even greater miracles than just the healing of this man. Then you really will be astonished.

As my Father gives those that he raises from the dead his life, in the very same way, the Son will also give life to anyone he wants.

Also, Father judges no one. However, he has given unto the Son absolute authority to decide judgments; therefore, all will honor the Son the same as they honor the Father.

Those who do not honor the Son are certainly not honoring the Father who sent him.

I tell you the solemn truth, those who pay attention and hear my message and in doing so have faith in God who has sent me. They have eternal life. And I will never condemn them for their sins; conversely, they have already passed from death into life.

Besides, I assure you the time is coming. In reality, it is here now. The dead will hear my voice, the voice of the Son of God. All of those who hear will live.

So as Father has life in himself, he has granted that same life-giving power to his Son.

He has also handed to him the authority to judge everyone because he is the Son of Man.

Do not be surprised! Without a doubt, the time is coming when all the dead in their graves will hear the voice of the Son of God. They will then rise again from the dead.

Everyone who has done the will of God will rise to experience eternal life, and all who have proceeded in evil will rise to encounter judgment. I can not do anything on my own I judge as God tells me. Because of that, my judgment is worthy and righteous since I carry out not my own, but he will of the one who sent me.

If I were merely testifying on my behalf, then my testimony would not be the truth. Yet, someone else also testifies about me. I assure you everything he is saying about me is correct.

You had yourselves sent witnesses to hear John the Baptizer, and his testimony about me was the truth. Of course, I do not need human witnesses, but I say these things so that you might receive your redemption. For you, John was like a burning, shining lamp, and his message attracted you for a while.

I have a far greater witness than John's, my teachings, and the miracles.

My Father has given me these works to accomplish; therefore, they prove he sent me.

My Father, who sent me, has also testified about me himself.

You have at no time ever heard his voice or seen him face to face; indeed, you have not his message in your hearts; it is the reason that you do not believe me, the very one he has sent to you.

You search through the Scriptures because you imagine that within them, you can find eternal life. However, all the Scriptures point to me! Nevertheless, you refuse to come to me so that you can obtain this gift of life.

I know that it is because you do not have a love of God within you. Your approval means nothing.

Because I have come to you in the name of my Father, and you have rejected me. If another comes in the authority of his own name, you will gladly welcome him. Is it any wonder that you are not able to believe! Because you willingly give honor to each other, at the very same time disregarding the recognition that comes only from the one who alone is God.

However, I am not the one who will accuse you before the Father. Moses will make accusations against you!

Yes, Moses, the one in whom you put your hopes because if you had actually believed Moses, you would likewise believe me because he wrote about me. However, given that you do not believe the things that he wrote, it is no surprise that you will not receive and understand what I say?" Jesus made his words clear to them, speaking in plain, precise language, which cut them to the core.

*Note: The testimony of two or more witnesses is required in the law, Deuteronomy 19:15, Numbers 35:30, Deuteronomy 17:6 (AMP) *[only] on the testimony or evidence of two or three witnesses shall a charge be confirmed.*

Here Jesus is giving a total of four:

(1). They had sent witnesses to hear John the Baptizer.
(2). The Scriptures that point to him.
(3). His teachings and the miracles.
(4). His Father, who sent him, has testified about him.

[Many prominent Rabbis had accurately predicted the time of the Messiah's arrival. This included Rabbi Nechuniah Ben Kanah, who had pointed to that current generation as the only possible allotted time.
The Prophet Daniel had given the timeline in great detail.
That he would have arrived in the rebuilt second Temple was told by Haggai.

In the second chapter, verses 6-9 (KJV) *'because thus says the Lord of hosts; yet once, it is a little while, and I will shake the heavens, and the Earth, and the sea, and the dry land.'*
And I will shake all nations, and the desire of all nations shall come: and I will fill this house with Glory, says the Lord of hosts. The silver is mine, and the gold is mine, says the Lord of hosts. The splendor of this latter house will be far greater than of the former, says the Lord of hosts: and in this place will I give peace, says the Lord of hosts.

In the writing of the Prophet Daniel, the ninth chapter has one of a few places in the Scriptures that give the specific word for Messiah - 'Moshiach' (The 'Anointed One').
In the twenty-third chapter, verses five to six, the Prophet Jeremiah wrote, "Look now, the days come, says the Lord, that I will raise up to David a righteous Branch. And a King will reign, prosper and execute judgment and justice in all the Earth. In his days, salvation will come to Judah, and Israel will dwell safely: and that name which he will be called by; is The Lord Our Righteousness (Yahweh-tsidkenu).

One of the earliest and most significant Prophecies for the coming Messiah had been presented by the patriarch Jacob to his son Judah. In Genesis, the forty-ninth chapter, the tenth verse. 'The scepter will not depart from Judah, nor a lawgiver from between his feet until Shiloh come and unto him, will the gathering of the people be.'

Also, with this event, two things of great importance would be made apparent, the right of Judah's lineage to govern and make judicial laws under its kings, including the power of capital punishment, which would remain unimpeded until after the Messiah's arrival.

Therefore, the Messiah, when he arrived, would have the authority to make and define laws.

Isaiah 33:22 (ASV) *For Jehovah is our judge, Jehovah is our lawgiver, Jehovah is our King; he will save us.*

Ezekiel 21:27 (ASV) *I will overturn, overturn, overturn it: this also shall be no more, until he comes whose right it is; and I will give it him.*

(The use of the term 'Shiloh' was long understood as being an idiom for the Messiah, said to be the peaceful one or He who is to be sent.

The scepter 'the right of the sword' the power or the right under the law to impose the death penalty as punishment for any capital crime, 'Jus Gladii,' also expressed as 'Potestas Gladii,' during the Roman Empire).

[Following the proclamation by the Persian King Cyrus the Great, allowing the Israelites captives to return to the land of Israel, accompanying their return from the Babylonian exile, the leaders had developed two tiers of the Supreme Court. (*Sanhedrin from the Greek' synedrion,' meaning 'sitting together' bet din, in Hebrew, "house of judgment"*), exercising broad powers in civil and religious affairs.

The 'great Court' was situated and centered on the Temple in Jerusalem, consisting of seventy-one men.

The priest was divided into two groups, the Pharisees and Sadducees, and comprised the three classes of chief priests, scribes, and elders, principally from influential families. The elders, like the Sadducees, were usually drawn from the wealthy sections of society.

The lower tier of the council operated with twenty-three members through Local synagogues in the larger towns and cities; smaller towns would have a smaller seven-man committee.

The council's authority, although it was limited to Judea, its control reached throughout the Nation. The Israelites had still possessed law-givers and judges even while they had been in exile.

Jewish leaders were allowed by the Roman conquerors to regulate the internal matters of their people.

The Romans found their interests were best served by not intervening in the internal affairs of the native provinces over which they ruled.

However, the legal power of the Sanhedrin had been suddenly restricted some twenty-three years before this period.

Herod Archelaus was the son and heir to the throne of King Herod. Through neglect of political wisdom in his dealings with the people, he was dethroned and banished to Gaul (France) and replaced by a Roman Procurator named Caponius.

Caesar Augustus removed the legal power of the Great Court that gave them judicial authority.

At that time, the Great Court realized its loss of legal, judicial power. They knew they had finally lost the scepter and were in dismay! There was a general cry of, "Woe unto us, for the scepter, has departed from Judah, and the Messiah has not come," with weeping and lamenting in the streets of Jerusalem over the matter.

However, in time, a significant degree of local self-government was approved. The Great Court then had restored to it some or partial control over leading the Nation in agreement with the Mosaic laws.

The Great Court was now reinstated in its appropriate place, in the 'Chamber of Hewn Stone,' beside the Temple.

So with this, a period of relative calm had returned. (*Except the return of the power to exercise capital punishment had not happened, the scepter had indeed permanently departed*).

As a result, all the Rabbis, learned men, and scribes recognized the long-awaited 'Messiah' should have been alive; and in the Temple, at this same period].

CHAPTER EIGHT

CLASH WITH THE LEADERS OVER THE SABBATH.

At about the time, Jesus and disciples proceeded from town to town, taking the Kingdom's message to the people.

They walked through some grainfields; this happened to be a Sabbath day.

The disciples were hungry, so as they went along, they broke off some of the heads of the grain and ate them. Some Pharisees saw them doing this and went protesting to Jesus, "Look how, your disciples are breaking the Sabbath law of work, by harvesting grain on the Sabbath." They exclaimed.

"Have you never read of King David in the Scriptures, what he did when he and his companions were hungry?" Jesus asked them. "He went into the House of God, where David and his men eat the sacred loaves of bread.

Set aside so that priests only may eat, in doing so, broke the law.

Also, did you not read in the Law of Moses that the Temple priests who are on duty may work on the Sabbath? I tell you, there is one here among you who is far greater than the Temple!

However, if you knew the meaning of this Scripture: I desire for you to show mercy, not offer sacrifices.' You would not be so keen in condemning my innocent disciples. Because, the Son of Man is Lord, even over the Sabbath," Jesus declared, refuting their idea of keeping the law.

"Yes, the Son of Man is the Lord, even over the Sabbath, not a slave to the Sabbath." He stated to the Pharisees with finality, sealing the matter.

On another Sabbath day, Jesus went into a synagogue, where he noticed a man with a deformed hand since it was the Sabbath day, the enemies of Jesus. The teachers of religious law, along with the Pharisees, kept on watching Jesus closely.

They had planned that should he heal the hand of the man, to accuse him of working on the Sabbath.

The Pharisees questioned Jesus, "Does the law permit a person to work by healing on the Sabbath?" They asked (*Hoping he would say yes, allowing them to bring charges of law-breaking against him*).

"If any of you had any sheep that fell into a well on the Sabbath, would you not work to pull it out?" Jesus asked.

"Of course you would. So how much more valuable is a person than a sheep! Yes, the law permits a person to 'do good' on the Sabbath." He notified them.

"Come over here and stand in front of everyone," Jesus told the man with the deformed hand.

Then he turned to his critics, "What does the Law permit on the Sabbath, the doing of good deeds, or is it a day for doing evil things? Is this a day to save or destroy life?" He asked, looking around at them all.

However, they were all silent and would not give him an answer.

He looked around angrily at them, deeply saddened by their hardened hearts.

"Hold out your hand." He finally said to the injured man.

So as the man held out his hand, the hand became fully restored!

Then the Pharisees were so enraged, they went away immediately. They met with the supporters of Herod to plot how to carry out their previous plan to kill Jesus.

Soon after that, the Pharisees called a meeting of all of their members to conspire to kill Jesus.

Jesus, as a result, left that area because he knew what they were planning. As he did, many of the ordinary people followed him.

He healed all those that were sick among them, and while doing so, he earnestly warned them not to disclose his identity.

There is a prophecy in the writings of Isaiah regarding this.

"Behold! My servant, whom I uphold,
My Elect One in whom My soul delights!
I have put My Spirit upon Him;

He will bring forth justice to the Gentiles.
He will not cry out, nor raise His voice,
Nor cause His voice to be heard in the street.
A bruised reed He will not break,
And smoking flax He will not quench;
He will bring forth justice for truth.
He will not fail nor be discouraged,
Till He has establishe d justice in the Earth;
And the coastlands shall wait for His Law."
(Isaiah 42:1-4 NKJV).

After Jesus had finished telling these stories and illustrations, he left that part of the country along with his disciples.

As evening came when Jesus saw the surrounding crowd still following, he gave instructions to his disciples to get a boat ready.

FREEING A MAN WITH A LEGION OF DEMONS.

"Let us now go across to the other side of the lake," Jesus stated.

So they all got into the boat with Jesus and set off, leaving the crowds behind *(although some other boats followed).

A fierce storm suddenly struck the lake in the middle of the journey, with waves breaking into the boat. Jesus was, by this time, sleeping at the back of the boat with his head on a cushion. The disciples went back, waking him up, shouting. "Lord, save us! We're going to drown,

"Teacher, do you not care that we're going to drown," they ask him?

When Jesus woke up, He reprimanded the wind and said to the waves, "Be Silenced! Be still," He commanded.

Suddenly the howling of the wind ceased, transferring an immense spread of instant calm.

The disciples, who a moment before was afraid of the storm, were now absolutely terrified; they were utterly amazed.

"Who is this man," they questioned each other. "Even the winds and waves obey him!"

Jesus turned to them, "Why is it that you are so afraid? Do you still not have any faith," He queried reassuringly?

(Psalm 65:7: *You who still the noise of the seas, the noise of their waves, also the commotion of the peoples.*

(Psalm 107:29 *He stills the storm; thus its waves are still*).

After this incident, they arrived in the region of the Gerasenes, across the lake from Galilee (*Gadara, an area southeast of Lake Galilee.*)

The very moment that Jesus was climbing out of the boat. There was an incident where two strange-looking men possessed by demons ran towards the little party of men to meet Jesus. As Jesus was walking and still some distance away, the men watched his approach and bowed low before him.

These men lived in a cemetery and were so violent that no one could go through that area. Day and night, they wandered among the burial caves and in the hills, howling and cutting themselves with sharp stones.

'Jesus Son of the Most High God? One of them began screaming at him, 'Why are you interfering with us. Why have you come here? Is it to torture us before the time appointed by God? The spirit said, speaking through the possessed man.

All this shouting was because by then, Jesus had already given a spoken command to the spirit in one man, "Come out of the man, you evil spirit," He told him with authority.

"Why are you Jesus, Son of the Most High God, interfering with me? In the name of God, I'm begging of you, do not torture me," this the second of the two men screamed.

"What is your name," Jesus demanded.

"My name is Legion," He replied, "because there are many of us inside this man."

*(This exchange was a battle of wills, first, by the demons calling Jesus' full name and title. This was not initially because of respect or acknowledgment of His authority, but was, in reality, an attempt at pure intimidation, [*we know all about you, we have power*].

Second by replying, 'my name is Legion' was not the whole truth. The demon is merely saying there are many of us, implying strength, [*we've built a stronghold here in this man*].

They knew that they would have to go but wanted to negotiate terms; they had already failed to kill or intimidate Jesus with the storm while he was in the boat.

Of the two men from the tombs that met Jesus, the demons had witnessed one man already delivered, rendering that or those demons subdued).

The evil spirits began begging him repeatedly not to send them out of the area to some distant place or into the abyss of the bottomless pit.

This man out of the two could no longer be restrained, even with a chain. Often he had been placed in chains and shackles; each time, he would snap and smash off the chains from his wrists as easily as he did those shackles. No one had been strong enough to subdue him.

Nearby on the hillside, a large herd of pigs was feeding.

"Send us into the pigs over there," the spirits begged, "Let us enter them.

Accordingly, Jesus permitted them. The evil spirits exited the man leaving without trouble, then entered the pigs. The entire herd of about 2,000 pigs became frightened, and stampeding, they ran headlong down the steep hillside, plunging into the lake and drowned in the water.

(*Note: Granting the request of the demons meant that they would leave the man without a fight, 'would not tear him,' this would have caused much damage and suffering as there was a vast number of demons).

We could think of the entire confrontation like this!

Demons to Jesus, 'we have power Jesus, as you can see, *(by that power), we recognize you, *(Son of the Most High God), and are ready for a fight.

Jesus to the Demons, "who are you? And what is your name?"

Demons to Jesus, 'we are very many, and we will put up such a fight it will badly damage this man in the struggle.

We admit you have the power to throw us into the specially prepared dungeon *(Abyss), where we will be tortured without hope of escape. Still, we won't go without a big fight.

Jesus to the demons, 'Oh, indeed?'

Demons to Jesus, 'if you don't send us out of the area, and allow us to take possession of those pigs over there. Then we will leave quietly, coming out of this man without making a fuss or any damage to him.

Jesus to the demons, 'as you wish, but go, right away,

When the herdsmen saw the pigs drown, they took off to the nearby town and the neighboring land, spreading the news as they ran. People from the area rushed out to see what had happened. A crowd soon gathered around Jesus. And by the time they arrived there, they saw the man who had been freed from the many demons. He sat contentedly at the feet of Jesus, fully clothed and perfectly sane, and they were all afraid.

Then those who had seen what had taken place told the others how the demon-possessed man came to be healed.

A great wave of fear swept over those people from the region of the Gerasenes that had gathered there, so they pleaded with Jesus to go away and leave them alone.

As a result, Jesus was about to return, crossing back to the other side of the lake. The man who was now freed from the many demons requested to go with him.

However, Jesus sent him home, "No, you go on back to your family, and let them know everything God has done for you," he instructed the man.

The man went ahead, visiting the Ten Towns, *(Decapolis; Greek: Deka, ten; polis, city). Of that region, and declared the great things Jesus had done for him. This witness from the man was the source of amazement to everyone that he told *(This work of evangelism would pay dividends later, after the day of Pentecost, as we see reported in Acts 8:40, **But Philip found himself at Azotus**) In the Decapolis' Ten Cities' area.

[The town Gadara and the city Gerasa were to the east of the Sea of Galilee and the River Jordan.

Gadara was a small town by the sea's eastern shore; Gergesenes was the wider country with Gerasa as its capital.

The small town is near the Sea of Galilee, and the larger City was Gentile areas occupied with Greek populations.

Having become possessed by demonic spirits, the swine behaved in a fashion utterly divergent from normal swinish behavior. Pigs rarely run far, yet the slope down into the sea facilitated them.]

Jesus then returned in the boat again to the other side of the lake. The people there were eagerly waiting for any news of him, and a large crowd gathered around him on the shore, where they excitedly welcomed him.

FAITH OF A WOMAN WITH AN ISSUE OF BLOOD: AND RAISING OF THE DAUGHTER OF JAIRUS.

Soon after his arrival there, a man named Jairus, a local synagogue leader, approached.

The moment he saw Jesus, he came and fell at the feet of Jesus; he pleaded fervently with him. "Please come home with me; my little daughter is dying," He said, "Lay your hands on her, healing her, so she will live.

This little girl was his only child; she was about twelve years old; Jesus set off with him as the people followed, crowding around him.

A vast jostling crowd again surrounded Jesus as he and the disciples started out, journeying along, going to the man's house.

A woman was among the crowd who had suffered for twelve years with an illness of constant bleeding. She had been suffering considerably from the attempted cures of many doctors. Although, over the years, she had spent everything she had to pay them, yet she had gotten no better. Instead, she had steadily become worse.

The woman heard about Jesus. As a result, she approached from behind him, pushing through the crowd, enabling her to touch the end of his clothes. Immediately as she did this, the bleeding stopped. And she could feel in her body her terrible condition was healed. This is because she thought to herself, "If I can just touch the fringe (*tassel*) of his robe, I will be healed.

(The scriptures from Malachi 4:2: prophesied this concerning the Messiah to come.

But to you who fear My name, The Sun of Righteousness shall arise, With healing in His wings (NKJV).

Believing the teaching that the Messiah indeed had healing in His wings or 'Borders,' she took action with faith and resolve even in her desperation).

In faith, she reached out for his *tzitzit*, namely ritual tassels placed on each corner (*kanaf*, in Hebrew).

Jesus, at once, realized that power for healing had gone out from him, "Who is it that touched my clothes," He asked as he turned around in the crowd of people.

"Look at this crowd pressing around you," His disciples protested, "how can you ask, who has touched me," they asked.

"Who is it that touched my robe? Jesus asks again, insisting on an answer.

Everyone denied it, and then Peter spoke up for the others, "Master, this entire crowd is pressing around you, He said.

Jesus kept looking about to learn who had done it.

"Someone deliberately touched me," Jesus announced, "because I felt healing power go out from me.

The woman then realized that she could not remain concealed. Though frightened and trembling at the realization of what had happened to her, she came and fell to her knees before him, telling him what she had done. The entire crowd heard her explanation, with the motive for holding his garment, resulting in her being immediately healed.

"Daughter," Jesus said to her, with warmth and tenderness accepting her into the family of the covenant. "Your faith has made you well; your suffering is over. Now go in peace."

(Her fear was justified because just being out in public was enough to get her stoned, and it was strictly forbidden for her to touch any person).

> Zechariah 8:22-23 (EHV) **Then many peoples and mighty nations will come to seek the Lord of Armies in Jerusalem and to plead for the favor of the Lord.**
> **This is what the Lord of Armies says. In those days, ten men from among the speakers of every language of the nations will take firm hold of the hem of a Jew's garment and say, "Let us go along with you, because we have heard that God is with you".**

While in the middle of this conversation with her, some messengers arrived from Jairus's home. "Your daughter has died." They announced to Jairus. "There is no further use disturbing the teacher now."

Jairus came and knelt before Jesus. "My daughter has just died," he said, "Yet you can bring back her life if you will just come with us and lay your hand on her."

Jesus had overheard their report to the child's father, and so he reassured Jairus, "Do not be frightened. Have faith, and presently, you will see that she will receive healing," He said.

Then he stopped the crowd from trailing and let no one follow him to the house except Peter, James, and John *(the brother of James).

They arrived back with Jairus at his home, and as they entered the place, Jesus saw much commotion and wailing. He moved through the crowds and went inside.

Jesus would let no one go in with him except Peter, John, James, plus the Father and mother of the little girl. Mourners filled the house; people were all around weeping and wailing.

"The child is not dead; she is only asleep," Jesus informed them.

The crowd, however, scoffed at him mockingly because they all knew she had died.

"All of you get out," He instructed them, "The child is asleep; she is not dead," He repeated.

After the crowd was removed to the outside, Jesus taking only the father and mother of the girl, along with his three disciples, went to the area where the girl was lying dead.

Then Jesus took her by the hand, "Talitha koum," meaning, "Little child, I command you to wake up, He commanded with a loud voice.

Then, her life returned at that moment, and the twelve-year-old girl immediately stood up and walked around! It overwhelmed her parents with amazement, but Jesus gave them strict orders insisting that they should tell no one what had happened; he told them to give her something to eat. However, the report of this miracle swept through the entire countryside.

After Jesus and his disciples left the home of Jairus and his family, two blind men followed along behind him, "Son of David, have mercy on us, They shouted, using the Messianic title to address Jesus.

They persisted until they entered right into the house where he went to stay. "Do you believe this? That I can make you see again," Jesus asked them?

"Yes, Lord, we do," they answered with total faith.

He then touched their eyes and said, "Because of your faith, it will happen. Suddenly their eyes were opened, and they could see! "Be sure that you do not tell anyone about this, Jesus sternly warned them.

However, they instead went out and spread his fame all over the region.

Later, when they left the house, people brought to Jesus, a demon-possessed man who could not speak. So Jesus drove out the afflicting demon, then after, the man started to talk. The crowds were amazed. "Nothing like this has ever before happened in Israel," They exclaimed with joy and excitement.

However, the Pharisees were unhappy, "He can cast out demons because the prince of demons empowers him," they claimed.

Jesus left that part of the country, returning to Nazareth, his hometown. The next Sabbath, he was found teaching in the synagogue. It amazed everyone when he taught there, "From where does he get this wisdom and such power to do miracles," they were asking?

"He is only the carpenter's son, and we know Mary, his mother, his brothers James, Joseph, Simon, and Judas. Also, his sisters live right here among us. Where did he learn all these things," they asked each other with disdain?

Just the idea deeply offended them, and they refused to believe in him; *(The use of his mother to identify his family was a way of insulting him, as men were usually only identified through the lineage from their father).

Jesus again reminded them. "They everywhere recognized a Prophet except his hometown, among his relatives and his own family, He said.

So great was their unbelief; Jesus could not do many miracles in their company, except only placing hands on a few sick people healing them.

Jesus was unusually and genuinely shocked at the level of their cynicism.

Jesus traveled around the area. He was going into all the cities and the villages, teaching weekly in the local synagogues. Proclaiming and teaching the Kingdom and its Good News, healing all the various diseases and sicknesses of the people.

However, when he saw the vast number of people making up a large crowd, it deeply moved him with great compassion over them because they were struggling and scattered, like sheep without a shepherd.

JESUS SELECTS AND SENDS OUT THE TWELVE TO TEACH AND PROCLAIM THE KINGDOM.

Jesus called all his disciples together to explain the task and the problem, "The harvest is certainly plentiful, and yet the laborers are few. Therefore, pray that the Lord of the harvest will send out laborers into his harvest, He told them.

Taking the twelve disciples apart from the others, Jesus gave them authority to cast out unclean spirits, with power over them, and with the ability to heal every disease and any sickness, then started sending them out two at a time. Their commission was to preach the kingdom and heal the sick.

So here are the names of the twelve chosen, which Jesus named apostles. The first was Simon, called Peter *(Stone), Andrew, his brother; then James and his brother John, who were the sons of Zebedee; along with Philip; Bartholomew; Thomas; Matthew, *(Levi) The tax collector; Judas

Iscariot, who became the betrayer; James the son of Alphaeus; Lebbaeus, *(Thaddaeus); and Simon, the Canaanite *(the Zealot).

Jesus gave them essential and needed instructions as he sent these twelve out, "Do not go among the Gentiles, or enter into any city of the Samaritans, He told them.

"Rather, go instead to the lost sheep of the house of Israel. As you go, proclaim this message and tell the people, 'The Kingdom of Heaven is near to you,

To confirm this truth heal the sick of their sickness, cleanse leprosy from people with the disease, and command demons to (come out) of the possessed. Be sure to do all this free, freely you received, so you also freely give.

Do not take any gold, silver, or even brass in your money belts.

Take no bag for your journey, or either two coats, or shoes, no staff, no bread: because 'the laborer is worthy of his hire, (*Or wage, an ancient adage.*)

Deuteronomy 25:4 "**You shall not muzzle an ox when it is treading out the grain**.

After entering a city or village, first, find out who is welcoming; then stay there until you go on.

Upon entering the house, greet it; if the household is worthy, let your peace rest on it. However, if it is not honorable, let your peace return to you.

If people do not receive or hear your words, shake the dust off your feet as you exit that house or city.

I tell you honestly; the land of Sodom and Gomorrah will have it more tolerable than for that city in the Day of Judgment.

* *(Note; there are levels of peace; one is the peace with God, there is also the peace from God plus the Peace of God. Here is an example of the peace from God; Jeremiah 16:5 I have taken away My peace from this people.*

When announcing the birth of Jesus to the shepherds, the Angel said, 'peace on the earth to all those with whom God is pleased.')

"Understand; I am sending you out as sheep's in the middle of wolves, therefore for that reason, be as wise as serpents, yet as harmless as doves.

Remember this, pay attention because the time will come when some men will bring charges against you in their meetings. They will roughly beat you in their synagogues. They will indeed bring you before governors and kings for my sake because you are a testimony to them and the nations.

However, when they persecute you, do not worry or be anxious about what you will reply. Since anything that is necessary for you to speak, you will receive it at that moment.

Since it is not you who will speak, instead, it is the Spirit of your Father who speaks within you.

Brother will bring accusations against brother, even though it will lead to their death and the father against his child. Children will rebel against their parents, causing their execution.

All men will hate you since you carry my name; however, the one who will want eternal rescue must continue to the end.
So be sure that when they persecute you in this city, escape into the next. Because I tell you assuredly, you will not have gone through all the cities of Israel until the arrival of the Son of Man." *(Brings Judgment.) Isaiah 13:2-5.

"Just as a disciple is not above his teacher, or a servant is above his Lord.

It is good enough for the disciple to be like his teacher and the servant as his Lord. If they call the master of the house Beelzebub, then the household members will also be labeled this and much more!

As a result, be not afraid of them because everything covered will be exposed. All hidden things will be known, so all I tell you in the darkness speak in the light; whatever you hear whispered in the ear, proclaim on the housetops.

Worry not even a little, or be fearful of those who kill the body yet cannot kill the soul; fear instead, He who can destroy both soul and body in Gehenna.

Two small sparrows sell for a coin of small value, are they not? Your Father ensures none of them falls on the ground outside his will. Down to the very hairs of your head are all numbered.

Then for that reason, do not be afraid; you are much more valuable than many sparrows.

As a result, everyone who will, without concern, declare me to others. I will also claim that person in front of my Father in Heaven.

However, those who deny me to others: before my Heavenly Father, I will also deny them.

Don't think that I came primarily to send peace into the Earth. No, I did not come to send peace, but alternatively a sword.

I am here putting a man and his father at variance—daughter against mother, as well, a daughter-in-law against mother-in-law.

The enemies of a man will be among those living in his household.

Those loving fathers or mothers more than me is not worthy of me!

Any loving son or daughter greater than me is not worthy of me.

A person not taking his cross and following me is not worthy of me.

The one pursuing only his life will lose it, yet he who loses his life because of my sake will ultimately gain it.

Those accepting you, accept me, as does anyone receiving me accepts him who sent me; the one who accepts a Prophet in the name of a Prophet will receive the reward of a Prophet. Everyone welcoming a righteous person because of their righteousness will share the same reward as that upright person.

The person giving one of these little ones just a single cup of cold water to drink in the name of a disciple; I tell you they will not lose their reward."

Jesus concluded the assigning of directions to the disciples he had chosen then sent them on the mission. Then, he and the rest of his followers set off in a separate course, teaching and preaching in the surrounding towns and cities.

The disciples left and started telling everyone they met to repent of their sins and turn to God. They forced out many demons and healed sick people, anointing them with olive oil.

Herod had captured and detained John the Baptizer at about this time, chained and placed him in prison, on account of what he had preached about the woman, whom Herod had married, by the name of Herodias.

This woman was already the wife of Herod's brother Philip. John had often preached against this, "It is not legitimate for you to be married to her." John had railed at Herod as he preached his categorical message of righteousness.

Herodias was angry with John over this, but Herod had guards posted around him, so she could not get her way! And though she increasingly wanted to kill him, John was, in fact, feared by Herod.

Herod lived in constant fear of the vast numbers of people who considered John to be a Prophet. And had it not been for this, he would have had John killed. He also kept him safe, knowing that he was a righteous and holy man from the many things he did and said. He was happy to go often and listen to John, yet would be very confounded hearing him preach, still did nothing to show a willingness to change.

There was an occasion when Herod made a big feast for his aristocratic friends and the High officials and the chief men of the Galilee region — gathering for his birthday tribute.
During this big party, the daughter of Herodias came into the room to dance in the middle of them; she delighted Herod and the others sitting with him with this dance. *(Most likely by the name of Salome, daughter of Herod Philip (son of Herod the Great and Cleopatra of Jerusalem) and Herodias, granddaughter of Herod the Great, the stepdaughter of Herod Antipas, tetrarch of Galilee).

In his state of vanity and inflated self-esteem, the King, looking to make a big theatrical display to his guests, told this young woman, "ask of me anything that you want, and I will give it to you," He said as a grand gesture. At which point he guaranteed it with an oath, "Regardless of what you will ask from me, I will give you, even if it is up to half of my kingdom."
Herod promised her this in what he thought was a witty move, as only through marriage could this be achieved. Hence, if she were to accept half of his kingdom, she would consent to the marriage and probably to the death of her mother as well.

The young woman swiftly left the dinner party, going out to seek advice from her mother, "What will I ask for," the daughter enquired?
"Ask him to produce the head of John the Baptizer." Her mother instructed.
Hurrying back immediately, she went to the King, "I want you to give me now, the head of John the Baptizer on a tray," she said.
The King was distressed over this, which made him highly regretful, yet, because of his grand bragging oath. Fearing losing face with those who sat at the dinner table with him, he did not see how to refuse her.

Herod straight away instructed a soldier of his guard, sending the officer to bring back the head of John.

Hence the soldiers went and beheaded John within the prison.

The head of John was fetched unto them on a tray and given to the young woman, and taking his head, she carried it to her mother.

JOHN'S DISCIPLES RECEIVED NEWS OF THE TRAGIC EVENT.

As a result, they went into the prison and got hold of his body, and went and placed it in a tomb.

After that, they went and informed Jesus of this sad news about John.

After Jesus heard the news about John, he crossed Lake Galilee in a boat to go to some remote area where he could be alone.

The crowds, however, having found out, followed him on foot from the towns. Stepping from the boat, Jesus, on seeing an immense crowd waiting, had compassion for them, healing those who were sick among them.

Shortly after this, when this same Herod (the tetrarch) heard the descriptions of Jesus and everything he was doing, Herod was very anxious, becoming confused and disturbed. Some people said that John had risen from the dead.

Others, that it was Elijah that had appeared, as this was the widespread expectation. Some others claimed it was one of the old Prophets that had appeared again.

Herod wanted to see Jesus and spoke to the people surrounding him. "I know that I have beheaded John, so who can this be, this man that I hear so many things about, Herod asked, somewhat nervously.

"This has to be John the Baptizer, returned from the dead, even though I had him beheaded. And is why powers like these are working in him," He declared to his servants.

CHAPTER NINE

DISCIPLES SUCCESSFUL MISSION: RETURNING TO THE SAD NEWS ABOUT JOHN.

The apostles who had gone on the mission finished and returned to meet again with Jesus.

They reported to him regarding the success of the things they had done and everything they had taught to those people of the towns where he had sent them.

The news of the death of John arrived to inform Jesus about the same time. So he assembled the disciples, "We need to separate ourselves from the crowds, and go into a quiet place so that we can rest for a time," He told them.

There was constant coming and going around them with so many people and so much activity, they often had no spare time, not even for stopping and eating.

The small party used a boat to take them over to the other side of the Sea of Galilee *(also called the Sea of Tiberias). They would try to find a more secluded area, away from the enormous crowds of people. They landed on the opposite beach near the City called Bethsaida.

Just the same, people saw them getting into the boat. And as usual, vast numbers of people followed them by whatever means that they could.

People had an appetite for more of the miracles they had witnessed Jesus performing. Since he healed all, they bought to him, every person who was sick or diseased.

As the group arrived near Bethsaida, the people recognized Jesus and also followed him on foot. The crowds grew as people came from the surrounding towns.

Jesus plus the disciples walked up a mountain, where they finally found a place in which the entire group could sit and rest for a time!

It was not long before Jesus saw that an even greater crowd of people was arriving to see him. As a result, he sympathized with them since they were like sheep lost without a single shepherd to lead and guide them.

Jesus explained many things to the people. So he welcomed them and caused all of them to be seated comfortably, then started telling them of matters relating to the Kingdom of God. He also healed each person who needed healing.

It was now near to the time of the Passover, one of the major feasts of the people of Israel (*Imperative for the people to leave and go to keep the Feast as commanded in the Torah*).

And as the day ended, the disciples began worrying about the welfare of the crowds. So they approached Jesus about it, "This is a deserted place, and it is already getting late in the day. And the people have nothing to eat, discharge them and allow them to go into the surrounding villages, and buy themselves food. And to local farms to find places where they can stay," they told him with concern.

"They will not need to go away," Jesus replied reassuringly.

He then turned and addressed Philip, "Where could we buy enough bread so that all these people may eat," Jesus asked him?

"Even if we were to spend two hundred Denarii on bread, that would not be enough food for them all, not for each person to receive even a little," Philip answered perplexed.

(*Note: One Denarii represented one day's wage for a skilled worker; hence two hundred Denarii would equate to over ten thousand dollars).

Jesus was testing the perception and faith of his disciples. He had given them many lessons of his absolute power over any situation, even nature. He wanted them to be sure that they could walk in the same authority.

Then Jesus called all the disciples, "You give them something to eat," He instructed them.

*(*They unsurprisingly took the directions literally and went searching through the crowds to find enough food to feed the people*).

Then, after searching through the crowds for provisions, Andrew, the brother of Simon Peter, came forward. "We have found a boy here with a little food he has with him five barley loaves and two fishes," Andrew reported. "Although that is far too small an amount, how could it feed so many people," He asked hesitantly?

The crowd was massive; counting only the men amid the people, the number would have easily been about five thousand people.

"Bring the bread and fishes here to me," Jesus instructed them.

They brought the food to Jesus, "Make all the people sit down, put them in groups of about fifty each," He directed.

The area had an adequate covering of grass, so the people all sat down in many groups, of sizes comprising roughly fifty.

*(Psalm 23, *The Lord is my shepherd; 'to feed, to guide and to shield me' I have everything I need 'will lack nothing' He lets me rest, 'makes me lie down in green pastures.*
He leads me beside the calm 'quiet' water.
He gives me new strength 'renews my soul. He leads me on 'righteous; or straight' paths for the 'sake' or 'reputation' of his 'good name').

Jesus picked up the five loaves and the two fish and looked up to the sky; he blessed them, then he broke them, after that, he gave them to the disciples.
The disciples then handed them out to the crowds, group by group, and kept giving to the people as much as all required.

Eventually, all the people were satisfied. Jesus then instructed his disciples, "Gather up all the broken pieces which are left over, so that there won't be a waste of anything," He said.

The disciples went through the crowds and gathered all the broken pieces left over from the five barley loaves and the two fishes. And from the remaining bits could fill, twelve baskets of those who had eaten.

(*Note: The number twelve symbolizes the government of the kingdom. The two items to be collected are bread and also the fish; Jesus had already said, 'I Am the bread of life.'

Representing the ones to whom Jesus came to give that new life. 'I will make you fishers of men.

These full baskets were a testimony to the extent of the miracle and only after the people were all wholly contented were the remains collected. The leftovers they gave to the poor among them).

> 2 Kings 4:42-44 (ESV) *A man came from Baal-shalishah, bringing the man of God bread of the First Fruits, twenty loaves of barley, and fresh ears of grain in his sack.*
> *And Elisha said, "Give to the men, that they may eat. But his servant said, "How can I set this before a hundred men," So he repeated, "Give them to the men, that they may eat, for thus says the Lord, 'They shall eat and have some left."*
> *So he set it before them. And they ate and had some left, according to the word of the Lord.*

*Note: The *entire week of the Feast of Unleavened Bread is also known as Passover. And this was the time of the Passover, where all able-bodied Israelite men were commanded to go to the Feast in Jerusalem.*

All your men shall arrive three on occasions in a year, to celebrate for seven days the Feast, to the LORD your God.

At the place, the LORD will choose (namely the Temple in Jerusalem).

On festivals of Pesah (Passover), Shavuot (the Feast of Weeks), and Sukkot (the Festival of Booths), they shall not arrive empty-handed. Each must bring his own gift, relevant to the blessing which the Lord your God has given you" Deuteronomy 16:16.

This meant the situation warranted the disciple's concerns because the people needed to first go home and begin arranging for the pilgrimage to and returning from Jerusalem, an arduous journey of above one hundred miles to the City through rugged country. This was usually slow and cumbersome, with entire families and neighbors traveling and camping in a group (*As with Joseph, Mary, and Jesus when he was twelve years old*). They were currently in the wilderness near Bethsaida on the shore of the Sea of Galilee.

Barley being the first grain harvested in the spring, and the Feast of unleavened bread celebrates the first fruits of the barley harvest.

Barley being cheaper than wheat made the bread the poor ordinarily ate, called barley loaves (actually small cakes).

As a result of this miracle produced by Jesus, the people became very enthusiastic and excited about his power. "He is with no doubt 'the very Prophet' for whom the world has been waiting." They were saying, referring to the promised Prophet foretold by Moses, for which all of Israel had eagerly awaited.

The LORD, your God. Will' elevate and establish' for you, a Prophet similar to me from among you, out of your brethren. Him, you will listen to. Deuteronomy 18:15-19.

Jesus knew then that they were on the verge of attempting to make him King. With great enthusiasm, the people were determined to take him by force and crown him King.

He took immediate action and compelled his disciples to get back down into the boat, sending them ahead of him to Capernaum on the other side of the lake. While they were doing this, he calmed the crowds, dispersing them and sending them home.

After directing all the people to go home, Jesus went up into the mountain alone to pray. Then when the night fell, he was there alone in prayer. His disciples, in the meantime, went down to the beach as directed. They had entered a boat in the early evening to go over the Sea to Capernaum.

They promptly departed as instructed. However, Jesus had still not arrived to join them. And it was now night. Jesus was alone on the land and now separated from them. And by this time, the boat was somewhere in the middle of the sea.

Suddenly a mighty blowing gale-force wind stirred up. And massive waves that had whipped up against them came from the opposing direction to the one they were rowing.

The men in the boat had been rowing, and rowing yet had not got very far. And it was now the middle and darkest part of the night.

So Jesus, perceiving the enormous challenge to the rowing they were having caused by the adverse conditions, went out towards them, walking on the sea.

Jesus looked as if he quite intended to be walking past the boat, except the disciples, when seeing him walking on the sea and moving closer and closer to the ship, they were anxious and somewhat uneasy, imagining that it was a ghostly apparition on the water.

They had become terrified. "It is a ghost," they cried out.

All of them saw him and were disturbed in the extreme by what they were seeing.

However, Jesus directly spoke to calm them, "Cheer up! I Am! Do not be afraid," He said reassuringly and with authority.

The sound of his voice gave them courage, and so Peter called out to him, "Lord, if it is indeed, you, command that I can walk over the water to you," He said rather courageously.

"Yes, come," Jesus replied, answering both the first question and the request.

Peter then stepped down from the boat, began walking over the top of the water to go to Jesus. Now, as he walked and saw how strong the wind was, he became fearful of the wind and waves. At this, he started to sink; as this happened, he had only one prayer, "Lord, save me," Peter shouted.

Immediately Jesus was there, stretching out his hand and seizing the hand of Peter with strength.

"Oh, you of such little faith, why did you have such uncertainties and disbelief," Jesus asked him?

Because of this incredible event, the rest of the crew were eager to receive Jesus along with Peter back into the boat.

As soon as they got into the boat, the winds died down, and all was calm again.

All of them were in awe and stunned at this. So much so that the disciples rushed over and worshipped Jesus, "You are truly the Son of God," They exclaimed.

The disciples managed to miss this truth during the miracle where Jesus multiplied the loaves and fishes. This Jesus said was on account of the hardness of their hearts.

The boat was immediately and suddenly at the land where they were going.

So now that they had crossed over, they landed at Gennesaret and moored to the shore.

*The loaves and fishes tested their understanding of whom he is and their authority (Jesus had said to them, 'you give them something to eat'). This likewise was an event testing the disciple's level of growth in faith.

Jesus appeared to be walking past at first. But note, he did not calm the storm when he had started from the shore. When the event was over, their boat was immediately at its destination.

After embarking from the boat and resting through the night, the people in the area recognized Jesus. They ran around that entire region telling the news. Therefore, people bought sick people on their mats to where they heard he was.

It was always the case wherever he went, whether into villages, cities, or the countryside.

It was usual for the local people to lay their sick in the market-places and pleaded to only touch the border of his garment. As many as reached him found they had been changed and made entirely well.

*Note: *The reference to 'border' is the tassels of twisted blue wool hanging off the corners of a cloak. The winding blue cord or hanging tassels memorialized the wearer's lineage and the family seal of authority. So important they could even be used as a family seal or pledge by pressing it into soft clay.*

Commanded in the Mosaic Law (Numbers 15:37–41), for men to wear the fringe as a reminder to obey the law. This grew to be the cultural norm to have long fringes tzitziot (Hebrew tzitzit), Interpreted as wings from the Hebrew kanaph, meaning the skirt or corner of a piece of clothing.

Following the extraordinary testimony concerning the woman with the issue of blood, who had received instant healing, spreading widely through the area, it inspired the people in the Galilee region to imitate touching Jesus' garment and received healing by faith.

SOME FOLLOWERS DEPARTED NOT BEING ABLE TO RECEIVE THE TEACHING.

On that next day, the crowd of people standing on the other side of the sea noted no other boat was there, only the disciple's vessel. Also, he had not entered the ship with his disciples, as the disciples had gone away alone. However, many of the boats from Tiberias came to where they had eaten the bread. After the Lord had given thanks and fed them.

Once the people saw Jesus was not there or indeed his disciples. They got into the boats themselves, coming over to Capernaum In search of Jesus.

When they eventually found him on the other side of the sea, they could not understand, "Teacher, when did you come here," They asked him, puzzled?

"You are hunting for me," Jesus answered, "I tell you in truth, it is not because you saw and believed the miracles, but only because you ate the loaves and were content with that food. *(believing the miracles would show they trust God).

Do not work for the food, which passes away, rather for the food that remains to eternal life, the life that the Son of Man will give to you since God the Father has sealed him." He told them as a warning to them, pointing out the importance of putting the Kingdom first.

"What will be the requirements for us to do, so we can perform the works of God," They asked?

"This is the true work of God that you believe in him, the one whom he has sent," Jesus answered.

"What then will you do for a sign so that we will see and believe you? What miracle will you do, they inquired with more than a bit of arrogance.

"Our fathers ate of the manna in the wilderness," They continued, "Just as it is written in the scriptures, He gave them bread out of heaven to eat," *(By this, they were asking Jesus for more miracles of the type that Moses had performed).

"Most certainly, I tell you," Jesus said, "it was not Moses who gave you the bread out of Heaven, but my Father gives you the real bread out of Heaven.

Since the bread of God is that which comes down out of Heaven and gives life to the world, He informed them, moving the focus of the subject back to the spiritual and the Kingdom."

"Lord, always give us this bread?" They asked with keen interest, now that the subject was about something that they really desired.

"I am the bread of life. Those coming to me will not be hungry, and those believing in me will never be thirsty," Jesus replied.

"Although as I told you, having seen me, you still do not believe me, all of those that Father gives to me will come to me. All those coming to me, I will not in any way throw them out.

Because coming down from Heaven, I am not here to do my will, but the will of him who sent me.

So this is the will of my Father who sent me. So that, of all he has given to me, I should lose not one, yet raise that person to life on the last day.

Also, it is the will of the Father who sent me so everyone who believes in the Son should have eternal life; therefore, I will raise him to life on the last day," Jesus said, reminding his listeners again of this vital teaching.

Some leaders took offense over this and were mumbling complaints about him since he said. 'I am the bread which came down out of heaven.'

"Is this not Jesus, whose Father is Joseph and is known to us along with his mother? Then how does he say, 'I have come down out of heaven?" They asked, complaining and murmuring to each other.

"Do not mumble among you," Jesus said to them, "None can come to me other than been drawn by the Father who has sent me, and I will raise them from death to life on the last day.

The writings of the Prophets say, 'God will teach them all. (Isaiah 54:13). So everyone who hears and learns from the Father will draw close to me.

Apart from the one who is from God, no one has seen the father.

I tell you truthfully; he who believes in me has eternal life.

I Am, the bread of life.

Your fathers died even though they ate the manna in the wilderness.

Here is the real bread that comes down from Heaven, and anyone may eat of it and not die.

I am that living bread coming to the world from Heaven. Anyone eating this bread will live forever. Yes, the food which I will give for the life of the world is my flesh," He Explained.

Jesus was teaching the people in Capernaum, some of these things he was saying, he said in one of the local synagogues.

The leaders disputed with each other, "How can this man give us his flesh to eat?" They were asking.

"I tell you positively," Jesus said, "Except for you eating the Son of Man's flesh and drinking his blood, you have not any life within yourself.

Any person eating my flesh and drinking my blood has eternal life, and I will raise him to life on the last day.

For my flesh is, in truth, real food, and my blood is, in reality, real drink; any person who eats my flesh and drinks my blood lives in me, and I in him.

The living Father has sent me; therefore, I live because of the Father; in the same way, the one who feeds on me will also live because of me, so this is the real bread, which came down out of Heaven; not as your fathers ate the manna yet died. Alternatively, those who eat this bread will live forever."

Many of his disciples grumbled when they heard this. "This speech is extremely hard-hitting and such difficult teaching! Who can bear to listen to it," They said antagonistically?

However, since Jesus knew within himself that his disciples grumble at this, he challenged them, "Does this cause you to stumble," He asked pointedly? "Then what if you witnessed the Son of Man ascending to where he was before? It is the Spirit that gives life. The flesh can achieve nothing for you; the very words that I am speaking to you are Spirit and Life, although some of you do not believe."

Since from the beginning, Jesus knew those who did not believe and the person who would betray him.

"For this reason," He told them, "I have said to you, no person can be drawn to me except being granted to him by my Father."

Many of his disciples departed from this point, and because of this, would not go any further with him. As a result, Jesus turned to the twelve, "What about you, do you also want to go away," He asks.

Simon Peter answered for them all, "Lord, to whom could we possibly go? You possess the words of eternal life.

We believe as true, trusting with faith that you are the Christ, the Son of the living God!" Said Peter with zeal.

"Did I not choose the twelve of you," Jesus asks them, "And yet, one of you is a devil," He stated.

He was referring to Judas, the son of Simon Iscariot, since although he was one of the twelve, it was he who would be the betrayer.

Sometime later, Jesus was walking in Galilee because he would not go into the Judean region for a time. Since the leaders over there were plotting and scheming how to kill him.

A delegation of Pharisees, as well as the Scribes, came from Jerusalem to observe him. In doing so, they sought an opportunity to find something with which to accuse Jesus.

As Jesus was teaching the people, one of the Pharisees invited him home for a meal. Jesus accepted the invitation; he went into the house and took his place at the table. After observing, it amazed his host that he sat down to eat without first performing the hand-washing ceremony required by Jewish custom.

So when they observed some of his disciples also eating bread with unwashed hands, they found the opportunity they were seeking.

((This is because the leaders, particularly the Pharisees, do not eat unless they wash their hands and forearms; this is in adherence to the tradition of the elders.*

They would never eat after coming from the marketplaces unless they bathe themselves; many other such traditions they insisted must be maintained: washings of cups, pitchers, bronze vessels, among many).

"Why do your disciples refuse to comply with the tradition of the elders, since they do not wash their hands when they eat bread?" The Pharisees and Scribes asked, challenging Jesus.

It did not impress Jesus; he rounded on them. "You carefully set aside the commandment of God, as you are clinging to the traditions of men, such as the washing of containers and cups. Yes, of course, you are quick to do many other such things.

You neatly reject the commandment of God entirely, so that all of your personal traditions. You can conveniently keep.

Therefore, by creating your traditions which you have handed down, that neatly cancels the word of God. You continuously do many things like this.

What is the reason for you to disobey the commandment of God, replacing it with your tradition?

Because God commanded, 'Honor your father and your mother,' and, 'the person who speaks evil of father or mother. Make certain that person is executed.

To make efforts to get around this, you have made a rule, stating. 'If a man informs his father or his mother, 'any profit you might have received from me is, in fact, a gift to be given to God. Then regardless of the kind of help you may have been able to receive from me, it is now made a gift devoted to God.

With this, you no longer allow that person to do anything for his father or his mother.

'So now he is no longer obliged to honor his father or mother,' this way, you have worked to make the commandment of God void because of your tradition.

You fraudulent play-actors," He denounced them. "The prophecies of Isaiah are about you and is fitting, where he had said, 'these are the one's drawing near to me with their mouth they are honoring me with their lips, yet their heart is far from me.

They are worshiping me in vain, teaching as doctrine the rules made by men," Jesus told them, speaking with an undeniable truth that convicts because it cuts to the heart.

Jesus continued, "You Pharisees are so careful to clean the outside of the cup and the dish, yet inside you are filthy! Full of greed and wickedness! Fools! Did not God make the inside and the outside?

Then clean the inside by giving gifts to the poor, and you will be clean all over.

What sorrow awaits you, Pharisees, since you are careful to tithe even the tiniest income from your herb gardens, yet you ignore justice and the love of God.

Yes, you should tithe; however, do not neglect the more important things.

What sorrow awaits you, Pharisees! Since you love to sit in the seats of honor in the synagogues and receive respectful greetings as you walk in the marketplaces. Yes, what sorrow awaits you! You are like graves in a field hidden neatly.

People walk over them all day without knowing the corruption they are stepping on."

"Teacher," an expert in religious law spoke up, "you have also insulted us in what you just said."

"Yes," replied Jesus, "What sorrow also awaits you experts in religious law since you overload people with unbearable religious requirements, even though you never lift a finger to ease the burden.

What sorrows await you! Because you build monuments for the prophets that your ancestors killed long ago. And you yourselves stand as witnesses, agreeing with the actions of your ancestors; they killed the prophets, and by building their monuments, you join in their crime!

God, in His wisdom, said this relating to you: 'I will send them prophets and apostles, yet some they will kill, and the others persecute.'

This generation will, as a result, be held responsible for the murders of all the Prophets of God, beginning from the creation of the world, even from the murder of Abel, to the death of Zechariah the Prophet. Some they killed between the altar and the sanctuary. Yes, it will undoubtedly be the incriminating charge touching this generation.

How great is the sorrow waiting for you, experts in religious law? Since you remove the key to knowledge from the people, you do not enter the Kingdom yourselves. Yet, you prevent others from entering,"

Jesus told them, spelling out and exposing the actual problems and issues of these outwardly pious people.

As he was leaving the Pharisees host's home, the teachers of religious law and the Pharisees became hostile. They tried to inflame him with many questions. They desperately wanted to trap him into saying something that they could use against him.

Jesus called the waiting crowds to come near him to explain the issue, "Hear me, all of you, and understand.

There is nothing that enters the mouth of the man. That can defile him. However, it is those things coming out of the man's mouth; this pollutes the man.

"Anyone having ears to hear," Jesus cried out, "let him hear, He advised them firmly."

The disciples found an opportune moment to approach him about what happened, "Do you know it truly offended the Pharisees when they heard what you taught," they asked?

"Every plant will be uprooted, which my heavenly Father did not plant," He answered.

"Leave them to continue; they are blind guides of the blind; when any blind leads another blind, both fall's into a ditch," Jesus told them as the conclusion of the matter.

Later, when he went into a house away from the crowd, Peter sought more clarity on the subject, "Explain the parable to us, Peter asked.

"Do you also even now still do not understand," Jesus asked him, "Do you not recognize that food that goes into the mouth passes into the belly? And then out of the body. So it cannot defile the person because it does not go into his heart. But into his stomach, then out of the body as waste. As a result, it purifies all foods!

Whatever proceeds out of the mouth come from the heart; they defile the man. Because from the heart emerges evil thoughts, murders, adulteries, sexual sins, thefts, false testimony, coveting, wickedness, deceit, lustful desires, an evil eye, blasphemies, pride, and foolishness.

These things all come from within, and they are the ones that defile the man, but to eat with unwashed hands does not pollute the man," Jesus explained, showing them the difference between physical food and spiritual truth.

CHAPTER TEN

MEETING A CANAANITE WOMAN WITH UNSHAKABLE FAITH.

The small party left that area entirely, trekking forty miles further into the northern region of Tyre and Sidon, on the very border of the coast. They selected a local house for privacy; this was a short time away from the crowds, as they did not want anyone to find out where Jesus was. Yet, he could not escape being noticed by many of the local people. A Canaanite woman hailing from close to the borders of that region arrived, standing outside the house. She repeatedly shouted, over and over! "Lord, Son of David! Have mercy on me; a demon that continually seizes her relentlessly disturbs my daughter; she kept pleading, using a clear Messianic title to address Jesus.

Jesus went outside but did not answer her.

As the woman was a Greek, a Canaanite/Syro-Phoenician by race, this was a remarkable display of faith. An unclean spirit possessed her little daughter, and as a result, of hearing about Jesus. She came and fell at his feet in the act of worship. And she pleaded he would cast the demon out of her daughter.

The disciples came out of the house and urged him, "Send her away; because she is drawing attention to us by constantly howling after us, they advised.

"I was only sent to the lost sheep of the house of Israel," Jesus told the woman.

Still, she came and worshipped him, "Lord, have mercy, please help me, She pleaded.

"Allow the children first to be filled. Since it is not right to take the bread of the children and throw it to the dogs, Jesus told her, measuring the extent of her faith. As this term was the way, 'southern Judean Jews' referred to all non-Jews.

"Yes, Lord," She replied, "Although even the little puppies eat the crumbs from the children, which fall from their masters' table.

"Woman, because of what you have said, you show that you have great faith! As a result, you go on back home.

And you will find what you have desired has been done for you. Indeed, the demon has gone out of your daughter, Jesus said, commending her.

She left and went back to her house, where she found her child was lying peacefully on the bed and the presence of the demon that had plagued her gone. Her daughter had been completely healed and made well from that exact moment that Jesus spoke of it.

(*Note: This woman, a Greek, or Canaanite/Syro-Phoenician from the area of Tyre approached and called, 'Lord, Son of David' this is remarkable in faith and discernment, she is a 'none Jew,' but has faith in Jesus, and calls Him Lord (Adoni, Master/Ruler/God).

After the news of John's beheading had reached them, Jesus had said that they needed to get away and rest. However, wherever they went, the crowds had mobbed them. And because of his compassion had healed and fed them. Then, large groups followed him across the Sea of Galilee from Tiberias to Capernaum because of the bread they were seeking. But having told them he was the real bread from Heaven, and they would need to eat and drink him, as Spiritual food. Many of his followers departed for good. They did not believe in him though they witnessed his many miracles and even asked him to perform miracles on demand.

Shortly after, there was a confrontation with the Pharisees. They had witnessed him and his disciples eating without going through all the elaborate hand-washing ceremonies insisted on by the Pharisees.

They had invited him to dinner to weigh him up; hence they couldn't care less about the miracles and only sought to dispute who he was. Jesus had to tell them the harsh truth and point out what was genuinely unclean and from where it came (*which was the inside, not the outside*). Also, the difference between spiritual and physical, which not even his disciples understood without more profound teaching from him.

Finally, after traveling over 30 miles further north to a secluded house for the needed rest, away from all the unbelief and strife, then arrives a woman with total faith who knew Jesus as Lord; knew that he is the son of David (The Messiah).

Like Ruth (the Grandmother of King David) and Jesus' ancestor, a Moabite, thus intermarriage was prohibited for the children of Israel (Nehemiah 10:31, Nehemiah 13:1-3, Deuteronomy 23:3, Ezra 9-10)

Yet unshakable faith in God and deep love had made a lasting legacy and an example of faithfulness to all women throughout the generations. Likewise, this Canaanite woman exhibited such faith that it is no wonder that Jesus went outside and did not answer her.

In stark contrast; to all that had happened over the recent weeks, this was wonderful and of such considerable difference that the Lord had to be in wonderment at her tenacious faith.

The only other time that he had encountered faith like this was with the Roman Centurion, also a Gentile, (who, unlike *Jairus*, the leader of the synagogue. Who had pleaded with Jesus to follow him home and lay his hand on his little child to make her well). This man said that; he did not even need to come under his roof, just say the word, and he knew it was done.

After all the play-acting of the Pharisees, all the unbelief of the people, after everything he had suffered and had to contend with, here is that unshakable faith of the kind that pleases God and draws a response from him. (Hebrews 11:6, Genesis 22:16)

Then the moment he tested her by parodying what southerners would say. That towering faith proceeds from her like a refreshing river; this was indeed an extraordinary, even unforgettable moment).

*Note: (Deuteronomy 23:3). (**No Ammonite or Moabite shall enter the congregation of the LORD; even to their tenth generation**: Yet Boaz was the son of Rahab the harlot (who entered through faith), the seventh generation from Judah through Perez.

Rahab married Salmon, an Israelite from the tribe of Judah. Ruth and Boaz fathered Obed, who had Jessie, the father of David the King, the tenth generation from the sin of Judah, and his daughter-in-law Perez (Genesis 38:12-26).

Deuteronomy 23:2 (NKJV) *One of illegitimate birth shall not enter the assembly of the LORD; even to the tenth generation none of his descendants shall enter the assembly of the LORD.*

This lineage of Jesus, son of David through Ruth and Rahab back to Perez, is one of immovable faith of these extraordinary women.

JESUS FEEDS ANOTHER MULTITUDE.

Once again, Jesus left the area of Tyre and Sidon. He was returning near to the Sea of Galilee. The route took them through the middle of the region of the Ten Cities. (Decapolis is a predominantly Gentile area, where the man with the Legions of demons had been set free and had evangelized, providing a powerful witness all over that region).

The little party went up into the mountain and sat and rested there.

Great crowds were arriving to see him, having with them the lame, blind, mute, maimed, and many others, putting them down at his feet. He healed them; then they brought to him someone who was deaf and had an impediment in his speech, pleading with Jesus to lay his hand on the deaf man.

Jesus took him to one side privately away from the crowd putting his fingers into his ears; he spat and touched his tongue.

Looking up to Heaven and sighing, he said to him, "Ephphatha, Meaning "Be opened,

The young man's ears immediately opened; the obstruction released from his tongue allowed his speech to return to normal.

All the things they were seeing amazed the people in the crowd. They had witnessed the mute speaking. Injured people made whole, those that had been lame now walking and those that had been blind seeing. Everyone was shouting, praising, and glorifying the God of Israel.

Jesus took careful pains to keep the people's rising zeal and excitement; from getting out of hand. He, hence, gave instructions while healing people for them not to tell about this. Yet, the more widely people publicize to others about Jesus.

The crowd of people was overflowing with awe and wonder; excitement rippled through the mass of people; they were saying, "He has done all things well. He makes even the deaf hear and the mute speak,

*(The leaders had long taught the people that this was one of the Messianic signs, which only the Messiah can execute when he arrived).

As the vast crowds continued to swell, Jesus signaled for his disciples to gather for a discussion. When they all were together, he voiced a problem. "I have sympathy for these people since they have been with me continuously for three days and have nothing left to eat.

Because they may even faint on the way, I do not want to send them away fasting and hungry; some of them have traveled a long way, He said, outlining the issue.

"We are in a deserted place; where would we get so many loaves to satisfy such a vast number of people," asked the disciples? Having forgotten what had happened just a few months before, with the feeding of another crowd.

Jesus asked them to go check on the current provisions, "How many loaves do you have, here, now?" He enquired after they checked.

"Seven loaves and also a few small fishes," they replied.

The crowds were of about four thousand men. In addition, there were women and children. Jesus gave orders for them to be seated on the grass right there on the hill; as they did, he took the seven loaves, after he gave thanks, broke them, and gave out the pieces to the disciples to serve the people.

He also blessed the few small fishes that they had, and then he issued them to the disciples to serve the people.

Everyone there ate all that they wanted until they were satisfied. Afterward, the disciples remembered to collect the leftovers and collected seven extensive full baskets of all the leftover broken pieces.

Having eaten and rested, Jesus discharged then sent the crowd home, then withdrew with his disciples in a boat for the borders of Magdala, the west side of the lake, *(The place of the watchtower) near Dalmanutha.

Having arrived in Magdala, the crowds also immediately gathered around him; the local Pharisees and the Sadducees came together. They then questioned him, and they kept searching for a way to weigh him up. *(These two separate groups though at odds with each other, were both well represented among the leaders, with members serving on the Jewish ruling council, the Sanhedrin).

In the religious leader's minds, the category of miracles Jesus had been performing; were all confined 'to the earth. Healings, exorcisms, and the like, which are considered signs on earth.

They taught the people and built a tradition that a miracle done on earth could be a counterfeit from Satan; they assumed signs done in the sky or from Heaven to be from God.

The major Old Testament Prophets had provided signs from Heaven; Samuel had called down thunder and rain from Heaven.

The people Moses led through the wilderness had manna from Heaven provided by God, also the pillars of fire and cloud.

Elijah, when confronting the Prophets of Baal, had called down fire from Heaven.

By this thinking, they conveniently ignored and excused all the astonishing miracles that Jesus performed. In doing so, they failed in correctly inaugurating the proper and essential seven-day silent investigation, which was to be used to determine that Jesus was the Messiah and King of Israel (*initially it was done to some extent, yet because of their own prejudice and jealousy, they were more critical than seeking truth*).

The people kept asking him to show them a sign from Heaven to prove who he was.

Jesus sighed deeply in his Spirit, "Why do the people of this generation look for a sign" He asked?

"When it is evening, you see a red sky and say, 'It will be fair weather.

'Today, it will be foul weather,' you say in the morning, 'because the sky is red and threatening. You hypocrites! You know how to distinguish the appearance of the sky, yet you cannot determine the signs of the times!

An evil and adulterous generation continuously searches for a sign. I tell you truly, no sign will be given to this generation, except for the sign of the Prophet Jonah," he said to them.

And with this, he left them, again using the boat, going back to the other side. During the journey, the disciples realized they had forgotten to take any bread. They found they had only one loaf between them in the boat. Jesus started teaching them about the Jewish leaders, "Watch out and be wary of the yeast *(leaven) of the Pharisees, the Sadducees and the yeast of Herod," He told them.

The disciples, having heard this, started a discussion among themselves, "It is because we brought no bread," they said.

Jesus, right away, knew about it; he knew what they were mumbling. Why are you discussing regarding having no bread among yourselves, do you not discern as yet, or able to comprehend," He asked?

"You of such little faith, 'you are saying it is because you have brought no bread, are your hearts still hardened even now,

You have eyes, do you not see, you have ears, do you not hear, do you not remember?

"On breaking the five loaves among the five thousand people, how many baskets full of leftover pieces you collected," he asks them?

"Twelve," They replied.

"When the seven loaves fed the vast multitude of people, with four thousand men also women and children, how many baskets full of leftover broken pieces did you take up?"

"Seven," they replied.

"Do you still not understand yet," He asked, trying to get them to see the spiritual beyond the physical.

"How is it you do not realize that I did not speak to you regarding bread? Instead, I am telling you to be wary of the yeast of the Pharisees and Sadducees."

Then finally, they realized he did not tell them to beware of the yeast of bread, but the puffed up teachings of the Pharisees and Sadducees.

*(Priests called The Sadducees controlled the Temple in Jerusalem; the name comes from the priest Zadok. 1st Chronicles: those that supported Solomon against King David's fourth son Adonijah's bid for the throne), (Adonijah or 'Ăḏōnîyāh, 'my lord is Yah.')

Although few in numbers, the Sadducees were wealthy and influential; they controlled the Temple, giving them the 'all-important' position of authority.

They rejected any idea of the Messiah, the reality of spirits, the resurrection, any miracles, the existence of Satan, or the supernatural.

There was also a group within The Sadducees known as the Herodians—working with King Herod to return 'the Herods' to complete control over Israel.

Annas, the Priest, was the father-in-law of Joseph Caiaphas, *(Yosef Bar Kayafa). A total of six of his sons and sons-in-law eventually occupied the status of High Priest of the Temple during his lifetime. They controlled the Sadducees. They held power at all costs. Any talk of Messiah as possible King threatened their status, greatly frightening them.

When the group arrived and came ashore at Bethsaida, they hiked to the local town. The people of the area brought a blind man to Jesus, requesting for him to touch his eyes and heal the blind man.

Jesus took hold of the hand of the blind man, making him follow him, all the way out to the edge of the village away from the crowds. Jesus then placed saliva on his eyes, and after laying his hands on him, asked the man if he saw anything.

He looked up, "I see men, but I can see them like trees walking," he replied.

Jesus once more laid his hands on the eyes of the man.

This time as he was looking intently, his regular sight was restored; now, he could see everyone clearly.

Jesus sent him back to his own house, "Do not re-enter that village, or tell anyone that is in the village," He instructed him.

TEACHING ON THE EKKLESIA'S POWER OVER THE GATES OF HELL.

They traveled next to Caesarea Philippi, an area about 25 miles north of the Sea of Galilee. On arriving there, Jesus found time alone to pray. Just a few miles from Caesarea, situated on the slopes of Harmon, is the ancient city of Dan; this city was known first by the name Leshem (Joshua 19:47) or Laish (Judges 18:29).*(The entire area around Caesarea Philippi, with its natural beauty and picturesque setting, had long been a center for false religion.

A city also blessed with cooling springs of water bubbling up to make yet another source of the Jordan River.

Unfortunately, during the days of king Jeroboam, the son of Nebat, who ruled the Northern Kingdom, they made Dan into a cultic shrine. Where one of the two notorious golden calves was set up. Of course, it was but a short step from the worship of a bull to the worship of Ba'al.

{King Jeroboam I, ruler of the newly breakaway northern Kingdom of Israel, established two sanctuaries to rival the Temple of Solomon in Jerusalem:

The two golden calves were commissioned, constructed, and installed, one at each shrine, one in Dan, one in Bethel (meaning House of God), Dan on the northern border, and Bethel on the southern border close to Jerusalem.

Jeroboam ordained a new priesthood and launched a pilgrimage festival to rival Jerusalem's holy convocations on his own chosen date.

These shrines are depicted as active places of worship in the scriptures (2Kgs 10:29, Amos 4:4, Amos 8:14) also continuing at Bethel, afterward (2 Kgs 17:24-28), extending throughout the time of the existence of the Northern Kingdom.

The locations of these cities were well calculated, as Dan was Israel's northernmost city, intending to attract worshipers from the far north areas.

Bethel being in Ephraim, was the southernmost border of Jeroboam's Kingdom and considerably close to Jerusalem.

Located on the primary route to Jerusalem, Jeroboam's designed this alternative worship strategy to attract those once customary to worship in Jerusalem}. (1 Kings 12:25-33; 2 Chronicles 11:13-17).

Ultimately, the beautiful site of Dan helped bring about the fall of Israel, or the northern ten tribes. These tribes have since been in dispersion from that time to the present because of their idolatry.

When Herod Philip built a city at the fountains of Jordan, 'Paneas' so named and dedicated to the Greek fertility god Pan, he had re-named it Cesarea. The area had been littered with temples of the ancient Syrian Baal-worship *(about thirty years before this period, Philip named it Caesarea Philippi in honor of Caesar Augustus).

This distinguished it from another city called Caesarea by the Sea. And was a place strongly associated with idols and rival deities from all over the Gentile world.

Sitting right at the foot of Mount Hermon, Caesarea Philippi was built on top of an enormous rock, a massive wall of rock over 100 feet straight up and about 500 feet wide.

These towering cliffs were known as the 'Rock of the gods,' alluding to the many shrines built against it.

One of these Shrines was dedicated to Caesar; additionally, a grand temple of white marble was also built to the godhead of Caesar.

Similarly, there was one to Pan, with a deep cavern located there; it was said to be the birthplace of Pan, the god of nature; there were assorted shrines to other gods.

A stream flowed from the center of a vast cave in the rock of the gods; and is the headwater for the Jordan River. This particular cave was known as the 'Gates of Hades' since the belief was that Baal entered and left the underworld through places of headwater.

'Baal worship involved many forbidding practices, including child sacrifice. The place was rightly repulsive to all the Jerusalem religious groups, who would never visit there.

> Isaiah 5:14 (ESV) *Therefore, Sheol has enlarged its appetite and opened its mouth beyond measure, and the nobility of Jerusalem and her multitude will go down.*

> Habakkuk 2:5 (ESV) *His greed is as wide as Sheol; like death, he has never enough. He gathers for himself all nations and collects as his own all peoples.*

So we can see that Jesus brought his disciples to the very gates of false religion, to the gates of Hades, for an important lesson.

The teaching is preparation for a more intense and urgent understanding of the nature of death and resurrection, even the power that Jesus has over both. Leading to their knowledge of what was to be the mission, in his returning to Jerusalem to die).

Later, when the disciples were again with him as they were walking on the road, in the full sight of the massive towering rock wall near the city. He posed a question to them, "who do men say I, the Son of Man, am?" He asked them collectively.

The disciples discussed it widely between them. "John the Baptizer, some are saying, some say that you are Elijah, and others, Jeremiah, or one of the old Prophets risen again." They eventually answered, itemizing what they had heard from different people, of their belief about Jesus.

Then Jesus directed the question to them, "And you, who do you, say that I am?" He said, asking for their individual opinion of the subject.

Simon Peter answered with a declaration, "You are truly the Messiah, Son of the living God."

"Blessed are you, Simon Bar-Jonah. Because it was not flesh and blood revealing this knowledge to you; it is from my Father who is in Heaven," Jesus replies approvingly.

"I will also tell you this; you will be called Peter *(*Little Rock*) and on this rock *(*Huge boulder, Bedrock.*) I will build my assembly or Ekklesia literally 'convocation' *(*Church*), and even the gates of Hades *(*Sheol.*) Will not endure and stand up against it."

*(Literally, the power of death will have no authority to hold the members of Jesus' assembly.

This place is not the lake of fire, HELL. Instead, it is the place where Lazarus and the rich man went to in death, Lazarus and all the righteous dead 'were' waiting in a section called 'paradise' or Abraham's Bosom. Until after Jesus' resurrection when he took them with Him, as He ascended.

The place had a huge divide (*Hades*) separated from paradise, which kept the people who did not serve the true God. And will continue doing so until the time of Judgment by Jesus).

> Revelation 1:18, "I am he that lives, and was dead; and, take note and consider, I am alive forever, Amen; and have the keys of 'hell' and 'death'"

Jesus continued, "I will give you keys to the Kingdom of Heaven. Then whatever you have bound here on earth will also be bound in Heaven. Likewise, whatever you release on earth will also be released in Heaven."
*(Isaiah 22:22 (KJV) **And the key of the house of David will I lay upon his shoulder; so he will open, and none will shut, and he will shut, and no one will open**).

This was Jewish legal language, whereby elders in the Synagogues, and The Great Court, made decisions. This process became known as 'binding and loosing' as they believed they were merely ratifying the decrees already made by the Heavenly Court.

*Note: First, Jesus tells them about 'gates' of Hades, representing the power of that place, as gates always refer to the power of a guarded city.

Then He tells them of keys, which have the power to lock or unlock in conjunction with Heaven.

He then cautioned and instructed the disciples to tell no one that He was Jesus the Messiah. *(*This necessity to remain quiet about this is essential because there was a 'set time' approaching when Jesus must 'be offered' as the King of Israel in Jerusalem*).

THE CRITICAL TEACHING OF THE ESSENTIAL MISSION ENDING IN JERUSALEM.

He started explaining to the disciples that he, the Son of Man, would need to go to Jerusalem and suffer many things. The leaders, Chief Priests, and Scribes will reject him; they will kill him, yet he will be resurrected after three days.

This entire speech he repeated to them often and bluntly. On one such occasion, Peter took him to one side and lectured him and to protest about it, "This is Impossible, Lord! That will never be done to you." He insisted.

Looking at his disciples, Jesus turned around and addressed Peter, "Get behind me, Satan! You are an obstruction to me because you have not placed your mind on the ways of God. But on those that are of man." He said firmly.

*Note: Jesus' first turned away from Peter and addressed Satan directly for the second time, with the same expression, "Get behind me, Satan" the first was in the desert. Here, Satan used Peter's passion and fear through emotions to deliver to Jesus, repeating his previous temptation.

Later Jesus told Peter, 'that Satan had requested to sift him like wheat, but he prayed that his faith does not fail.'

Jesus called the crowds to gather near, telling them all, including the disciples. "Anyone desiring to be my disciple will need to deny himself, taking up his cross, and then he can follow me.

Because anyone who is seeking to save his life will lose it, and anyone who will lose their life through persecution for my sake, or the Good News, will not only find it, but you will also save it.

What is the use to a man if he achieves the entire world and loses or sacrifices his own self?

Is there anything that he can give in exchange for his life?

Anyone who will be ashamed of me and my words in this sinful and adulterous generation likewise the Son of Man will be ashamed of him also upon his return. The Son of Man will return in his own glory, also in the glory of his Father and with his Angels, each person will receive the reward he has earned by his actions.

I tell you truthfully: some of you standing here will certainly see the Son of Man appearing in the glory of his Kingdom with power. Long before you will see death." He explained.

JESUS IS TRANSFIGURED ON A MOUNTAIN.

Then, just eight days later, he traveled up to a high place on a mountain to pray; he took only a few of the disciples with him on this occasion. These were Peter and the two brothers James and John.

While Jesus was in the middle of praying, the appearance of his face was transformed by light, changing him into dazzling brightness before their eyes.

Jesus became transfigured.

His face shone like the full sun. His clothing also became dazzling white with light, extraordinarily white, like snow. Yet, whiter than any brightener on earth can wash clothing.

Suddenly, Moses and Elijah appeared next to Jesus and talked with him as he was shining in glory.

They were there discussing with him concerning the substance of his upcoming departure. And the completion of his purpose that he was near to achieve in Jerusalem.

Peter James and John, who had journeyed with Jesus, were fatigued and unable to stay awake while Jesus was praying. Though the moment he was transfigured, they became immediately wide awake. And being fully awake, they saw his glory; they also saw the two men standing with him, who were also glorified.

When it was clear that Moses and Elijah were going away from Jesus, Peter spoke, "Master, it is surely good for us to be here." He exclaimed.

We can make for you three booths, if you want, one for you, and one for Moses, and one for Elijah!"

Peter, James, and John were terrified. And Peter did not know what to say.

Suddenly as he was still speaking, a bright cloud appeared over them. It envelops them, causing them to be terrified as they entered the cloud.

Immediately, they heard a voice from the cloud, "This is my beloved Son, in whom I am well pleased. Him, you must hear."

(Here Peter was speaking out of fear, and the issue is simple, though it may be a good idea, there is only one Lord and God, it is his word and only his word that is needed. As great as Moses and Elijah are/were as prophets, they are only servants of the living God; they are not and cannot be placed on the same level as Jesus. He is God!)

("The LORD your God will send to you a prophet, this prophet will be like me, emerging from among your own Israelite people. You must listen to him"*). Deuteronomy 18:15.

When they heard it, the disciples fell on their faces; It terrified them. After the voice ended, Jesus reassured them with a touch, "Get up, and do not be afraid." He said to them encouragingly.

As they lifted their eyes and looked around, they suddenly realized that they were again alone with Jesus, Moses, and Elijah had left the mountain.

*(Note: *This fulfilled what Jesus had told them the previous week, 'some of you will positively witness the Son of Man appear in the glory of his Kingdom with power.'*)

As the four of them journey back down from the mountain, Jesus instructs Peter, James, and his brother John, "tell no one of the vision you have witnessed till after the Son of Man has risen from the dead." He urged.

Accordingly, they remained silent because of this instruction, keeping all to themselves and telling no one about what they had seen on that occasion.

They were searching for an understanding of what Jesus meant by "rising from the dead."

As they came slowly down the mountain, the disciples questioned him, "In that case, why do the Scribes say that Elijah must first appear?" They asked.

"Elijah indeed appeared first so that he can restore all things," answered Jesus.

"How is it also written about the Son of Man that he must suffer many things and be despised?" He asked them, trying to remind them of the scriptures and the Prophecies.

"Yes, I tell you that Elijah has already appeared; but was not recognized. Instead, they treated him in whatever way they wanted, just as was written about him. And it is just the same way they will also make the Son of Man suffer." He assured them.

The disciples then understood that he was referring to John the Baptizer.

CHAPTER ELEVEN

CONTENDING ABOUT STATUS: FROM THE INNER AND OUTER CIRCLES AMONGST THE DISCIPLES.

The following day, when they had arrived back, coming down from the mountain.

As they were re-joining the other disciples who had remained behind, Jesus saw a large crowd of people surrounding them, being intensely questioned by Scribes.

When the people saw Jesus was returning. They were astonished and amazed at how he looked; they straightaway ran towards him from all over the hill to greet him.

He went straight to the Scribes and asked, "Why do you question my disciples? What is it you are asking them?"

A man that was within the vast crowd stepped forward and kneeled to him, "Lord, will you have mercy on my son because he is my only child? I beg you to look at him. He has a fearsome spirit.

He is a lunatic 'Moonstruck' epileptic. He suffers dangerously; he often falls into the fire and often into the water.

And wherever that spirit grasps him, it throws him down, making him suddenly cry out as it convulses him. So he foams at the mouth and grinds his teeth. Bruising him severely and making him waste away, and it scarcely ever leaves him.

So I brought him here to your disciples and pleaded with them to cast it out, but they could not; they could not cure him." The father explained.

"Oh Faithless, Unbelieving, and perverse generation, how long will I be with you, how long will I put up with you?" Jesus asked, dismayed at the lack of faith he found.

"Bring the child here to me." He instructed them.

The man went to fetch his son, and as they were bringing the child, instantly as he saw Jesus.

The demon straight away threw him down, and the child convulsed violently, falling on the ground, shuddering and foaming at the mouth.

"How long has it now been since the first time when he started having this?" Jesus asked his father.

"Since he was a small child," the father replied. "Often, it throws him into the fire or the water, to destroy him; however, if you can do anything for him! Will you have compassion on us, and please help us."

"If you can believe and have faith," Jesus replied, "then, all things are possible to him who believes." He told him, building his faith.

The father of the child unashamedly cried out, "I believe Lord." He affirmed.

"Please, will you help me with my unbelief?" He prayed, asking for help, this he said with tears.

The people were still running to see Jesus from all over the hillside.

So when Jesus saw that a crowd would quickly form around them, he rebuked the unclean spirit, "You mute and deaf spirit, I command you, come out of him, and never enter him again!" Jesus commanded; after the boy had howled and with great convulsions, the demon finally left the child.

This left the boy looking like he was dead, to where most of them said, "He is dead."

However, Jesus took the child by the hand, compassionately lifting him up, the child got to his feet completely normal. Jesus then gave him back to his father, who saw that his son was cured.

*Note: Jesus knew it was a 'mute and deaf spirit,' everyone else, including the disciples, was thinking it was a lunatic spirit because the father had said so.

Later, when they had gone into a house, Jesus' disciples came and asked him privately, "Why were we not capable of casting out that demon?"

"Because of your unbelief," He told them, "since I tell you truthfully, even if you have faith only as small as a grain of mustard seed. You will tell this mountain. 'Get up and move from here to there,' and it will move. Then you will find that nothing will be impossible for you.

"However, this kind will not leave except through prayers and fasting," Jesus explained.

He states that without prayer and fasting, they will not replace unbelief and lack of faith. (Faithless, Unbelieving, and perverse generation, regarding the father and especially the disciples, is the issue. The father had it; they had it. Prayer and fasting are also essential in correctly discerning the nature of any hindrance been faced).

Then as they finally understood, they were all overwhelmed at the Grace and the majesty of God.

[*Note: Jesus had already commissioned them and sent them out; he had already given them power and dominion over all spirits. Recently he told them of the keys to the Kingdom, which had control over the domain of the evil spirits. So he fully expected them to handle this or any other demon. The issue was their lack of faith. And this had surfaced and had been addressed several times before, *(Example, when Jesus had told them to beware of the leaven of the Pharisees. And they assumed it was about not having enough bread, even after the two miracles of feeding the vast crowds. He had admonished them for their lack of faith, again after he had stilled the storm, after them waking him from sleeping in the back of the boat).
The smallest amount of faith was more than enough, along with an unshakable belief in God.

All lack of power is perverse in God's Kingdom, stems from unbelief and lack of faith, and is cured simply through prayer and fasting].

They left that area and were heading towards Capernaum, so they passed through Galilee. Jesus tried to make sure that the people did not know that they were staying in Galilee; even so, people found out. There was widespread awe and excitement about all the things that Jesus was doing.

As a result, he warned his disciples, "Pay close attention and do not forget these words. Let them sink into your ears, understand that the Son of Man is about to be betrayed; then turned over to the hands of men.

To be killed, and when he is killed, on the third day, he will be 'raised up' again." He told them, reminding them of what he had been teaching them.

All the disciples were deeply unhappy, even though they did not understand what he was telling them. It was concealed from them, so they could not take it in, and they were afraid to ask him what it all meant.

While they were again traveling on their way to Capernaum, as they journeyed, a dispute began raging among the disciples; the argument was about which of them was the greatest.

Eventually, they took the dispute to Jesus, trying to get him to settle it in a roundabout way by asking, "Lord, which person then in the Kingdom of Heaven is the greatest?"

Jesus had already perceived the way they were reasoning within their hearts. So after they had arrived at a house, he questioned them about it, "What is it you were arguing about among yourselves while we were on the way?" He inquired from them. *(This was most likely Peter's house and was a rest stop).

Since the argument had been over this issue, which one of them was actually the greatest and had flared up among them several times before, none wanted to speak up, so everyone remained silent.

The resolution to this question was placed on hold by the people responsible for collecting the Didrachma coins for the Temple Tax. Who at that moment approached Peter as the group was on their way into the house. "Does your teacher not pay the Didrachma?" They asked.

"Yes," Peter answered without a pause.

The Census Tax, later the Temple tax.

*Note: This was not just any random man-made tradition but an actual command from the scriptures.

> Exodus 30:11-16 ...Each person who is counted must give a small piece of silver as a sacred offering to the Lord.

> ...it should be used for the care of the Tabernacle.

When Peter came into the house, Jesus anticipated him, "What do you think, Simon? Where do the kings of the earth receive toll or tribute, from their own children or strangers?" He queried from Peter.

"From strangers," Peter replied.

"Then, for that reason, the children are exempt," said Jesus. "However, in case we should cause them to stumble, go down to the Sea, and cast a hook in, draw up the first fish that comes up. Then when you have opened its mouth, you will find in it a Stater coin. Take that it to them and with it pay the Temple tax for you and me." Jesus instructed him.

(*A Stater coin, two days wage. Equivalent to one Greek stater, or tetradrachma, also Shekel' Jewish silver coin.'*)

*Note: Peter was in a dilemma since, by his own admission, he had declared Jesus as the Son of the living God, then if so, the tax was being collected on behalf of Jesus' Father, who is God, whom Jesus represented. Peter failed to think this through, and although he referred to Jesus as Lord *(*Adoni or Lord; my Ruler*), he was remiss to ask Jesus what he should do.

The very first incident where Peter had recognized Jesus as Lord, *(*Adoni*), and involved a massive catch of fish. 'When the net was breaking, where Peter had fallen to his knees and admitted that he was a sinful man.' This fishing trip would be a vivid reminder of that moment.

Having to 'go a long way down to the sea, casting in a hook,' on this occasion. 'Waiting for the first fish' is going to take a lot of time, effort, and patience and will give time for reflection to a man who needs it.

It was also a beautiful lesson in God's Grace and provision because here is the Son of God. Who is exempt from and does not need to pay this ransom. And here is Peter, who represents 'sinful' man, who needs to pay this to God but has not paid. Still, Jesus is volunteering to provide the payment for them both; this wonderfully foreshadows his mission. Paying the ransom, he did not need to pay for all humanity, who was unable to pay it for themselves.

Later after the tax incident, as He sat down, he called all twelve men to pay attention, "If any man wants to be the first, he must be prepared to be last of all, and the servant of all." He told them.

Jesus called over a little child, standing the child in the middle of the disciples; he picked up the child in his arms. "I tell you truthfully," He said, "Unless you change becoming like little children, you will never enter the Kingdom of Heaven *(*This is the earthly Kingdom, spanning a thousand years, the disciples' dispute was about ruling with Jesus*).

The one who, as a result, humbles himself like this little child, that same person is the greatest in the Kingdom of Heaven.

The one who receives this little child in my name welcomes me. Anyone receiving me receives him who sent me because anyone who is least among you all, this person will be great." Jesus reminded them of this principle of the Kingdom.

"Master, we saw someone who does not follow us casting out demons using your name: we banned him because he is not one of us," John said, still thinking of the disciples' place and standing.

"Do not forbid him," Jesus replied, "as no person doing a mighty work in my name will be hasty to speak evil of me since he who is not against us; is for us.

Therefore, the person who will give you a cup of water to drink in my name, because you are my followers, I tell you, that one will in no way lose his reward.

However, the one who causes one of these little ones who believe in me to stumble. Better having a millstone hung around his neck, sinking in the depths of the ocean.

How terribly unhappy for the world that there are things that make people stumble, losing their faith! Such things will happen as the occasions always come! Except, how terribly unhappy for the one who causes such!

If the cause of you stumbling is your hand or foot, cut it off, casting it from you. Better you enter life maimed or crippled, rather than having two hands or two feet; been thrown into *(Hell), into the eternal, unquenchable fire.

'Their worm there does not die, nor is the fire quenched.'

If your foot causes your stumbling, cut it off. You are better entering life lame, rather than having your two feet then be cast into Gehenna, 'where their worm does not die, or the fire ever quenched.'

If your eye causes your stumbling, pluck it out, casting it from you, it would be better for your entering life with one eye, rather than having two eyes yet been thrown into the fire *(of Hell.)

'Their worm there does not die, nor is the fire quenched.'

Salt is good for seasoning and preserving, but if the salt has lost its ability to season, how will even the salt be preserved?

Because everyone is going through a testing refining fire, you will eventually be well preserved and protected from the eternal flames. Hence you are the preservatives that maintain the peace.

Be sure that you do not despise even one of these little ones because I tell you their Angels always look at the face of my Father, who is in Heaven.

It is that which was lost that the Son of Man came to save.

(*Note: *Although Jesus is using here a child to represent 'humility and simple faith,' the 'little ones' referred to are any of the children of God who are entering the Kingdom*).

What do you think? If a man has one hundred sheep, where just one of them goes astray, will he not leave the ninety-nine and go seek in the mountains to recover the one that has gone awry?

If he finds it, I tell you; without doubt, he will rejoice more over it than over the ninety-nine, which has not gone astray.

In the same way, it is not your heavenly Father's will that one of these little ones should perish.

If another believer hurts you, go to him and tell him! So that you can work it out between the two of you. You will have gained back your brother if he listens to you. If he does not, take one or two others along to determine the truth in the presence of witnesses.

Should he refuse to listen to them, tell it to the assembly; if he refuses to hear the assembly, treat him as an outsider, which you do not associate with!

I tell you truly, anything you secure on earth will have been fastened in Heaven, and whatever things you have released on earth will have been released in Heaven.

When you get together about any matter on earth, two being the minimum, making a prayer request, my Father acts on your request in Heaven. Also, as two or three of you are together because of me, you can be confident that I will be there."

Peter, who by then had begun to get the vital connection of Grace and unity, questioned Jesus on the matter. "Lord, then how often do I forgive my brother who has sinned against me, even up to seven times?" He asked, hoping that he had the gist of this. For a people who are taught, 'An eye for an eye' retribution. This was a huge step and a breakthrough for Peter.

"No, I am not telling you, 'up to seven times,' instead even up to seven times seventy," Jesus replied, astounding the men.

*(This number which is four hundred and ninety, occurs throughout the Scriptures and is ten times the number of the Jubilee, which itself is every 'forty-nine' years.

The redemption and forgiveness period will endure covering the full extent of the history of Israel or seventy times, 'the Great Jubilee Cycles,' of four hundred and ninety years, 'written as seven times, seven times, seventy years.' Or three thousand, four hundred and thirty years in total, and stretched to the entire history of the people of Israel.

The Scriptures presented a total of five distinct Great Jubilee Redemption Cycles.

The first Great Jubilee of Israel was from Adam to the birth of Abram.

This was on the fortieth Jubilee from Adam.

Then from Abraham (*after God had changed his name* from Abram to Abraham' father of many' or 'multitudes') to the time of the Exodus, this was the Fiftieth Jubilee, which overran by fifteen years, *(Minus the fifteen years, from the birth of Ishmael to Isaac's birth, making a perfect number. Genesis 16:16, *Abram was 86 years old at Ishmael's birth and 100 years old at Isaac's*).

Then from the Exodus to the Dedication of the Temple built by Solomon, this was on the sixtieth Jubilee, which overran by one hundred and thirty-one years. 'Minus one hundred and thirty-one years, where the nation was under the yoke of foreign nations for their sins, throughout the period 'of the Judges,' making a perfect number.'

Then from the Dedication of the First Temple to the Decree of the Persian Emperor Artaxerxes to restore Jerusalem, this was on the seventieth Jubilee, which overran by seventy years. 'Minus the seventy years, they were in Captivity in Babylon, making a perfect number.' Ezra and Nehemiah returned at that time; and had rebuilt the City of Jerusalem, *(Ezra. 7.) These first four periods were the exact fulfillment of the distinct divisions that God had determined for his historical purpose, using these wonderful Cycles.

Seventy sevens of years would have been a meaningful saying to any Israelite.

In Leviticus 25: 3-9, God divided their calendar, into seven-year periods, with every seventh year being a 'Sabbatical Year.'

This then represents the number seen as the perfection of forgiveness.

Four hundred and ninety years was also the time given to Daniel until the Messiah's arrival.

*(Daniel 9:24, Subtract a final seven years, yet to come near the end times, relating to Israel and the city of Jerusalem, thus making four hundred and eighty-three).

Which had started the prophetic clock, four hundred and forty-five years before the birth of Jesus; this was precisely on the eighteenth Jubilee.

This Decree to Restore Jerusalem was the fifth, 'Great Jubilee Redemption Cycles,' which took the nation to the very exact day of the Messiah of Israel's arrival. (Riding in on a donkey, offered to the nation as a King of peace)

Appreciating the wonder of this, as well as its magnificence, meaning, and impact, cannot be overstated).

THE KING IS COMING.

Zechariah 9:9 (EXB) **Rejoice greatly, people of Jerusalem [Daughter Zion]!**
Shout for joy, people of Jerusalem [Daughter Jerusalem]!
[Look; Behold] Your King is coming to you.
He does what is right [is righteous/just], and he saves.
He is gentle [lowly; humble] and riding on a donkey, on the colt [a colt, the foal] of a donkey.

THE YEAR OF JUBILEE.

Leviticus 25:8-13 (NKJV) **'And you shall count seven Sabbaths of years for yourself, seven times seven years; and the time of the seven Sabbaths of years shall be to you forty-nine years. Then you shall cause the trumpet of the Jubilee to sound on the tenth day of the seventh month; on the Day of Atonement, you shall make the trumpet to sound throughout all your land. And you shall consecrate the fiftieth year and proclaim liberty throughout all the land to all its inhabitants. It shall be a Jubilee for you, and each of you shall return to his possession, and each of you shall return to his family.**
That fiftieth year shall be a Jubilee to you; in it, you shall neither sow nor reap what grows of its own accord nor gather the grapes of your untended vine.

For it is the Jubilee; it shall be holy to you; you shall eat its produce from the field.
'In this Year of Jubilee, each of you shall return to his possession.'

"Understand that the Kingdom of Heaven is like a kind of king, who wanted to settle accounts with his servants." Jesus continued, expanding the teaching.

"When he had reconciled accounts, they brought one to him, who owed him ten thousand talents, *(Estimated to be approx. multiple hundreds of millions of dollars.)*

However, because he could not pay, his lord commanded him, his wife, and children to be sold, along with all he had and payment made as settlement.

The servant, as a result, fell to his knees before him, 'Lord, have patience with me, and I will repay you all!' he said.

Being moved with compassion, the lord of that servant released him and forgave him the debt.

But that same servant went out, finding one of his fellow servants, who owed him one hundred Denarii's, and he grabbed him and took him by the throat, 'Pay me what you owe!' He demanded, *(One hundred Denarii's: = approx. several thousand Dollars.)*

"So his fellow servant fell down, begging him, 'Have some patience with me, and I will repay you!' He pleaded.

He would not. He instead went and threw him in prison until he could pay back all that was due.

Therefore, when his fellow servants saw what was done, they were exceedingly sorry and came and told their lord all the details.

Then his lord called him in, 'you are a wicked servant! I had forgiven you all your debt because you begged me.

Should you not have also had mercy on your fellow servant, just as I had compassion on you?' He asked him.

His lord was angry, turning him over to the tormentors until he would pay all that was due to him.

So my heavenly Father will also do to you if you do not forgive your brother from your hearts for his misdeeds."

Jesus continued, "Also, I sincerely tell you, if you can come into agreement with each other on earth, then Heaven is moved. So if two of you will agree on earth regarding any matter you ask about, my heavenly

Father will do it for you. Because wherever two or three assemble as one in my name, I am there along with them," He told them, concluding the excellent teaching of the principals of the Kingdom, *(Godly Kingdom.)

As they went on the way from Capernaum and were on the road traveling to Galilee, many people approached them, claiming to want to be disciples of Jesus.

One was a Scribe, who said to Jesus, "Teacher, I will follow you wherever you go."

"The foxes have foxholes, and the birds of the sky have their nests, but the Son of Man has nowhere that he can lay his head," Jesus told him.

One of his followers asked him, "Lord, will you allow me to bury my father first and then come follow you?"
*(This could also be a matter of settling a family estate. This may not necessarily mean the father had already died. It could even be many years yet, 'as with Abraham and his father, Terah' Genesis, 11:31.)

"Follow me," replied Jesus, "and leave the dead to bury their own dead; you go instead and make the Kingdom of God known."
(*Note: *This 'Kingdom of God' is not the future earthly rule of Jesus, but the Father's Kingdom. And no one that belongs to the Father is dead, even if their physical body ceases to function, and all that rejects the Father's offer of salvation is already dead*).

"Lord, I do want to follow you," Another person said, "even so, will you first allow me to go say farewell to the people who are part of my household?" He asked.

"Anyone who, after putting his hand to the plow, then looks back, he is not suitable for the Kingdom of God," Replied Jesus, reminding him of his need for prudence.

Arriving back in the Galilean area, the hometown of most of the disciples and Jesus, It was soon time for another important national feast; this one was 'the Feast of Booths.'
*(They were to live in these booths for seven days as a vivid reminder of the days living in tents during the wilderness journeying. 'Numbers 26:65, 32:15.'

Also, when they came to the Temple, they would carry an etrog, which was a citrus fruit, symbolizing the fruit of the Promised Land.

The Sekhakh roof should be left relatively loose, not tied together, or tied down. Preferably the families should make it from something grown from the ground and then cut off, such as branches, corn stalks, bamboo reeds, sticks, or two-by-fours. Then it must be constructed so the wind will not blow it away.

Sekhakh must be placed sparsely enough that the elements, notably rain, can get in, and preferably thinly sufficient that they could see the stars. Yet not so sparsely that over ten inches are open at any point or give extra lighting above the shade.

A lulaw was also used, made from the branches of palm trees, myrtles, and willows tied together with a golden thread. This lulaw would be waved during the celebration in the Temple and at suitable times during the service).

[Messianic expectation was at its highest about this time. The common assumption was for the Messiah to suddenly appear at the Feast of Tabernacles and then be crowned as the Davidic King at Passover six months later.

In addition, this was a unique sabbatical year. There was the regular sabbatical year every 7th year; then the distinctive year of Jubilee after 'seven weeks of seven years,' or after 49 years, making it the fiftieth year, the highest time for the Messiah's arrival.

Jeremiah 23:5-6 said that the Messiah would be a "BRANCH FROM DAVID'S LINE."

Zechariah prophesied that 'the Branch' would wipe away our guilt, *(Zechariah 3:9 (ASV) *For, behold, the stone that I have set before Joshua; upon one stone are seven eyes: behold, I will engrave the graving thereof, saith Jehovah of hosts, and I will remove the iniquity of that land in one day.*)

That he will build the Temple of the Lord and have royal dignity *(Zechariah 6:12-13), **And, "on that day," the LINE OF DAVID will be, "like the ANGEL OF THE LORD, going before them."**

*(Zechariah 12:8.) Then "**that day**" as Zechariah 14:16, Said is when all nations are commanded to celebrate "**that day.**" It will be the Feast of Tabernacles!]

Now that Jesus was back home, his brothers James, Joseph, Simon, and Judas started questioning him about whether he would go to the celebrations.

"Why do you not leave from here and go into Judea; because if you are doing all these things, it is your opportunity to proclaim yourself to the world?" They asked, somewhat skeptically.

"Your disciples will then also see all of 'your miracles' that you are doing.

Because when someone seeks to be known openly, he does nothing in secret," They said, advising him cynically.

His brothers spoke to him in this manner because they did not believe in him. They were also imagining that Jesus was only seeking fame from the people.

"It is not yet my time," Jesus replied to them, "but it is always your time. You, the world, cannot hate; however, it hates me because I give evidence that its actions are evil.

You go on ahead to the feast. I am not yet going to this feast, and the reason is that my time is not yet ready." He explained cordially.

After telling them this, Jesus remained where he was there in Galilee.

Psalm 69:8 (ESV) *I have become a stranger to my brothers, an alien to my mother's sons.*

CHAPTER TWELVE

MISSION TO JERUSALEM: THE PEOPLE OF SAMARA REFUSED TO HOST HIM.

Eventually, as the time approached to complete his mission. He intently and resolutely set his face to go to Jerusalem, making all necessary arrangements knowing this was now his last fall festival.

His brothers had already left, going on to Jerusalem to take part in the feast; as a result, Jesus started his journey quietly and with careful preparations.

He sent people to go to various villages and make arrangements for his arrival.

> *(Malachi 3:1 (ISV) **"Watch out! I'm sending my messenger, and he will prepare the way before me. Then suddenly, the Lord you are looking for will come to his Temple. He is the messenger of the covenant whom you desire. Watch out! He is coming**!" **Says the Lord of the Heavenly Armies**) (*Yahweh Tsebaoth, Adonai-Tzva'ot.)*

The pace set by Jesus was now both steady and urgent. Leading the way, going increasingly ahead of his disciples, reports were coming back from the villages.

In one village, their people did not want him to lodge there. The reason was, Jerusalem and not their village was his destination; this was the village of Samara.

*(*The countryside around Samara by this time had almost certainly received the enthusiastic report of the people of Shechem*). Except now, the strong religious prejudices surfaced.

Previously when Jesus entered their village, they were happy to receive him, as he was traveling north away from the city because he had left the area of Judea.

Now he was heading for Jerusalem; most people were sure in their thinking that he would be crowned King there. This included and was undoubtedly fuelled by his enthusiastic disciples. As a result, the Samaritans were very unreceptive.

Given this, two of the disciples, the two brothers James and John, named sons of thunder/ Boanerges, approached Jesus. "Lord, do you want for us to destroy them by commanding of fire to come down from the sky, just as the prophet Elijah did?" They asked a little over-enthusiastically.

*(The notorious incident involving the Prophet Elijah and the Samaritans, having once taken place within that location in the past, was in their thinking. A miracle from Heaven would convince people, as this was one of the sure signs of the Messiah, as the Jewish leaders taught the people.

The political Kingdom of the Messiah ruling from Jerusalem was firmly in the minds of the disciples.

And the determined and relentless pace of Jesus to get there; was focusing their thoughts on this idea.

By constant debating, pondering, and general bickering about who would be greatest, together with Jesus' resolved purpose in reaching Jerusalem. Such ideas designed to show they had what it takes; were surfacing from among the men.

John wanted to forbid the unknown follower of Jesus. He had been casting out spirits in his name, claiming that it was because the man 'was not one of us.' Peter's notion of 'forgiving seven times,' being a great deal).

> *(2 Kings 1 *Then Elijah answered the captain of fifty men, if I am a man of God, then fire from Heaven will descend, and destroy you and your fifty. So then fire did descend from Heaven, destroying him and his fifty.*
> *Ahaziah again sent to him another captain along with fifty men. He told Elijah, "Man of God, 'Come down quickly,' says the King,"*

Elijah again answered, if I am a man of God, then fire will descend from Heaven, consuming you and your fifty men. Suddenly the fire of God fell from Heaven, destroying the captain and his fifty).

Jesus turned and spoke sharply to them to challenge the idea, "You do not recognize or do you know of the spirit that is in you. Given that the Son of Man is here to save the lives of men, and not in fact to destroy them." Jesus told them firmly.

After this, the party of travelers simply moved on and found and stayed in another village.

As a result, after all of this, the Lord selected and appointed seventy of his followers.

To send out in two's, going ahead of him into every city, town, and area he would travel, giving the towns and cities the chance to know that the Kingdom and the Messiah had arrived.

(*This was known as issuing a Yoke, it called the people to follow the light and graceful teaching of the Messiah, giving them new hope*). 'Jeremiah 27:2-8.'

"The harvest is certainly plentiful, yet the laborers are few in numbers." He told them encouragingly.

"Therefore, pray and ask the Lord of the harvest to send out laborers into his harvest.

Go out on your way. And be watchful, as I am now sending you out as lambs among wolves.

Be sure not to carry a purse, wallet, or spare sandals. Do not be interrupted by stopping to greet anyone on the way.

In every house you would enter, first say, 'May this house rest in peace.'

In this way, if a son of peace is there, your peacefulness will rest on him; however, if not there, your peacefulness will then return to you.

Stay there in that same house, eating and drinking the things they give, since the laborer is worthy of his wages.

Do not travel from house to house seeking what is best or profitable.

Go into a city, and when they receive you, eat the things that they provide for you.

And in that city, heal the sick, and notify them, 'The Kingdom of God has come near you.'

However, when you are not received in a city, you will go out into its streets and say, 'even the dust clinging to us from your city, we brush off as a testimony against you, despite that, know that the Kingdom of God has come near to you.'

I tell you, it will be even more endurable for Sodom than for that city on that day in the judgment." Jesus declared giving explicit instructions and directions to the followers he had selected to go out in pairs.

Then he turned and gave a severe warning to some cities, which considered themselves lofty and notable.

He continued, "And to you, Chorazin, watch out! And take heed! Also, to you, Bethsaida!

Because of the mighty miracles performed in you, had I done in Tyre and Sidon the same, they would have repented long ago, sitting in sackcloth and ashes.

Yet, it will be more bearable for the cities of Tyre and Sidon in the judgment than for you.

You, Capernaum, who is so exalted to Heaven, will be brought right down to Hades." Jesus declared, as a prophetic warning about the future of those cities.

Again he instructed the disciples as he sent them off on the mission, "The one who listens to you hears me, and the one who rejects you rejects me. The one who rejects me is rejecting him who sent me." He concluded.

Later, after completing the mission, the seventy disciples sent out returned jubilantly and with exhilaration. They gave their reports to Jesus, "Lord, in your name, even the demons are subject to us!" They said, full of excitement.

"I was watching, and I saw Satan suddenly fall like lightning from Heaven. Jesus told them.

And now observe, you have the authority I give to you. Enabling you to tread on serpents and scorpions, and I give you the power to overpower all enemy forces; therefore, nothing will hurt you.

Do not, however, rejoice that spirits are subjected to you; instead, be elated and glad that your names are written in Heaven."

When he finished explaining the importance of the victory, Jesus expressed joy in the Holy Spirit, saying, "I thank you, O Father, Lord of

Heaven and earth, since you have hidden these things from the wise and prudent. Yet you gave the revelation of them to little children. Yes, Father, since it was well-pleasing in your sight."

(With this, Jesus declares the successful mission of 'the seventy,' as the evidence of the defeat of Satan).

Jesus turned to his disciples, "My Father has put all things in my power." He said, "No one can know who is the Son, only the Father, and who is the Father, only the Son, and to any, I give that revelation of the father."

"Happy and Bless are your eyes because of the things you see," He told the disciples privately. "Many of the Prophets and kings wanted to see the things that you see and hear and did not see them or hear them."

In Jerusalem, the Feast of Tabernacles had begun, and people were looking for Jesus with Intense excitement, "What do you think, where is he?" They were asking each other eagerly.

Within the crowds of people, various groups were whispering and talking impatiently about him. "Without a doubt, he is a good man." Some said.

"No, do you not see, he is just leading the people astray." Others were claiming.

People did not dare speak about him openly, as they all feared the Chief Priests and Leaders. Who had issued commands and made threats against any person who proclaimed that Jesus was the Messiah!

Then suddenly, in the middle of the time of feasting, Jesus arrived in the Temple and started teaching with power.

This amazed and frustrated the Chief Priests and Leaders, "How does this man know letters with this knowledge and learning, having never been educated?" They questioned each other, trying to demean him with the crowd.

Jesus having full awareness of what they were thinking and saying, spoke boldly, "My teaching is not from me, it is from the one who sent me.

If anyone desires to do the will of God, then he will know about the teaching and whether it is from God or if I am speaking just from myself.

The one speaking from himself is merely seeking his own glory. Still, the just messenger seeks only the glory of the one who dispatched him. Therefore, no wickedness is found in him." He said, answering them.

"Were you not given the Law by Moses, and yet none of you keeps that law? Why then do you look for a way to kill me?" Jesus asked pointedly.

"We think that a demon haunts you! Who do you think is looking to kill you?" They asked disdainfully.

"After I did just one miracle, and all of you are astounded because of it," Jesus answered truthfully, ignoring their mocking tone.

"Moses gave the law of circumcision to you; as a result, you will circumcise a boy on the Sabbath. *(Even though the law is not in reality from Moses, on the contrary, the Father gives it).

If they carry out the operation of circumcising a boy on the Sabbath, so they may not break the Law of Moses. Then how is it you are angry with me for making a man completely healthy on the Sabbath?

Judge not only according to the appearance, but your judgment should be sincere and upright." Jesus told them, silencing his opponents and putting them to shame.

This exchange caused some of the people of Jerusalem to speak up openly, "Is this not the same man whom those rulers want to kill?" They ask each other, now with new boldness.

"Look how openly he is speaking, and they are not doing anything to him. People were asking, suspecting the truth of the matter. Could it be possible that the Chief Priests, in reality, do know that he is truly the Messiah?"

"What we were told about the Messiah is that when he appears, 'where he comes from, no person will know,' yet this man, we do know where he is from." Some supporters of the establishment had other opinions. They were speaking with enough doubt to quieten down the enthusiasm of the rising confidence in the crowd.

"Yes, you may indeed think that you know me and that you know where I am from," Jesus affirmed, raising his voice.

"I was sent here; it was not through my own decision, the one who has sent me is true, but Him you do not know, I, however, have come from Him, and I do know Him," He said with total authority, the words falling like the blows of a hammer.

As soon as Jesus voiced this, some of the people attempted to seize him. Yet, not even one person could touch him because the appropriate moment for him to be arrested had not yet arrived, and he controlled the timing.

The people were divided over Jesus. Some accepted that he was the Messiah and spoke up boldly. They asked with conviction. "The Messiah when he arrives, will he be able to do any more miracles than those that this man has done?"

The Pharisees overheard this, so they stormed off in frustration and joined forces with the Chief Priests. Then, having got together, sent some Temple guards to creep into and mingle with the crowds and suddenly arrest Jesus.

Jesus, who, although knew, was unmoved by the actions of the Chief Priests, spoke with power, addressing their plan, "Just a little time longer I will be here with you, then I will return to him who has sent me.

You will look for and not be able to find me, and the place where I will be, you cannot follow me there." Jesus told his opponents.

"Where is it that this man will go, and we will not be able to find him? Will he go to the Greek's townships and teach those Jews that are spread out in the middle of the Greeks?" They ask each other.

'You will then look for and not be able to find me, and the place where I will be, you cannot follow me there,' "these words that he spoke, what could be the meaning of them?" They asked, puzzled.

Something amazing happened in the Temple on the last day, which was the main day of the feast; Jesus stood and called out with a loud voice, "If anyone is thirsty, they should get the real drink from me!

As written and told in the Scriptures, 'whoever accepts me as true, out from within him will flow multiple rivers of living water." The impact and timing of this moment were superbly and amazingly beautiful.
*(The Last day is another Sabbath, called Shemini Atseret, 'final Sabbath day').

> *(Isaiah 55:1 (EXB) **The Lord says, All you who are thirsty, come and drink [to the waters; John 7:37]. Those of you who do not have money, come, buy and eat [Prov. 9:5]! Come buy wine and milk without money and without cost.**)

> *(Jeremiah 2:13 (EXB) **My people have done two evils: They have turned away from [abandoned; forsaken] me, the spring [fountain] of living water [17:3]. And they have dug their own wells [cisterns], which are broken wells [cisterns] that cannot hold water [the idols, like the wells, are useless**].

Jesus was speaking here about the future pouring out of the Holy Spirit and the gift of the Spirit.

That would be given to those who believed in him. This event had not yet arrived and would await his death and resurrection.

Large numbers of the people, who knew that Jesus was their Messiah, spoke up,

"This man is beyond doubt, 'The Prophet.'" They exclaimed with joy.

"This, in fact, is the Messiah," Said others.

Some people were mocking, "What do you think? That Galilee could produce the Messiah!

Has the Scripture not said that the Messiah comes from the seed of David, the King, and from David's own village of Bethlehem?" They asked critically.

*(The Season preceding the wonderful and elaborately joyous 'Feast of Tabernacles' in Israel was long, with hot, dry months with no rainfall, so they offered many prayers for rain at the feast.

Often the first shower of rain was expected at this time, bringing an added dimension to the great joy of the occasion and confidence for the coming seasons.

This all cumulated in the 'Water-drawing Festival.' The Priests split into three separate groups. The leading group would remain in the Temple, worshiping with songs accompanied by Flute music.

At the very moment, one of the young Priests' Cohen' took a golden pitcher accompanied by high-pitched flute music to the Pool of Siloam and filled it with water.

'On Sabbaths, since they cannot travel, they stored it inside the temple the day before.'

The young Priest led a large procession carrying lighted torches as they made their way back up to the Temple.

A separate procession went from the pool of Siloam over to the Kedron valley to a place called Motza. To collect and bring back willow branches, their function was to decorate the altar of sacrifice.

The chosen procession went around the altar with the worshippers carrying the palm leaf *(Lulav), seven times with the trumpets sounding, as they acted out 'the walls of Jericho event.'

The Lulavs were vigorously shaken to give up praises and as a prayer for Thanksgiving and hope of the long-awaited salvation from God whenever the choir reached a certain point in the worship.

The golden jug with the water from Siloam enters through the 'Water Gate' just as the sacrifice is complete. The Priest then walked up to the rise of the altar, where there were two silver basins with narrow holes, one for the wine offering and the other for the water offering.

The Priest then ceremoniously pours the wine and the water into these respective holes allowing the liquid to filter down to the bottom of the altar.

Just before they poured the water upon the altar, there was complete silence so that the sizzling sound of the cold water on the hot alter; would be the signal for the people to break out into jubilant song and dance.

The ceremony was an appeal for abundant rain. And the rabbis have connected this celebration with Isaiah 12 *ESV* where it is said, (*'with joy, you will draw water from the wells of salvation!'*)

This was the exact moment when Jesus shouted, "If anyone thirsts, let him come to me").

Because of this, it created a division in the people over their belief in him.

The Temple guards, if they could, would have arrested him, yet no one could attempt any arrest of him.

The Temple guards had to report back empty-handed to the Chief Priests and Pharisees.

"Why did you not bring him back to us?" They were asked.

"We have heard no man who has ever spoken like this man," answered the guards tentatively.

"Are you also deceived and led astray by this man?" The Pharisees snapped back angrily.

"Have any of the rulers or the Pharisees believed he is the Messiah, other than this crowd that does not know the law and is accursed?"

One of the Chief Priests named Nicodemus, *(who had previously visited Jesus under cover of darkness)*. Spoke up, "In our law, where does it judge a man unless he is first heard in person: and what he is doing is clearly identified?" He asked the others.

"Are you also one of these Galileans? Go search for yourself through all the scriptures, and you will find that no Prophet will come up out of Galilee." They answered angrily.

(*Here, the Pharisees were noticeably wrong, as the Prophet Jonah was of the village of Gath Hepher; its location is some three miles north of Nazareth in lower Galilee. Nahum and Hosea were also from Galilee. For these highly learned men not to know this, it was virtually impossible, but they intended to conceal the facts*).

This protest from Nicodemus was of considerable and defining importance; not only did it result in halting the council's proceedings. The frustrated leaders comprising the Chief Priests, Sadducees, and Pharisees disbanded, each going off to their own homes. The rulers could not carry out their purpose of condemning Jesus without a hearing. However, though defeated for a short time, they now had to find a new strategy involving discrediting him with the people.

About this time, as they were in the Temple during the day, he taught his disciples about what would occur after he was no longer with them.

This is what he said to them. "Know that nation will grow in opposition to nations and Kingdom in opposition to kingdoms. There will be great earthquakes, famines, plagues, and troubles in a variety of places. There will also be panic and cosmic signs from Heaven.

However, these things are only the beginning of the birth pains.

Watch and be on your guard because you will be arrested, handed over to tyranny, and be killed. Because you carry my name, people of all nations will hate you. They will beat you in synagogues and prisons; they will then drag you in front of councils and before kings and governors because you carry my name as a witness to them.

For you, it will turn out as a testimony.

When they lead you away and arrest you, do not be concerned in advance or premeditate on what you will speak. Yet say whatever will be given you in that hour, since it is not you who speak, but the Holy Spirit.

As a result, determine in your hearts not to meditate in advance on how to answer. Since I will give to you a mouth and wisdom that all of your opponents cannot resist or contradict.

The world will hate you because you carry my name; even your parents, brothers, relatives, and friends will betray you. Brother will betray brother and the father his child even to death. Children will rebel against their parents, causing them to be put to death.

All men will hate you because you carry my name.

However, not even one hair of your head will expire. Still, anyone enduring to the end will be rescued. Through your endurance, you will win your lives.

Many will weaken and will betray one another, hating one another.

Many false prophets will arise, leading the majority into deception.

Because of the increase in iniquity, true love will grow cold in many people. However, those who continue to the end will be rescued.

The time will come when you see armies surrounding Jerusalem; you then know that it is the time of its destruction.

Those in Judea must then escape into the hills. People in Jerusalem must leave; no one out in the country should return to the city.

It is the days of God's vengeance, which will fulfill his prophetic words from the Scriptures.

In those days, it will be dreadful even for pregnant women and for nursing mothers as there will be great tragedy and fury against the people of this land.

With the sword, some people will die; others dispersed into captivity all over the nations of the world. As for Jerusalem, the Gentiles will trample it down until the end of the Gentiles era of control."

He gave them this illustration: "Notice," He continued, "the fig tree and all the other trees. When their leaves sprout, you unmistakably know that summer is almost upon you.

Likewise, these events will let you know that the time approaches for the Kingdom of God.

I tell you that this generation will endure until all these things have taken place. Though Heaven and the earth depart, yet my words will never disappear."

JESUS LEFT THE TEMPLE AND HEADED FOR THE MOUNT OF OLIVES.

The Mount of Olives is on a long sloping hill on the east side of the Temple Mount. Rising about half a mile out of the Kidron valley, this lay between the Temple Mount and the Mount of Olives and contained many caves and tombs such as that of Absalom, the third of King David's sons.

Then very early the following day, he arrived back in the Temple, where all the people gathered to him.

Jesus sat down in the middle of them and began instructing them. He was teaching in the forecourt of the Temple, which was part of the court for women.

A group of Scribes *(Lawyers) along with some Pharisees were ready to execute a plan they had come up with overnight. They searched for a method of accusing him of breaking the law, thinking they had found the perfect plan.

They brought a woman into the Temple court. Who they said was caught in the act of adultery, dragging her into the center of the enormous mass of people. Addressing Jesus, they said. "Teacher, we discovered this woman committing adultery; we caught her in the actual act."

"Now the command in our law, which is from Moses, is that we should stone such. What do you command then and say should be done concerning her?" They asked pompously.

Because they regarded and taught the people, a woman's testimony was not legally valid. This was a convenient method of using the law to condemn her. Even as they were actually breaking the law by not presenting both parties' caught as they claimed.

(Jeremiah 17:9-10 (NKJV) *The heart is deceitful above all things and desperately wicked; who can know it?*
I, the Lord, search the heart; I test the mind, even to give every man according to his ways, according to the fruit of his doings).

Jesus did not bother to answer them; *(just as if he had not even heard them)*. He stooped down, writing with his finger on the ground.

Frustrated, they continued asking him over again.

Then looking up, Jesus told them, "The one among you who is with no sin, let him throw the first stone at her."

Stooping down again, he continued to write on the ground with his finger.

Psalm 90:8 (EXB) *You have put [set] the evil we have done [our guilt/iniquity] right in front of you; you clearly see our secret sins [our hidden/secret sins in the light of your face]*.

*(None of these scholarly 'men of letters' standing there could have missed the connection with the writings of the Prophet Jeremiah in the scriptures.

> Jeremiah 17:13 (ERV) *O LORD, the hope of Israel, all that forsake thee shall be ashamed; they that depart from me shall be written in the earth, because they have forsaken the LORD, the fountain of living waters*).

Scripture presents one test of adultery,

> Numbers 5:16-18 (EXB) *'The Priest will bring in [near] the woman and make her stand before the Lord. He will take some holy water in a clay jar, and he will put some dirt [dust] from the floor of the Holy Tent [Tabernacle] into the water. The Priest will make the woman stand before the Lord, and he will loosen her hair [perhaps signifying ritual uncleanness; Lev. 13:45]. He will hand her the grain [tribute; gift] offering [Lev. 2:1] of remembrance, the grain [tribute; gift] offering [Lev. 2:1] for jealousy; he will hold the bitter water that brings a curse.*

> Numbers 5:23 (CEB) *The Priest will write these curses in the scroll and wipe them off into the water of bitterness. Then he will make the woman drink the water of bitterness that brings the curse. And the water that brings the curse will enter her, causing bitterness.*

They acted out all this in 'The Water Ordeal,' where three elements needed are. Living *(or Holy water). Dust from the Temple and the writing of the 'name of the Lord' used as an oath, where the ink or letters, the dust, and the water were mixed.

Then the Priest made the woman drink the mixture.
*(Though they did not hear and understand, Jesus had declared that he was living water, and right there showed the fulfillment of the genuine three elements needed).

Their conscience convicted each one when they heard it, so they silently left one after the other, starting with the eldest, down to the very last.

They knew the people could stone them for claiming no sin under the law *(the specific crime here was false wittiness). Also, in Jewish Law, witnesses to the capital offense began the stoning.

So it had to be the one who witnessed this crime because it said the witnesses must be the first ones to start the execution of the guilty *(Deut. 13:9: Deut. 17:6-7). And the husband must be one of those present and a participant.

So for them to carry out this plan, the plotters would have to admit publicly to be hypocrites, having been the actual witness to the crime. Therefore, breaking the law by not bringing the other party also caught in the act, as they had said.

Of all the people who had tried setting the trap evaporated, Jesus and the woman were the only ones left there in the middle of the amazed crowd.

Standing up, Jesus saw none of them; the woman alone was standing there. "Woman, out of all those that accuse you, where are they? Did no one condemn you?" He asked.

"No, no one, Lord," She replied.

"I also do not condemn you. Go on back home. From now on, do not sin anymore," Said Jesus, breaking yet another of their made-up rules, namely, any Rabbi addressing a woman in public, this applying even to members of that Rabbi's family.

The condemnation of any person in such cases needed a requirement of two or more witnesses *(Deut.19:15).

Therefore, the accusers had all left; there was now no legal case to answer. Consequently, the issue of adultery could not be addressed. As a result, Jesus called for her to cease general sinning. *(He did not condemn her or pronounce any judgment).

> Jeremiah 17:14-18 (KJV) *Heal me, O LORD, and I will be healed; save me, and I will be saved: for you are my praise.*
> *Look, they say to me, where is the word of the LORD? Let it come now.*
> *As for me, I have not hastened from being a pastor to follow thee: neither have I desired the woeful day; you know: that which came out of my lips was right before you.*
> *Be not a terror to me: you are my hope in the day of evil.*
> *Let them be confounded that persecute me, but let not me be confounded: let them be dismayed, but let not me be*

dismayed: bring upon them the day of evil, and destroy them with double destruction.

*(Thru high expectations that electrified the people about the expected Messianic arrival, and as there was a division among the leaders, most thought the promised Messiah would come as a national leader, who would free the Jews from Roman, and all foreign occupiers.

With this in mind, the Jewish leaders had asked Jesus to make a civil ruling as a magistrate. Doing this was an attempt to force his hand in several ways; the very least would bring him to the attention of the Romans, who importantly had removed the power enabling the Nations' authorities to carry out any death sentences. Besides, it could place him in a poor light among the ordinary people, for which he also could be stoned.

Although the woman, as it was supposed, had sinned against God, the matter the Scribes and Pharisees presented to Jesus was a matter of executing civil law).

While the stones were not for the woman alone, they fully intended to use them for her or Jesus that day.

*(Psalm 57:6 *"**They have arranged a net for my feet; my soul is grief and misery. They have dug a pit in front of me; they themselves have fallen into the middle of it**"*).

"I am the world's only true light!" Jesus exclaimed with a loud voice.

"Anyone who walks in my path will not walk in the darkness; they will have all the light that gives life." He explained the perfect and wondrous meaning and fulfillment of the festival they had just concluded by extinguishing the temples Candelabras.

*(A total of four giant candelabras stood within the Temple, in the court of the women.

At the ending of the first day of the Feast of Tabernacles, these four golden amazing lamps were lit in the Temple, remaining lit for the duration of the feast.

Each of the four golden candelabras stood well over fifty feet tall. Each candelabra ended in four branches, and at the top of every branch was a large bowl for oil, making sixteen in total.

Oil-filled the four golden bowls on each candelabra. After that, the oil in those bowls was ignited.

They kept the four golden lamps lit and only extinguished as the day dawned following the last night of the feast).

The remaining Pharisees in the crowd, having recovered from their latest setback, found a voice as they saw how the people could recognize the connection and were rightly impressed. "You are now giving evidence about yourself. Therefore, this witness of yours is not valid." They challenged, hoping to salvage their pride.

"Even if I were to give evidence about myself, my witness is indeed still true," Jesus answered, "for I do know where I came from and where I am going. You, however, do not know where it is I came from or where I am going.

You can only judge concerning the flesh. I, however, judge no one.

Yet, if I were to judge, my judgment is correct since I am not alone, but I am always with the Father who sent me.

It is also a written matter of record in your law that the evidence of two people is valid.

I am one who is giving evidence about me, as the Father who sent me also confirms me," Jesus exclaimed with authority.

"Your Father, where exactly is he?" They asked, trying to make a rude insinuation.

"You do not know me, or do you know my Father, yet if you knew me, you would also know my Father," Jesus told them flatly.

All this took place in the Temple treasury in the middle of the Temple complex, where Jesus was speaking, specifically, the Court of Women.

Still, none of the leaders dared to arrest him because his timing was not ready, and he was setting the pace of the events.

CHAPTER THIRTEEN

THE LEADERS GROW INCREASINGLY FRANTIC TRYING TO STOP HIS POPULARITY.

Jesus continued during the day to teach and preach, "I am going away, then you will die in your sins, searching for where I am. The place where I am going, you can in no way follow there." He told them firmly.

This confused the Chief Priests and Leaders, "Will he kill himself that he says, 'Where I am going, you can in no way follow there?'" They asked each other.

"You are from here on this Earth below the heavens. I am from a place far above." Jesus told them.

"You are the product of this world. I am not part of this world.

As a result, I said you would die in your sins; because unless you are prepared to accept as truth that I am he, you will indeed die in your sins."

"Who then are you?" They asked.

"Precisely as I have been telling you from the very beginning, concerning you, I have many things to speak about and judge; however, the one who sent me, He is faithful and true! The things that I am hearing from my Father, only those things I preach to the world." Jesus replied.

[*Note: The statement made by the leaders about 'killing himself' was an attempt at mocking Jesus by condemning him to Hades. While seeing themselves as being very devout Jews, they would undoubtedly be in Heaven in their reckoning.

These opponents of Jesus, by an act of their own will. Still blinded by their unbelief, they scornfully concluded he must be talking about suicide, which was they deemed a sin without redemption. Since he said, 'they could not go where he was going.'

They were altogether sure of their righteousness and therefore going to Heaven, which as they saw it. Their blessing of great wealth and status reflected this fact.

They were pretty confident that Jesus must have been talking about committing suicide and condemning himself.

Jesus pointed out 'that there was enough to judge them.' But his only interest was in following unerringly all he heard from his Heavenly Father. Yet this did not excuse or condone them].

They did not comprehend that it was about the Father He was telling them.

"Later following the time that the Son of Man will have been 'lifted up' by you, then will you recognize I am he, I say these things as my Father taught me, and I by myself do nothing without him.

The Father who has sent me is with me and has never left me alone. That is because I always do the very things that are pleasing to him within his will." Jesus told them.

Among the vast crowds, large numbers of the people believed in Jesus that he was Israel's Messiah, and as he was speaking, more was added to that number.

Jesus addressed those who had believed him, "By remaining and continuing in these words of mine, then you are beyond a doubt, my disciples.

You will know and recognize the truth, and the truth will make you free." He told them.

"All of us are from the seed of Abraham, and we have never yet been a slave to anyone. Then how can you say, 'You will be given freedom?'" His rivals asked, incensed.

"I tell you truthfully, every person who commits any sin is, in reality, the slave of sin," Jesus retorted.

"A servant," He continued. "Is someone who will not live in the master's household forever; however, a son is one of the family; he remains forever.

As a result, if it is the Son who makes you free, you assuredly will be free!

Yes, you are descended from Abraham, this I know; yet because my word can find no place in you, you try to find a way to kill me.

Those things I have seen with my Father are the things I speak, in the same way; you also do those things you have seen with your father."

"Our father is Abraham." The Pharisees shouted.

"If you were, in fact, children of Abraham, then the things that Abraham did you would also do," Jesus told them sternly.

"Instead, you now want to kill me, a man who has told you the truth, that truth that I heard from God. Abraham never did this.

All the things that you do are from your father." He warned them.

"We at least have one Father; we were not born because of some sexual immorality. Our Father is God." They said, trying to mock him.

"If your father truly were God, you would love me, since I am here from God and have arrived from God; I am not here because of myself; instead, he sent me."

"What is the reason that you do not understand my speech?" Jesus asked rhetorically.

"Because you cannot hear my word, you are the very image of your father, the devil, and you want to do the same desires as your father.

From the beginning, he was a murderer. Therefore, he will never stand in the truth since there is no shred of truth in him. Every time he speaks a lie, he speaks on his own since he is only a liar; and the father of lies.

Yet, since I tell the truth, you do not believe me.

Which one out of you can convict me of sin?

If I then am telling the truth, why do you not believe me?

Those who are of God hear the words of God; this is the root of why you do not understand because you are not of God." He said decidedly.

At that moment, The Chief Priests and Leaders shouted, "Are we not correct to say you are a Samaritan and have a demon?"

"I do not have a demon! However, I have always honored my Father, and you dishonor me," Jesus answered firmly.

"Yet I do not seek glory for myself. There is one, however, who looks and judges.

I tell you truthfully, any man who will keep my word, he will never see death."

"Now for sure, we know that you have a demon. Abraham he died, and the Prophets they all died, and yet here you are saying. 'Any man who will keep my word, he will never see death.'

Are you now claiming to be greater than our father, Abraham, who died, or the Prophets who died; who then do you make yourself out to be?" The leaders challenged him.

"If I would elevate myself, my praise would be nothing. Jesus notified them. It is my Father whom you have said that he is our God who honors me."

"You have not known him; however, I do know him. If I were to say, 'I do not know him,' I like you would be a liar. However, I know him, and I always keep his word.

Abraham, whom you say is your father, was glad when he saw my day. He saw it and was grateful." Jesus declared firmly.

The Chief Priests and Leaders were stunned, "You are not yet even fifty years old, and you have seen Abraham?" They asked, shocked.
"I tell you most positively before Abraham even came into existence, I AM," Jesus stated powerfully. *(To Jewish ears, the sentence I AM, is the sound YHWH, or Yahweh, which they would not speak, it been the revered, revealed reference that God gave about Himself to Moses, The **TETRAGRAMMATON**. "God said to Moses, in Exodus 3:14, **'I AM WHO I AM**. Or, **Yahweh** generally translated "**LORD**," **So say to the Israelites:** "**I AM has sent me to you**).

Because of this, they were so angry that they rushed to grab stones to throw at him. Except they found Jesus to be totally hidden from them; as he calmly walked through the middle of them in their rage and passing by all of them, he left the Temple.

After this confrontation with the leaders, Jesus was on his way out of the Temple. He was passing a man who was blind and had been in this condition from his birth.
"Rabbi," Said his disciples, in a sudden reversion to calling Jesus, Teacher, instead of 'Lord' *(Adonai). "Who was it that sinned, that as a result he was born blind, was it this man's own sin or his parents?" They asked him.

[*Though there was some scriptural basis for this thinking, such as Numbers 14:18 (*punishes the children for the sin of the parents*) and Psalm 51:5 (*I was sinful at birth*.) Etc.

The teachings of the Pharisees largely influenced this question. Believing the sick and lame were in that condition because of their fault through sin. This teaching was a form of reincarnation *(Bought with returnees from the captivity in Babylon) where any sins of a past life were re-lived with the punishment of disease and sickness in the present life].

"This is not through the sin of this man, or even because of his parents. Yet here is a wonderful opportunity for the power and wonder of God to be known through him," Jesus told them firmly, putting paid to the false notion.

"While it is the day, I must labor, performing the miracles of him who sent me. There is night approaching when no person can work.

While I remain in the world, I am the light of the world." Jesus warned his disciples with authority, reminding them of who he, in fact, is. (*This sudden relapse to addressing Jesus as just teacher rather than Lord was because of their perception of the situation. If he was Lord and Messiah, he had power and could overcome these Pharisees with force if necessary.*

If he is running away from a confrontation, then he may not be the Messiah after all.)

After this, he spat on the ground, and with his hands, made mud with the saliva. Next, anointing the blind man's eyes with the clay, then instructed him, "Go to the pool of Siloam and there wash your eyes." He said. The name Siloam means sent.

SIGNIFICANCE OF THE POOL OF SILOAM.

Here was another living parable and the seventh Messianic miracle (among many others) that should have been a conclusive witness to the leaders.

- Healing of a leper after the sermon on the mountain.
- Raising a widow's son in a town named Nain.
- Raising Jairus' daughter (ruler of a synagogue in Galilee).
- Healing two blind men who call Him the "Son of David."
- Healing a mute demon-possessed man. When the people had exclaimed, (nothing like this was ever seen in Israel).
- Healing a blind man who said, "I see people; they look like trees walking."

Isaiah 35:5–6 (NKJV) fulfilling the prophecies: ***The eyes of the blind shall be opened, And the ears of the deaf shall be unstopped.***
Then the lame shall leap like a deer, and the tongue of the dumb sing.

The pool of Siloam was instrumental and integral in the Water-drawing Festival, connected to the festival of lights that had just concluded. Jesus had declared to the people that he was the light of the world, the one who the Father had sent into the world; the expected, anticipated Shiloh to come, spoken of by Israel before his death, Genesis 49:10.

The one sent into the world was sending a man born blind to a pool called sent (Siloam) to receive sight; the true and the only light of the world, the Shiloh, who gives light to all who are blind and in darkness.

Doing as instructed, the blind man went off to the pool by faith; he regained his sight after washing. Later, he returned, clearly walking with his full eyesight.

Many of the people who knew him, including his neighbors also others who knew that he was blind before when they saw him walking, talked about it, "This man walking, is he not the same man who always sat and begged, being blind?" They were asking excitedly.

Some of them were saying, "Yes, it is him," and others, "He only looks something like him."

"Yes, I am the same man." He told them all.

"How is it that your blind eyes were opened?" They started asking him, knowing that this was the proof of the Messiah.

Every person who attended a Synagogue knew this was to be one of the major miracles of the eagerly awaited Messiah.

"A man called Jesus anointed my eyes, with some mud that he made, and then told me, 'Go wash in the pool of Siloam.' He answered. So I went down to the pool and washed, and I received sight."

"Where is the man Jesus that healed you?" They asked with anticipation.

"I do not know," was the man's only reply.

The nature of the miracle meant the man couldn't know where Jesus was, as he first had to go to the pool before he could see.

The people swiftly took the man who had been blind to the Pharisees with excitement. *(As this was one of the clear signs of the Messiah, the leaders were required to activate the process of a week-long investigation, authorized by the Great Court, verifying that the Messiah of Israel had indeed arrived).

The Pharisees then questioned the formerly blind man, asking him to repeat how he could now see.

"He put some mud he made on my eyes, and after I went and washed, I can see." He replied briefly.

It was on a Sabbath day that Jesus had made the mud and opened his eyes because they considered the making of clay a matter of working on the Sabbath, so breaking the Sabbath Laws.

"This man he is not from God, because as you can hear, he does not keep the Sabbath!" Some faction of the Pharisees immediately exclaimed.

"How then can a man who is just a sinner be able to do such wonders?" Others asked.

Because of their focus on their own tradition of the Sabbath laws, this miracle caused a massive division between them; they were unsure what to do.

They decided to consult the man who was healed, "What do you have to say about this man since it was your eyes that he opened?" They asked him.

"Clearly, he is a Prophet." He promptly replied.

This did not help their dilemma; therefore, they held any further conclusions until the formerly blind man's parents were bought into the Temple. To be questioned about him.

For them, it was easier to discredit the formerly blind man as a faker than to accept the miracle.

(*Note: *This demonstrates the level of power and control the leaders' wielded over the lives of the ordinary people. They had the means of quickly getting relevant information relating to the man's family and his immediate parents.*

The leaders could summon his parents, requiring prompt presenting of themselves to the leadership in the Temple, with the confidence of them being there.

With this measure of authority, their ability to exclude a person from the Temple or barring them from Synagogues was equal to being excommunicated. It would spell the end of virtually all social interactions, including the ability to trade in any local market, etc.)

When the parent arrived, they questioned them, "Is this man your son, whom you say was born blind? How then is it he can see now?" They ask cynically.

His parents chose to be very careful with their answer, "We know that this is indeed our son and that yes, he was born blind and has never been able to see.

However, how he can see now, we do not know. Moreover, we do not know who it is that had opened his eyes. He is old enough to tell it all to you. So you ask him was their cautious reply. He will be able to speak up for himself."

The reason for their hesitant answer to the Leaders was because there was a general word out. The authorities had already decided 'we would put them out of the synagogue' if anyone acknowledges (or confesses) Jesus as Messiah.

Still unsatisfied, the leaders once again recalled the man who was once blind, "In this miracle give the praise only to God. Because we know that this man could only be a sinner." They stated, trying to intimidate him.

"If, in fact, he is a sinner of any manner, I do not know. I know one thing; however, although I was once blind, I now see." He answered firmly.

"What was it he did to you? How did he open your eyes?" They asked him again, almost shouting.

"I have told it to you already, and you did not listen then. Why do you want to hear it all over again?

Is it because you are also now trying to become his disciples?" He asked, with scathing contempt for their behavior.

They resorted to insulting him, "You are the one that is his disciple, but we are only disciples of Moses.

We know for sure that God has spoken to Moses. However, with this man, where he comes from, we do not know." They said, trying to regain the upper hand.

"How utterly amazing," said the man fearlessly.

"You know not where he comes from, yet he has opened my eyes.

All of us know God does not listen to sinners. Yet anyone who is a worshipper of God, and does his will, God will listen to him." He said, strikingly quoting well-known scriptures.

(Psalm 66, *'If I have hidden evil in my heart, The Lord will not hear...'* and Isaiah 1:15 (CEB) *When you extend your hands, I'll hide my eyes from you. Even when you pray for a long time, I won't listen. Your hands are stained with blood*).

"And since the world began, never has it been heard that anyone has ever opened the eyes of someone born blind.

This man could do nothing if he was not from God." The formerly blind man said with spirit and conviction.

"You who were completely born in your sins, you now dare to educate us?" They asked him with disdain. Then unceremoniously, they threw him out of the Temple.

News that the man, who had been healed of blindness, had been abruptly thrown out of the Temple reached Jesus, so Jesus went and found him and spoke to him, "Do you believe in the Son of God?" Jesus asked.

"Who is he, Lord, to make it possible that I will believe in him?" The man enquired.

"You have been blessed to see him, and it is he who speaks with you," Jesus told him.

"Lord, I truly do believe!" He said, and right away, he fell to his face and worshipped Jesus.

"It is for this judgment that I am here in this world, ensuring any who do not see will see, while all those who do see will become blind." Jesus declared forcefully.

Some of the Pharisees who were there heard this, "Then are we also to be considered the blind?" They asked mockingly.

"If you were, in fact, blind, you would then have no sin; however you say, 'we see.' As a result, your sin will remain with you." Jesus replied.

"I tell you most truthfully, anyone who does not enter the sheepfold through the door; instead they climb up some other way, that one is a thief and a robber.

The shepherd of the flock is the only one who will enter by the door. The gatekeeper will open the gate for him, and it is his voice that the sheep identifies.

His very own sheep he will call by name, leading them out of the sheepfold.

Each time he brings his sheep out. They are not driven out; he leads them from the front, and the sheep gladly follow him because they know his voice.

They absolutely will not follow a stranger; they will instead flee from him; since they do not know the voice of strangers."

(Ezekiel 34, **Son of man, prophesy against the shepherds of Israel. That do feed themselves! Should not the shepherds feed the sheep**?)

They did not grasp the parable that Jesus told them, so as a result, Jesus repeated, "I tell you most positively, I am the only door for the sheep.

All those before me came as thieves and robbers, so the sheep did not listen to them.

I am the only door. Anyone entering through me, that person will be saved and will have access to the pasture, having entrance or exit at will.

The thief only ever comes to steal, to kill, and destroy. I am here that everyone can have life and may have it more abundantly.

I am the good shepherd. The good shepherd is the one that gives up his life for the sheep.

The hired hand is not a true shepherd, he is not the sheep's owner, and this one sees the wolf coming, so he escapes leaving the sheep.

The wolf then goes among and grabs the sheep and scatters them.

As only a hired hand, the hired hand escapes because he does not care for the sheep.

I am the good shepherd. My own, I know, as I am also known by my own, even as the Father knows me, and I know the Father. And I surrender my own life for the sheep.

I also have other sheep, which are not part of this fold. Those I will also carry, and they will hear my voice. Then they will all become one flock with one shepherd.

The Father has loved me since I surrendered my life to retake it.

No one has any ability to take my life away from me; I of myself surrender it. I have the power to relinquish it, and I have the power to recover it again. I have received this decree from my Father."

Instances of Shepherds throughout Scriptures.

- Genesis 31:38-40; Psalms 78:52-53; Jeremiah 31:10; Amos 3:12; Luke 2:8 'One who cares for flocks.'
- 1 Samuel 17:34-35 'David, the shepherd, defends his flock against a lion and a bear.'
- Psalms 23:2; Song of Solomon 1:7; Jeremiah 33:12 'Causes the flock to rest.'
- Leviticus 27:32 Jeremiah 33:13 'Numbers the flock.'
- John 10:3-5 'knows his flock by name.'
- Genesis 29:2-10 Waters the flocks.'
- Numbers 32:16; 1 Samuel 24:3; 2 Samuel 7:8; John 10:1 'Keeps the flocks in folds.'
- 2 Chronicles 26:10; Micah 4:8 'Watchtowers of the flocks.'

Recorded occurrences detailing the tending of flocks.

- Genesis 4:2 Abel.
- Genesis 29:9 Rachel.
- Exodus 2:16 Daughters of Jethro.
- Exodus 3:1 Moses.
- 1 Samuel 16:11; 2 Samuel 7:8; Psalms 78:70 David.
- Zechariah 11:17, Zechariah 10:2 The idol shepherd (*Antichrist.*)
- Isaiah 44:28 He is my shepherd: Name given to Cyrus.
- Jesus is the good shepherd.

When the Pharisees and Leaders heard all that Jesus said, they became sharply divided over his credentials, "He has a demon, and is insane! Why do you even listen to him?" Many of them said.

"This is not the speech of one possessed by a demon. Is it in any way possible for a demon to open the eyes of one who is blind from birth?" Some others replied with equal force.

Jesus left them there in a dilemma that constricted them. They had their duty to proclaim him as Israel's Messiah. They had the evidence; no person in history had ever opened the eyes of any person born blind.

They had the teachings of the great Rabbis, who had laid down clear listings of things that only the Messiah could perform, yet they refused to act.

A religious scholar, one scribe, stood up with a question intending to test Jesus, "Teacher, what will I need to do to inherit eternal life?" He asked.

"What do you find written there in the Law of Moses? How do you interpret it?" Jesus asked.

"You will love the Lord, your God. With your whole heart, your soul, all your strength, and your entire mind; also love your neighbor just as you do yourself." The religious scholar answered.

> Leviticus 19:18 (ESV) ***You shall not take vengeance or bear a grudge against the sons of your own people, but you shall love your neighbor as yourself: I am the Lord.***

"You have answered correctly. So then do this, and you will live." Jesus told him.

"Who though is my neighbor?" The religious scholar again asked, still desiring to prove or vindicate himself.

JESUS ANSWERED BY GIVING THE AUDIENCE A MEMORABLE PARABLE.

"Once there was a particular individual; who, while traveling down from Jerusalem to Jericho. This man was attacked by robbers, who took his clothes and beat him, then departed, leaving him half dead," Jesus explained.

"It happened; a priest was on his way down the same road, the Priest, seeing the injured man, passed by him on the other side of the road.

A Levite also came by the place; he passed by on the other side of the road on seeing the injured man.

Now, as a certain Samaritan, traveled and came where the injured man lay.

When he saw the wounded man, it moved him with compassion. And approaching him, he bandaged up his wounds, bathing them with oil and wine.

After that, the Samaritan set him on his own animal, bringing him to an inn, where he cared for him.

The next day on the departure of the Samaritan, he took some money and gave it to the innkeeper, telling him, 'Take special care of this man. Should you spend any more than that amount, I will repay you on my return.'

Now, what do you think, which one of the three is a neighbor to the man attacked by robbers?" Jesus asked the scholar in conclusion.

"He who showed mercy on him," the religious scholar answered.

"Then go do the same," Jesus instructed him.

Earlier, they had accused Jesus of either having a demon or being a Samaritan; to this, Jesus had replied. 'I do not have a demon.' but had said nothing about 'a Samaritan' until now.

Now Jesus has flipped their hatred of the Samaritan with this parable in which He said, "A certain Samaritan, journeyed and came where the injured man lay."

[This parable could be viewed in this way. (*A Samaritan being only a half-Israelite, having a Jewish mother and a none Jewish or foreign father, Jesus qualifies as his father is God*).

Jesus is that traveler who finds the injured person.

Each of 'His people' represents the injured man, the individual attacked while on a journey 'going down' from Jerusalem (*Heaven*), Yireh the abiding place, and Shalem (*Place of Peace paradise*) Jericho, (*Jericho representing the fallen state*).

Jerusalem signifies the place of peace, lost to all humanity through Adam.

Set upon by 'the thief' (coming only to steal, kill, and destroy) who took (or stripped him of) his clothes.

(Genesis 3:7 '***Then the eyes of the two of them were opened, and knowing they were naked, they fastened fig leaves together making themselves coverings***').

Although Priests and Levites (*selected to be mediators between man and God*) had been since the Tabernacle of Moses entrusted with the tasks of bringing the law to the lost people.

Or the later Temple duties, even the sacrificial system, none, in the end, could help redeem and restore the lost.

Only the one who was so despised and rejected is the very one who came and ripped his own clothes (As well as flesh).

ISAIAH 53:5 (KJV) **'But he was wounded for our transgressions, he was bruised for our iniquities.'**

*(Then they, after they crucified him, divided up by drawing lots for his garments among them.

Matthew 27:35. This realized the prophecy of Psalm 22:18, **"They divide my clothes among them"**).

He then dressed our wounds and poured in 'oil and wine' (*anointing by God's Spirit*). Isaiah 53:5: **'We were healed because of his stripes.'**

Leaving a deposit in (*lieu*) or place of full payment (*redemption*) until he would return from his urgent but long and necessary journey, he took us (*the rescued from the world*) to a place of safety (*Ecclesia*). He charged temporary shepherds (*Keepers*) to care for us].

CHAPTER FOURTEEN

JESUS AND THE DISCIPLES CONTINUED TO TRAVEL FROM VILLAGE TO VILLAGE.

A s they continued on their way, they entered Bethany, a village about two miles from Jerusalem.

This was the hometown of the sisters Martha and Mary.

Jesus and the disciples rested in the home of the sisters for a time.

As Jesus was teaching, Mary decided to sit attentively at Jesus' feet and listen to all that he was saying.

Martha, however, was preoccupied with a significant number of tasks. Serving and making food preparations for everyone. After some time, she approaches Jesus. "Lord, do you not care seeing my sister has left me to do the serving alone?" She asked with evident fretfulness.

"Ask her to help me then." She continued peevishly.

"Martha, Martha," Jesus answered softly, "You are anxious and troubled about so many things."

"However, there is only one thing that is needed. Mary, she has chosen that one good part, which will not be taken away from her."

Later as Jesus was praying in a private location, the disciples waited. So when he finished praying, one of his disciples asked him, "Lord, will you teach us how to pray, like John taught his disciples?"

Jesus replied, explaining this way, "When you pray, this is the pattern for what you should say, 'Our Father in Heaven, may your name always be held holy.

Allow your Kingdom to become manifest. Allow your will to be done, as in Heaven, likewise upon the Earth.

Give unto us today our daily bread.

Forgive us all our debts, as we also forgive everyone indebted to us.

Take us away from all temptations, delivering us from the evil one.

Since yours are the Kingdom, the power, and the glory forever. Amen.'

Jesus continued with an illustration about asking, "Any one of you, if having gone to a friend at midnight, to ask of him, 'my friend, lend me three loaves of bread.

Because I have nothing to set before a friend of mine who has arrived from a long journey,'

The friend from within the house will answer, 'Do not bother me. I cannot get up to give provisions to you.' I have now shut the door, and I, as well as my children, have retired to bed.

I tell you, while he will not rise to help him even because he is his friend. Yet, the friend will eventually get up and give him all the necessary provisions because of his persistence.

"Keep asking, I tell you, it will be given to you. Keep seeking, and you will find. Keep knocking; it will eventually be opened to you.

Because every person who asks will receive, he who seeks will find, and to him, who knocks, it will be opened.

"Which of you fathers, if your son were to ask you for bread, will give him a stone? Or if he were to ask for a fish, you would not give him a snake instead of a fish, will you?

Or if he asks for an egg, you would not give him a scorpion, will you?

So if being evil, you know how to give your children good gifts. Imagine how abundantly your heavenly Father gives those who ask of him the gift of the Holy Spirit?" He explained.

From within the crowd that followed him, a young man approached Jesus, "Teacher." He said, acknowledging Jesus as a Rabbi, "Will you advise my brother that we should divide the inheritance between him and me?" He Pleaded.

"Man, who has appointed me to be a judge or an arbitrator over you?" Jesus asked him.

(*It would be expected for teachers considered a Rabbi to apply their own interpretations, where the application of some particular law found in the Torah is concerned. And as in this case, to settle disputes*).

"Be alert!" Jesus warned, "Be sure that you keep yourselves from covetousness and understand that the life of a man does not amount to the great number of things which he possesses."

Jesus told the people a parable to illustrate the importance of focusing on the priorities of the Kingdom.

"There was an individual who was a rich man, and the land he owned produced lavishly and in large quantities.

Reasoning to himself, he said, I do not have enough room to store all of my crops, so what am I to do?

'This then is what I will do.' He said, 'I will demolish my existing barns and then build for myself, greatly improved ones, allowing me to stockpile all my grain and my goods.'

I will then say to my soul. Soul, now you have much supplies and provisions for many years. So from now on, take it easy, eat, drink, and be merry.'

"However, God said to that man, 'you foolish man, this very night you die, and your soul is required from you.

Then who will own all the things which you have arranged for yourself?' Similarly, is the one who collects treasure for himself, yet cannot be rich toward God."

(Psalm 49:10, "*Wise men die; the fool and the common die alike and leave their wealth to others.*")

Jesus addressed his disciples, "I tell you, as a result, do not be worried about your life. Not what you will eat, or even for your body, including clothing that you will wear.

Life is so much more than mere food, and the body is much more than any clothing.

Reflect on the Ravens and their splendor, yet God provides for them without ever planting or ever having to harvest with no warehouse or barn. You are very much more valuable than birds!

By you being worried, can any of you add a cubit to his height?

If you cannot do even the least and smallest things, why then be concerned about the rest?

Reflect on how the lilies grow. Without working, never making clothes, yet I can tell you as splendid as Solomon was, he was never displayed in splendor approaching one of these.

Yet, if God clothes the grass in this fashion, existing only for today and burnt tomorrow. How much further will he clothe you! O you children, why is your faith so small?

Do not hunt for what you will eat or drink, or allow yourself to be concerned.

Because these are things, the people in the nations of the world look for. However, your Father already knows that you require these things.

Instead, try to gain God's Kingdom, and then all these things you will also have.

Be joyful and never be fearful, little flock, since it is his good pleasure of your Father to give you the Kingdom.

All that you possess, go sell it and then give gifts to those that are deprived.

This way, you are making purses that do not grow old; treasures that never fail in the heavens; no thief can come near and never destroyed by any moth.

Since the place where you store your treasure, that's where you will also have your heart.

"Be fully clothed and ready for the work and have the correct and adequate light.

You should be like men alert and waiting for the return of their lord from the marriage feast, and then they can instantly open to him the moment he arrives and knocks.

That lord, when he arrives and finds that those servants are alert and waiting, they will be approved.

I tell you most certainly; the lord will put on the waiters' uniform, allowing them to sit at ease, while he will be their waiter.

Even at a very late hour, if he arrives unexpectedly and finds them alert and aware, they will be most exalted.

However, be sure of this. Had the master of that house known what hour the thief was coming, he would have watched, not allowing his house to be broken into.

As a result, be ready also, for the Son of Man is arriving at a time that you do not expect him."

"Lord," Peter spoke up, "Are you only telling this parable to us, or everybody?" He asked.

"Who is the guardian considered loyal and wise?" Jesus replied, "The one his lord has set over his household to run the house, supplying the provisions to all the others when necessary.

Happy and exalted is that guardian, after finding that he did it all and well at his lord's return. I tell you truthfully; his lord will promote him to manage all things." The Lord continued to explain.

"However, if that appointed guardian should say in his heart, 'My Lord delays his arrival,'

Then use this to mistreat the others that he is in charge of, using his time to party and to get drunk, and then the appearance of his lord will be in a day when he is not expecting, and in an hour not known to him.

Then the lord will order that guardian punished. Sending him away to be with the hypocrites who only pretended to serve their master, to the place where people will cry loudly, gritting and grinding their teeth with pain.

That foolish custodian, knowing his lord's will, and did not see its seriousness and prepare or ensure what the lord wanted was done. He will be beaten with many stripes.

However, another who did things that deserve punishment except he did not know will be beaten with few stripes.

When one is given a significant amount, a great deal will be required of him. To any entrusted with a lot, they will expect more of him." He said, making the teaching clear to them.

"I am here to set in motion the launching of fire on the Earth. I would have desired for it to have already been lit and ablaze now.

I, however, have a baptism with which I must first be baptized. And how impatient and distressed I am until it is consummated!

Do you imagine I am here to give the Earth peace? No, not peace, instead I say division.

Because from now on, there will be divisions in one house of five, three uniting against two. The father will be against the son and the son against the father.

Mother against daughter, mother-in-law, and the daughter-in-law against one another," Jesus informed them, explaining the urgency of the teaching to his disciples.

He turns to the crowd, "On seeing a cloud rising from the west, you directly say, 'There is a shower on its way,' and then it occurs.

On feeling a south wind blow, you exclaim, 'There will soon be a scorching heat,' and then it occurs.

You are such fine hypocrites! Knowing how to read the appearance of the Earth and sky, yet how do you not understand these times?

Why are you not able to judge for yourselves what is right?" Jesus finishes by asking rhetorically.

Then he reminded them of the actual judgment he will bring. "Realise when you are on the way with an adversary," Jesus continued, "Going before the magistrate. Try urgently to reconcile with your opponent, or he perhaps drags you in front of the judge, the judge handing you over to the officer, who will throw you in prison.

I am telling you; by no means will you be set free until payment of the entire due fine."

Some people from the crowd approached Jesus with news of the incident involving some Galileans being killed in the Temple by Pilate's soldiers at the time of one festival. Resulting in mixing their blood with the Temple sacrifices!

"These Galileans, do you imagine that since they suffered these things, that they were any worse sinners than all the other Galileans?" Jesus asked them.

"No, I tell you," He continued, "Yet you will all, in the same way, perish unless you repent.

Or even those eighteen people, on whom the tower in Siloam fell, killing them.

Do you believe they were worse wrongdoers than all the men who live in Jerusalem?

No, I tell you, however, unless you will repent, all of you will also perish."

JESUS CONTINUED WITH ANOTHER MEANINGFUL PARABLE.

"There was a man who had a vineyard where he planted a fig tree, and from which he arrived looking for fruit on it, but found none.

He said to the vinedresser. 'Consider, for three years, I have sought fruit from this fig tree and have yet to find any. Chop down the tree right away; there is no reason for it to be wasting the soil?'

The vinedresser replied, 'lord, let us leave it alone for this year also; until I can dig around it, with intentions to fertilize it.

If it then bears fruit, very well; however, if after that it does not, you can then cut it down.'" Jesus concluded, sending a clear message to the people on the theme of judgment.

On a Sabbath day, Jesus was teaching in one of the synagogues.

There among the congregation was a woman who for eighteen years she had been suffering from a spirit of infirmity; this caused her to be bent over so that she could not straighten herself up.

Jesus called her when he saw her, "Woman, you are released from your infirmity." He said to her.

Jesus simply laid his hands on her, and then she immediately could stand up straight, then praised and acknowledged God.

The ruler of the synagogue became angered for the reason that Jesus had healed on the Sabbath.

He said to the crowd, "Men have six days in which to work. Hence come and be healed on those days, but not on the day that is a Sabbath!"

"You hypocrites," The Lord exclaimed.

"Each one of you, do you not untie your ox or donkey from the stall on the Sabbath, leading the animal away to water, this woman, a daughter of Abraham who has been bound by Satan eighteen long years, should she not be released from this bondage on the Sabbath day?" He asks the whole synagogue, incredulously shaming all his disappointed opponents. At the same time, all the astonishing things he did, delighted the crowd.

"The Kingdom of God, it would be similar to what? To what will I equate it?" Jesus asked.

"The Kingdom would be similar to a single tiny grain of mustard seed, taken by a man and placed in a garden he owns.

It became a large tree when it grew, allowing the birds of the sky to come live in its branches."

"What will I compare to the Kingdom of God?" He again asked rhetorically.

"The Kingdom is like a small amount of yeast taken by a woman making bread, hiding it in three measures of flour. Eventually, it all becomes leavened" (*raised by fermentation.*)

(Inexplicably, the flames returned to the candelabra during the period of the Maccabees, expressing the miracle of God's presence in the Temple.

The flame once lit miraculously burnt for many days, without supplies of the necessary oil needed for the purpose, and was reminiscent of the eternal flame of God, which burned for the people of Israel.

Jesus became the tangible, physical expression of the very presence of God, the Light of the entire World, who came to dwell among us and give us the eternal light of the life from God).

The time of 'Hanukkah' marks the historical defeat of the considerable, more powerful Greek-Syrian army by the determination of the Maccabees after the Greeks had invaded and conquered Israel; However, with just a small group of Jewish rebels led by Mattathias and his five sons, including Judas Maccabeus (Known as the Hammer.)

The Maccabees managed to shape themselves into a capable rebel army, and with God's help, triumphed over the dominating invaders.

The Maccabees; allowed the Jews to rededicate the Alter that had been defiled and worship freely in the Holy Temple in Jerusalem.

In the wintertime, during the time of the Feast of the Dedication at Jerusalem, Jesus was walking within the Temple complex called the Solomon's porch area, which had remained from the destruction by Babylon of the old Temple when Judah was taken into exile. And had been left there essentially intact, following the rebuilding and expansion of the second Temple.

The porch was *'The Porch of Judgement'* attached to the original Temple of Solomon. King Solomon had constructed a large hall a hundred feet long and sixty feet wide—marked with distinctive massive cedar support columns from floor to ceiling. This was the hall of judgment where the King would make judicial laws, legal decrees, and exercise justice.

The reconstructed Herod's Temple had three huge "Porch" or "Portico" situated on the east side of the outer court.

The Levites inhabited parts of these premises with rooms located there. It was also here that the doctors of the law met to hear and answer questions.

(*Jesus' parents had once discovered him here, asking and answering questions, when he was twelve years old*).

Near two hundred years before, in the time of the Maccabees, after raiding the Temple, the Greek general *Antiochus* Epiphanes took a Pig, then proceeded to sacrifice it to his god on the Altar, in defiance of the God of the Hebrews.

Then after he was defeated by Judas Maccabeus, and the Temple was rescued and rededicated. The old defiled Altar was pulled down, and new stones were commissioned, hence the Festival of 'The Rededication,' which later became known as the 'Feast of Lights.'

The stones from the old Altar were sanctified so they could not be thrown away, and as they were now defiled, neither could they reuse those stones for the Altar. The stones were taken instead and stacked in one corner of Solomon's Temple; they had now been there for over one hundred and sixty years, awaiting a solution.

The Rabbis had finally concluded it was best to leave the decision, saying, 'when the Messiah came, he will tell us what to do with these stones from the altar.'

Jesus was often seen here, speaking and teaching the people or just walking. On one occasion, as he walked.

The Chief Priests, Rabbis, and Levites suddenly surrounded him, and they anxiously challenged him, "How much longer are you going to hold us in suspense? If you are indeed the Messiah, then tell us openly." They demanded with evident frustration.

"I have told you, yet you do not believe. The very miracles that I do in the name of my Father, they give evidence about me." Jesus replied coolly.

"Yet you do not believe, as I said since you are not of my sheep.

I know my sheep; they hear my voice and follow me.

I give eternal life to them. Therefore, they will never die! From my hand, no one can ever seize them.

My Father, who is much greater than all, has given them to me. No one is then able to take them out of my Father's hand.

The Father and I are one." He concluded, reminding them of his previous message.

The Leaders were so enraged. They went and grabbed some of the stones from the pile to throw at him.

(Having been put aside, awaiting 'his' the Messiah's final decision on arrival. Now, for telling them the truth, that he was God! The people finally found how to make use of the desecrated stones of the Altar, ruined by Antiochus. They were to be used to throw at the very one for whom they had waited.

The very stones that had been torn down because of the Temple's desecration, by a past abomination, stood the likelihood of being used against the Messiah, who was the Temple made without hands.

Despite what they were looking for in a savior for Israel, the defeat brought by Jesus was against the tyranny of sin, not over the Roman conquerors).

"I have shown you many wonderful miracles from my Father, on account of which one of those miracles do you, stone me?" Jesus asked them.

"We do not stone you for any miracle, but for blasphemy: since you, who are a man, make yourself God." They replied.

"In your law, is it not written, 'I said, you are gods?'" Jesus asked, quoting Psalm eighty-two, a Psalm of solemn judgment.

"If God called those whom the word of God came to, gods, (and the Scripture can never be broken), do you then dare to say of him whom the Father sanctified and sent into the world, 'You blaspheme,' for saying, 'I am the Son of God?'"

Do not believe me if I don't do the miracles of my Father.

However, if I do them, even if you do not believe me, believe the miracles; so you may know and believe the Father is in me, and I in Father." He told them loud and clear.

Again they wanted to get hold of him, yet found they could not; Jesus just walked away and left the area.

Jesus left with the disciples and set off to the place where John was baptizing initially; this was beyond the Jordan into the eastern Judea area. They remained in that area for some time.

There had to follow a six-day separation. (*Because the Leaders had failed to do what was legally required, in their own rules. Jesus left the area until the statutory time expired*).

Psalm 82, God presides over the court of Heaven; He stands as judge among the heavenly judges:
Saying, "How long will you judge making unjust decisions, showing the wicked special favors."
"Defend the poor and orphans giving them justice; protect the rights of the oppressed and the needy.

Rescue those who are poor and helpless; save them from the grip of evil people.

However, these oppressors know nothing; they do not recognize what is happening; they are so ignorant!

They wander about in darkness, not knowing what they are doing, while the whole world is shaken to the core.

I, God Most High, say, "You are gods, my very own sons; all children of The Most High.

Still, you will die like mere mortals. You will die, your life' ending like that of any ruler."

Jesus set off from Galilee and went into the borders of Judea and beyond the Jordan (Perea). Herod Antipas, who had beheaded John for preaching against his divorce and remarriage to the wife of his still-living brother, ruled in this region.

Enormous crowds assembled around him here as well. As he regularly did, he again taught them.

Jesus healed the people as they were following him.

The Pharisees, who were followers of the Oral Law of the Rabbi's, approached with a question they hoped would be a test to determine which of their various positions he would endorse.

(In the Mishnah, 'Their Oral Torah' was various instructions, arrived on from the positions of several rabbis.

Rabbi Beth Shammai declared a man who finds his wife guilty of some improper conduct 'interpreted as adultery.'

Rabbi Beth Hillel - declared a man who finds his food even simply ruined by his wife, 'interpreted as any reason.'

Akiva Ben-Joseph, Rabbi Akiba - announced a man who finds another woman more beautiful than his wife, 'interpreted as a no-fault divorce.'

King Herod had already killed John the Baptizer over the question of his divorce; they were hoping that Herod would also imprison or kill Jesus).

"Is there any lawful reason for a man to divorce his wife?" They asked.

"Have you not read there in the Scriptures, how he who made them, at the creation he made them male and female. And declared, 'on this basis a man shall leave his father and mother, joining to his wife; the two then become one flesh?' Jesus asked them.

"As a result," he continued, "they are in fact one flesh and not any longer two separate people. So then, what God has joined together, do not let any man tear apart."

"Why did Moses decree for us to give her a written announcement of divorce then, and so divorce her?" They asked, hoping to salvage something using the law.

"Moses," Jesus replied, "given the fact of the hardness of your hearts, allowed you to divorce your wives, although, from the beginning, it has not been so.

I tell you; the one who divorces his wife, except for the cause of sexual immorality. Marrying another commits adultery, and he who marries her when she is divorced commits adultery."

"That which God joined together, do not let any man tear apart." He told them.

Later, when Jesus and his disciples went inside the house, they enquired about it, "If this is the state of the man with his wife, it is not practical to marry." They stated.

"The man divorcing his wife, to marry another, commits adultery against her.

If a woman herself divorces her husband and marries another, she commits adultery." Jesus repeated to remind them.

"Not all men can accept this teaching, except those to whom it is granted, because some are eunuchs, born that way from the womb of their mother. And some are eunuchs who were made eunuchs by human actions. Some have even made themselves eunuchs for the sake of the Kingdom of Heaven. They, who can receive it, let them accept it."

Vast crowds of people came to him. The people were full of praises and were saying things like, "John, in reality, did not do miracles, although everything John said about this man is true."

Many people in the area believed in Jesus, knowing that he is Israel's Messiah and King.

As he walked day by day through the small cities and villages, teaching and healing the people, he steadily traveled on his way back towards Jerusalem.

One person following him approached with a question, "Lord, the ones who are saved are they only very few in numbers?" asked the man.

Jesus addresses the crowd, "Try hard to enter in by the narrow door, because I tell you, many will search for the entrance, and will not be able to enter." He told them.

"After the master of the house has got up and closed the door, and you then having arrive standing outside knocking at the door, calling, 'Lord, Lord, open up the door for us!'

He will then answer, telling you, 'I do not know who you are or where you come from.'

You will then say, 'We are the ones who ate with you and drank in your presence, and you even taught in our streets.'

He will insist, 'I tell you; I do not know from where you've come. Get yourself away from me, all you workers of iniquity.'

On that day, there will be great gnashing of teeth by you seeing all the Prophets in the Kingdom of God, Abraham, Isaac, Jacob, and you yourselves being thrown outside.

From the east, west, north, and south, will people come to sit down in the Kingdom of God!

Take note, some are last who will be first, and some are first who will be last." Jesus cautioned.

CHAPTER FIFTEEN

JESUS TEACHES AS HE TRAVELS TO JERUSALEM.

Later during the day, some Pharisees arrived to speak with him, "Get out of this area, and go elsewhere, seeing as Herod wants to kill you." They were claiming.

(*This had been their hope all along and the reason they tried to involve Jesus in speaking out about divorce, as John had done*).

"Go back and tell that fox" (*The lawless one.*) 'See, I am casting out demons and performing cures today and tomorrow also, and then on the third day, I will complete my mission." He replied.

(*Jesus used a common saying, of 'today tomorrow and the third day.' A widely used adage that all Jews knew meant we must complete the work regardless*).

"However, I must continue on my way today, tomorrow, and the next day, pressing on since it cannot be that a Prophet is killed away from Jerusalem.

JESUS' LAMENTATION OVER JERUSALEM.

"Jerusalem, Jerusalem! You who kills the Prophets, stoning the Prophets and those messengers sent to her?

How very often have I wanted to gather your children together, as a mother hen gathering her brood hiding under her wings, and you refused!

Observe then how your house is left to you desolate (*the Departure of the Lord's Glory*), I tell you with solemn truth; you will not see me, until you say, 'Blessed is he the *One* coming in the name of the Lord'" (*Baruch ha-ba b'shem Adonai*). Jesus warned, with the scripture from the well-known Psalm 118:26, speaking of the Messiah's arrival.

One ruler of the Pharisees invited Jesus to dine on a Sabbath meal. The Sabbath meal is the most important meal of the week, carefully prepared in advance.

Arriving at the home of this chief Pharisee, the people there, including the lawyers, were all intensely scrutinizing him.

They had arranged the placing of a man there who was ill and had the bloating water condition called Dropsy, in the opposite position to Jesus at the dinner party.

The placing of a man there, who was ill with Dropsy (*in this condition, he would be in considerable suffering and distress. Keeping him sitting there for their purpose would prove to be absolute agony for him*).

After observing their behavior, Jesus turned to the lawyers and Pharisees, "If we make someone well on the Sabbath, does the law allow or do not allow?" He asked, point-blank and forcefully.

However, none of them committed themselves; they all remained silent.

Jesus called the man with the condition and purposely held him. After healing him, he compassionately allowed him to leave.

(*The people involved in setting this trap for Jesus being so intently concerned about 'ritual purity' that this would be the most unlikely of all dinner guests. And although he did not necessarily need to touch the man, Jesus purposely made physical contact to show their hypocrisy*).

[The Pharisees held to their teachings, saying they permitted no physician to work his trade on the Sabbath unless it was to save the life of the patient.

Among Rabbis, it was commonly taught that people with this kind of disease had committed some grievous sin, which, according to their wisdom, could have even been in a past life.

This condition of Dropsy is the old term for *edema* (*or Oedema*), the swelling of the soft tissues because of an abnormal accumulation of excess fluid caused by congestive heart, liver, or kidney failure, resulting in swelling limbs and bloating of the face and body.

An extremely uncomfortable illness only relieved in the short term by puncturing the patient's skin with a hollow needle to siphon off the excess fluids. However, whenever this was done, the person would become ceremonially unclean].

"Each of you men, if your own son or even an animal such as an ox, was to fall into a well to drown, would you not pull him out without delay even if it was on a Sabbath day?" Jesus demanded of them.

Not one of them could reply to this.

After observing their attitude to the preferred positions they strived to sit for the dinner, he told them a parable to illustrate the principles of the kingdom concerning courtesy and humility.

"If you receive an invitation to be a guest at a wedding celebration, do not seat yourself in the best seat.

Since by chance, the host may have invited another more honorable than you and would have to approach and tell you, 'Leave this position and give the space to this person.'

Then you, with shame, will have to take a lower place.

Instead, when you are invited, go to find the lowest place to sit, then when the host arrives, he will approach and inform you, 'Friend, follow me, and I will move you up to a higher placing.' This will ensure that you receive honor among all the other guests at the table.

Because every person promoting himself will be reduced and demoted, while the one with humility is the one that will be celebrated." He explained to his audience.

Then turning to the Pharisee who had invited him, "when you make a dinner or a supper, do not just ask your own family, close friends, brothers, or rich neighbors to attend; otherwise, they doubtless will also return the favor, and in so doing, they then have paid you back.

When you make a feast, however, by you inviting those that are poor, maimed, lame, or the blind, you will be blessed; since they are the ones that do not have any resources to repay you. Yet, you will receive repayment in the resurrection of the righteous." Jesus instructed him. (Note: They only invited the man with the Dropsy condition as a trap, not through wanting to help the poor or unfortunate).

(Proverbs 25:6: *Do not push for status or boast in an audience with the King, pretending you belong among the great.*

Proverbs 27:2 *Never call attention for the praise of yourself, Let the praise come from the mouth of another*).

One guest sitting there with them spoke up, having understood the significance of 'the Kingdom' in the story that Jesus used. "It will be an enormous blessing for anyone who will eat at the banquet in the Kingdom of God!" He exclaimed.

"The master of a prominent household made a grand feast, for which he invited many people," Jesus replied, using another example.

"He sent out messengers from his household to those requested guests when the time came for the festivities. 'All is now ready for you, and your presence is required.' They were informed.

Each of them started making excuses for not attending.

'Unfortunately, having just bought a field, I need to go and attend to it; please send my regret,' said the first in reply to the messengers.

"Another told the messengers, 'I have just purchased ten farm animals, oxen's that need to be yoked in pairs, and I will need to go try them out. Please send my regrets.'

'I have just gotten married; my wife is waiting, and as a result, I cannot come,' another said.

"That courier returned and told his lord of all the messages of regrets.

This treatment very much angered the master of the house, 'Quickly now go and bring in the poor, maimed, blind, and lame from the streets and lanes of the city.' He instructed the couriers.

'Lord, we now completed all as you instructed, yet there is still space available.' The messengers later told him.

'Go out even into the highways and hedges and force any of them there to enter. In that way, my house will be filled because I tell you that not one of those men who were initially invited will taste anything of my supper.' The lord of the house Commanded," Jesus explained, as a dire warning against being complacent where the Kingdom is concerned.

Later as Jesus traveled to towns and villages, sizeable crowds followed him. He turned, addressing them, "To follow me, I will expect you to relinquish your father and your mother, your wife, children, brothers, sisters, and indeed your own life. If you do not, then you cannot be my disciple.

Unless you are prepared to bear your very own cross and follow me. You cannot be my disciple," he announced, explaining the actual cost of discipleship.

Jesus gave a memorable illustration to help them grasp the truth, "If one of you, desiring to build a tower. Would you not first sit down and count the project's cost to know whether you will have enough to complete it?

Or, it is not just conceivable that having first laid the foundation and then been unable to complete it. That will cause everyone to mock you when they see you, saying, 'look, this is the man who embarked on building something that he could not finish.'

Consider the action of a king who goes to engage in a war with another king. Will he not first sit down and judge if he can meet with only ten thousand troops, the other King coming in opposition to him with forces of twenty thousand?

And having found that he is not able, he will swiftly send a delegate to the other King before that King enters his land, asking for conditions of peace.

So, accordingly, any of you who do not abandon all he has cannot be my disciple.

Salt is good for taste and seasoning, yet should the salt ever become flat and tasteless, what will you use to re-season it?

It is not fit for the soil or even for the compost pile. It will be thrown out. Whoever has ears and can hear, let them hear," he invited them to judge their actual intent.

Jesus was attracting people from a wide category, incorporating those considered as being the outcasts of society, including people who collaborated with the Romans and collected the tax, those the leaders deemed the worst of all sinners.

Nevertheless, more and more people wanted to hear him.

The Pharisees and Scribes had much to say about this. "This man is welcoming and eating with sinners and the rabble." They murmured about him.

JESUS TEACHES WITH THE PARABLE OF THE JOY OF THE LOVING FATHER.

If any of you men here had one hundred sheep and found that one of them became lost, would you then, not leave the ninety-nine others in the wild, to go and try to find the one that was lost?

And you, when you have found it, carry it on your shoulders as you celebrate, then calling to your friends and neighbors on arriving back at your home. You would say to them with joy. 'Let us celebrate, now that I have found my lost sheep!'

I tell you, just the same way. More joy will be in Heaven over only a single sinner repenting than over ninety-nine upright people not needing repentance." Jesus exclaimed, to the great delight of the people.

He also addressed a part of the parable to the women in the crowd. "Or any woman, if she, having ten gold coins, and lost just one coin. Would she not get a light, search thoroughly through the house, looking until she found it?

Upon finding it, she calls to her friends and neighbors, 'Come celebrate with me, I have now found that gold coin of value, which I had lost.' she says.

I tell you, there is the same joy in the presence of the Angels of God because of just one sinner finding repentance."

Jesus continued with another extraordinary illustration of the principles of the kingdom, "A particular man had two sons.

The younger son of the two asked his father, 'Father, divide your property and give me my share.' The father divided his assets between them.

Then just a few days later, that younger son assembled everything and traveled to another country.

On arriving there, he spent his assets on constant rowdy living.

After depleting all the resources, a relentless famine came to that country, and he found that he was now in great need.

He became a hired laborer to a native of the country, who sent him to his farm to feed the pigs.

He became hungry enough that the husks that were eaten by the pigs looked palatable, but none was given to him by anyone.

However, when he eventually came to himself, he said, 'in my father's house, how many of the servants and hired hands have more than enough bread to spare, yet I will die with hunger!

I will get myself up and return to my father and say to him, 'Father, against Heaven, and in your sight, I have sinned.

And do not any longer warrant to be called a son; hire me as one of your servants.'

He left that country and returned to find his father. However, his father already saw him approaching, even when he was still a long way away.

The father was so stirred with compassion; he ran to his son and hugged him by the neck, kissing him.

The son started to speak, 'Father, against Heaven and in your sight have I sinned. I no longer warrant being called your son.'

However, the father instructed his servants, 'Go and bring back the best coat and dress him in it. Place on his hand a ring, and on his feet, new shoes.

Take the best calf and kill it, then we will eat and have a celebration, because I have regained a son who, although was dead, is again alive. And even though he was lost, he is now found.'

The household all got together and celebrated.

At that time, his elder son was out in the field. As he approached the house, he could hear music and dancing.

He signaled to one servant, asking what was happening.

'Your brother has returned, so your father has killed the best calf since he has received him back safe and sound.' The servant reported.

But, the elder son was so angry; he refused to go in. As a result, his father had to come out begging him.

Still, he protested to his father, 'Consider, these many years I have served you without disobeying one of your instructions. Yet you have never given even a goat to me, so I might call my friends and celebrate.

Yet just as soon as this, your son, who has devoured your living with prostitutes, arrives here, you killed the best calf for him.' He replied, murmuring to his father.

The father replied. 'My son, you are with me all the time, and all that I have belongs to you.

However, it was fitting to celebrate and be thankful since this your brother was dead and is again alive. Although he was lost he is now found.' Jesus declared to his stunned and delighted listeners.

(Note: *The 'joy that's in the presence of the Angels because of just one sinner finding repentance' is not just the joy of the Angels, but more so of the father. And to emphasize this point, Jesus told of the wayward son who is searched for continuously and finally welcomed back by a wonderfully loving father. He then throws a lavish party accepting the lost son back to the family. The father's amazing love extended similarly to the older son to whom he showed grace rather than irritation at his refusal to enter the residence).*

JESUS DIRECTED THE NEXT ILLUSTRATION TO HIS DISCIPLES.

"A certain wealthy lord," He began. "Who had a manager received an accusation brought to him about the manager wasting his assets.

He called him and asked, 'what is this that I hear about you? Give a final accounting of your management because you can no longer be a manager.'

'What will I do, the manager contemplated, considering that my lord is taking the management position from me?

I do not have the strength to dig. And I am humiliated to beg.

I know what to do, he thought! So after I am removed from management, they will accept me into their homes.'

After making a list of each one that was in debt to his lord, he summoned them,

'How much do you currently owe, my lord?' He asked the first.

'I owe a hundred containers of olive oil.' The merchant replied.

'Quickly take your bill, sit down, and write fifty containers.' The manager instructed.

'What is the size of your debt you owe to my lord?' He then asked another.

'I owe a hundred stacks of wheat.' This merchant replied.

'Take hold of your bill, and now write eighty.' He instructed him.

His lord highly praised the dishonest manager since he had done wisely." Jesus finished with a startling conclusion.

"Given that within their own generation, the children of this world are so much shrewder than are the children of the light.

I tell you, use the unrighteous mammon as a means of making friends for yourself. So that when you expire, they will also accept you into the eternal tents," Jesus confirmed to the disciples.

(Jesus told the disciples to use 'the unrighteous mammon' to do whatever possible while still in the world, not for the world's sake, but the kingdoms, very different from the conclusion given to the Pharisees).

"The one who is reliable in a very little is also reliable in a great deal." Jesus continued.

"The one who is dishonest in the little things is also dishonest in a large amount.

As a result, if you could not be reliable with the unrighteous mammon of this world, who will charge the true eternal riches to your care, if you have not, been dependable with things belonging to others, who will give you the things that belong to you?

No one can be a servant to two masters; because one will be hated and the other loved, or one will be accepted, and the other derided.

You can never serve God and mammon." He told them categorically.

The Pharisees were listening intently to this. They then scoffed at and openly mocked Jesus over his teaching about money. They loved and believed that their money was a sign of blessings from God.

Jesus turned to them, "You are the kind of people who endorse and approve yourselves in the sight of men. However, God knows your hearts since that which is celebrated among men is detestable in the sight of God.

The law's proclamation, the Torah, and the teachings of the Prophets continued until John. Then from that time, the Kingdom of God and the Good News it brings is preached; and everyone is receiving and vigorously fighting their best to get into the kingdom.

However, regarding the law, it remains whole and intact it will never change. Far easier for Heaven along with Earth to expire than for one tiny stroke of a pen among all the law to fall," Jesus informed them, dealing with the root of their problem. Their external show of righteousness stops them from seeing the kingdom's message, accepted by all those who had changed hearts towards God.

"Whoever, after divorcing his wife, marries another, is engaging in adultery, as he who after marrying any woman being divorced from a husband, causes adultery," Jesus stated. Silencing the Pharisees, showing them they were not keeping the law as they thought, but by reinterpreting them, actually broke them.

Jesus now took them back to their dealings with and love of money to show its actual end. As they were sure that their riches, along with their keeping of external rules, which they consistently made up. It was not only a sign of God's blessings but would usher them straight to Heaven.

A WARNING INSTEAD OF THE USUAL PARABLE: WITH A TRUE STORY NAMING AN INDIVIDUAL.

"Now, there was a particular person who was very rich. This rich man was sumptuously dressed, wearing the best in purple and the most excellent linen; his everyday living was luxurious.

And set down outside the rich man's gate was a beggar by the name of Lazarus; this man was covered in sores; he desired to be fed even from crumbs discarded from the wealthy man's table (*Much like a puppy*).

Yes, the dogs even approached him and licked his sores.

Then Lazarus finally died, and then the Angels came and took him away to the side of Abraham.

That rich man died also and was buried.

The rich man now in Hades, in agony, raised his eyes and saw Abraham a great distance away, and with him, Lazarus comforted at his side.

With intense agony, he cried, saying. 'Father Abraham, have compassion for me, and send over Lazarus so that he could help me by dipping his fingertip in some water, just to cool my tongue because I am suffering great torment in these flames.'

However, Abraham replied, 'Son, you remember that in your lifetime, how you received the beautiful things, while Lazarus received all the awful things. Yet here he is; now comforted, and you there in anguish.

Also, there is fixed, a great impassable gulf between us here and you, which prevents any who desire to pass from here to where you are. Besides, none of you can cross over to us from there.'

The rich man in Hades said, 'Father, for that reason, I ask you. Send Lazarus instead to my father's house because there I have another five brothers, and it will give evidence to them.

Then they will not also end up into this place of torment.'

However, Abraham replied, 'They have the complete witness of Moses and the Prophets. Let them take note of them as evidence.'

'No, father Abraham,' He called back, 'except if there was one that was to go to them, back from the dead, then they will repent.'

'If they do not pay attention to Moses and the Prophets, Abraham told him, 'it will not convince them even if one rises from the dead.'"

Jesus concluded as a very stern warning of their position.

Jesus turned back to the disciples. "There will be many incidents that will cause some to falter and stumble. It is not possible to have no occurrence; however, let him who causes the faltering of others, watch out!

He would be better off being thrown into the sea with the weight of a giant millstone hung around his neck rather than he should be the cause of one of these little ones to stumble.

So be cautious, and if you find a brother who offends you, then reprimand him, and forgive him if he apologizes.

You will forgive him even if he comes back seven times in the day saying sorry, after offending you each time."

After Jesus finished explaining that both sin and forgiveness must be taken extremely seriously, his selected followers, having previously been granted powers when they were sent on a mission, and are now called apostles, were shocked at what they understood from this. The apostles made a request to the Lord, "Lord, Increase our faith." They asked?

Jesus took them past the notion of faith working by its size and explained that what was needed was obedience and humility along with gratitude, which always brings true faith in God.

"The size of your faith, if it is only the size of a grain of mustard seed, it is still enough for you to tell this sycamore tree, 'Uprooted now, and go to the sea and be planted there,' and it would obey you." The Lord said, dealing first with the issue of their idea of faith.

"However, would any of you who have a servant working in the field, digging or minding livestock?

And the servant comes back at the end of the day, will you tell him, 'Go sit comfortably at my table and take it easy,' or more likely, 'Get changed, then prepare my food and serve me, as I dine. Then later, you can eat.'

Is the servant given any thanks because he carried out orders? No, I know that he is not.

You also, having done all the things that you are commanded to do, then you should say, 'we are servants that are undeserving, all that we have really done is only performed our duties and obligations.'" He told them, expanding on the need for faithfulness, humility, and gratitude.

A message arrived for Jesus, telling him that his friend Lazarus was ill.

Lazarus and his two sisters Mary and Martha were from the village of Bethany. (At this time, Jesus had still only spent a few of the required six days away from the Leaders in Jerusalem).

Mary was the one who had decided to sit and listen attentively to the teaching of Jesus.

The message came from the sisters, "Lord, your friend that you love dearly is ill." They reported, without actually saying his name, as a precaution.

However, on hearing the message, Jesus told the disciples. "It is not to the death that this sickness will lead. Instead, it will be to the glory of God, and by it, God's Son will be exalted."

Although Martha, Mary, and Lazarus were a family of close friends that Jesus cared for, when he heard the news, he stilled remained where he was another two days.

Then after the two days, he called the disciples, "We will now once again return to Judea." He told them.

"Rabbi, just a short time ago in Judea, The Chief Priests and Leaders were trying to stone you, and now you are going there again?" The disciples asked, suddenly reverting to calling Jesus just a Rabbi.

(*As in the Pool of Siloam incident with the blind man, after recognizing Jesus as Lord' Adoni,' this sudden demotion to just, teacher, for the second time, was inexcusable. Again misreading the situation, thinking Jesus was there hiding out*)!

"Are there not twelve hours of daylight?" Jesus asked them in return.

"Any man who walks in the day sees by the light of this world and does not stumble.

However, the man stumbles if he walks in the night since there is no light in him." Jesus countered, reminding them he is the light of the world. (As he also had done at the Pool of Siloam).

"Lazarus, our friend, has fallen asleep. However, I am going so that I will wake him out of sleep." He said.

"Lord, if Lazarus has only fallen asleep, then he will recover!" The disciples declared with some relief.

It was in actuality the death of Lazarus that Jesus was speaking of, though they had taken it to mean natural sleep and rest.

"Our friend Lazarus is dead," Jesus told them bluntly.

"Because this will be beneficial to you to help you believe, I am happy that I was not there.

However, let us now go to him."

Thomas, known as Didymus (*Greek for the twin*), rallied his fellow disciples, "Let us also go so that we can die along with him." He told them in a misguided act of sheer daring.

Death is an enemy; Jesus is Life. (*Note: Jesus being one with the Father, always sees death as sleep, and he frankly did not want to use death to describe Lazarus's condition. In actuality, Lazarus clearly had died about the same time as the messenger's arrival to inform Jesus, and he had been well aware of that fact. 020

There was a two-day journey to get from Bethany to the area beyond the Jordon, where Jesus and the disciples were staying. Had Jesus left right away, the only difference would have been, when he got back to the sister's Mary and Martha, Lazarus would still have been dead, but two days instead of four.

Yet as Jesus said, it was for their benefit that he was not there so that they could witness the Glory of God.

By Jesus expressing, 'let us now go to him,' after saying plainly, Lazarus is dead. Sounded like he was ready to go and die as well.

This bought about Thomas's brave reaction; the disciples thought the death was possibly connected to the hostilities from the authorities).*

When Jesus and the disciples eventually made the two-day journey from the area beyond the Jordan, arriving on the outskirts of Bethany, they found Lazarus had been placed in a stone tomb; he had already been dead some four days.

Because the neighborhood of the village of Bethany was within easy walking distance from Jerusalem, a significant number of Leaders from the city joined the women around Martha and Mary to comfort them regarding their brother.

Martha received word that Jesus had arrived in the vicinity, so she left Mary in the house and went out to meet him.

On arriving where Jesus was, she was distraught, "Lord, if only you could have been here, my brother would have lived and not have died." She said.

Just the same, I know that anything that you will ask from God, you will be given it by God."

"Your brother, he will rise again," Jesus declared softly, comforting her.

"Yes, Lord," She replied. "I know he will rise again on the last day at the resurrection."

"I AM the resurrection as I AM the life. Anyone who believes in me will still live, even if they die.

And the ones who are alive and place their faith in me will never die. Do you accept and believe this?" Jesus asks her firmly.

"Yes, Lord. I accept as true and have faith that you are the Messiah! The Son of God, of whom the world has been waiting." She replied with faith.

Martha left after this conversation and headed back to the house, where she quietly signaled to her sister, Mary. "The Teacher has arrived and is inquiring about you." She told her.

On hearing this, Mary quickly got up and rushed out to meet with him.

Jesus was still there on the outskirt of the village, in the same location where Martha had met him.

Then when Mary got up quickly and went out, the Jewish Leaders and others who were with her consoling her in the house followed her, "She must be going to weep at the tomb." They said.

(*In Jewish custom regarding death and burial, after a person dies, the body would be prepared for burial and then placed in the grave soon after death. It was usual to bury within two days. Loved ones, friends, and neighbors would bring condolences to the family for up to one week, as the family grieved in the house; this was known as Shiva*).

Mary, having then arrived back where Jesus was, and seeing him, she fell at his feet, weeping, "Lord, my brother would not have died, had you been here." She said.

Jesus saw her weeping, and those who followed her also weeping; he was troubled and groaned in the spirit, "Can you show me where you have laid him?" He asked them.

"Lord, come and see." They replied.

The Lord Jesus wept.

The people who mourned with the sisters commented on this, "Look how much obvious love he had for him!" Some were saying, "This man who opened the eyes of the man who was born blind, could he have not also kept this man from dying?"

As he arrived at the tomb, this caused Jesus, who was full of compassion for them, to groan within himself again over their lack of understanding and belief.

The people placed Lazarus's body in a cave on the side of the rock with a large stone placed at the entrance.

"Remove the stone," Jesus instructed them.

Martha commented to him on this. "Lord, there is a stench by this time since he has been dead now for four days!" She exclaimed, very much surprised.

"Did I not tell you how you would see the glory of God if you believed?" Jesus asked.

They removed the stone from the mouth of the cave where the dead man was lying.

Lifting his eyes and looking up to Heaven, Jesus prayed, "Father, for hearing me, I thank you. I know you always listen to me.

Yet on behalf of the crowds of people who are standing here, I say this! That they would have faith and believe that you send me."

At the end of this prayer, Jesus spoke in a booming voice, "Lazarus, come out!" He commanded.

Splendidly, the dead man emerged out of the cave with renewed life, his face, eyes, hand, and feet all still bound with the burial wrappings.

Because he could not walk or move, Jesus commanded them, "Unbind him, and allow him to be free." (*Note: *This miracle did not require Lazarus to walk out of the cave*).

Of those Chief Priests and Leaders from Jerusalem, who visited the sisters and saw what Jesus did, many believed that he was the Messiah.

However, some of them went to report back to the Pharisees, telling them of this miracle of Jesus.

[All the people were awaiting Israel's Messiah, and the Leaders knew and taught details of the miracles the Messiah was expected to perform in the synagogues, including making the blind see, casting out a demonic spirit from a deaf and dumb man, whom no person could interrogate, healing a leper, among many. And the final one, which they spoke about and taught in the synagogue, was the 'rising of the dead.' And, importantly, the person had to be well known with the death manifestly attested to (*This meant it needed to be more than a few days since the death. Because it was commonly held, the dead person's spirit hovered near the body for up to three days and could, by some uncertain means, re-enter the body*).

The Prophet Elijah was supposed to arrive just before the event and blow a mighty trumpet, which would alert the world. Then the Messiah would raise the person back to life.

With any evidence of these Messianic miracles, The Great Court was to assemble a delegation to follow the candidate for seven days. During that time, they were not permitted to speak. Then follow this period with another fact-finding length of time, where various questions would be fielded to the candidate. At the end of which, they would make a pronouncement through official and sanctified channels. (*All of these assorted ideas were their own laid down rules*).

A notable feast of the Lord in Israel is called "Yom Teruah, the Day of Blowing," distinctive for the blowing of the trumpets as its enduring feature and known as the Feasts of the Trumpets. No specific reason for observing the Feast of the Trumpet was cited. Still, it was understood that this feast called the people to prepare to stand before the judgment of God.

The picture was of a Day of Judgment. On which all mortals pass before the Father's 'Heavenly Throne.' Giving an account for their deeds and receiving the promise of mercy.

Although the blowing of the trumpets was understood to be a call to repent, preparing oneself to stand trial before God. They missed the point that the Call of John the Baptizer could itself be seen as the blowing of a great trumpet, the very thing that they awaited].

The Pharisees had split into two main factions, holding vastly divergent views. This again differed from the Sadducees, who were adamant that there was no Spiritual life and no resurrection!

On the other hand, the Lawyers only cared about carrying out the legal requirements of the law and adding oral traditions to the written commandments.

In this way, they had all come to convince themselves that these miracles, of the type that Jesus performed, were earthbound miracles, which could be counterfeited by the devil; instead, what they needed was a miracle from the sky, such as the Manna in the wilderness or the calling down of fire from Heaven (*this is the reason why they repeatedly ask Jesus to give them a sign from Heaven*).

The leaders arrived at the early conclusion since they could only comply rigorously with their oral law and customs, and could not understand the mercy of making someone well on the Sabbath, that the power behind the miracles of Jesus was derived from the false god Baal (*Beelzebub*), Israel's ancient enemy.

With this as their verdict, they also resolved to kill the Lord; this reality became widespread, prompting his brothers' hastily devised rescue mission, which also included their mother, to the packed house where he was teaching. The family had attempted to counter the Pharisee's claim by declaring that Jesus was only overwhelmed (Beside Himself). Therefore, they thought that would be enough to save his life.

With each of the notable miracles that Jesus performed, with only the exception of the first leper after the sermon on the mountain, the Great Court failed to follow up with any fact-finding.

(*This was to commence with a 'seven day' intense, silent investigation, then followed by a period of questioning, ending with the conclusion and the proclamation of the High Council*).

This failure to legally proceed, according to their own rules, prompted Jesus to leave their area of influence. As a result, he left for a secluded place for the ensuing six days, remaining there until the prescribed period expired.

That is why Jesus withdrew to the area beyond the Jordan after healing the man born blind. And why he had to wait there a further two days after receiving the message of Lazarus' illness.

There were several reasons for the withdrawal. The first was to allow the complete required seven days to expire and for the leaders to cool off and instruct the disciples in the crucial impending end of the ministry in Jerusalem.

Back in Jerusalem, there was a hastily-convened meeting of all the Chief Priests and the Pharisees; they were perplexed over the latest miracle; "What are we in reality doing? Since this man is performing many miracles. They asked each other. (*Though factions had plotted to kill Jesus in the past, this was now the actual official meeting of the Sanhedrin - The Great Court. Yet Jesus still had some supporters and followers among its members*).

"Should we continue to leave him alone like this, all the people will believe in him; then the Romans will come and remove us from our position and take away our nation." They were saying, which had already happened.

The Romans had taken away the nation from them. They were worried about their position of power over the people and the wealth it bought for them.

Caiaphas, who was that year's High Priest, addressed the group. "Plainly, you do not discern what is involved here, nor do you judge it to be beneficial for us. It should be one man's death on behalf of the people rather than the whole nation should end." He told them.

Caiaphas made this immense prophecy, not of himself but being the High Priest; God used his position to declare the truth through him.

Jesus would die not only for the entire nation but also for all the children of God, gathered together into one, from all those who are scattered abroad throughout all the nations.

So they took seriously the view that Jesus had to be put to death and looked for a way to accomplish it from that day onwards.

CHAPTER SIXTEEN

Jesus left that area and went to a city called Ephraim, which is in the country near the wilderness. He and the disciples stayed there for a time.

They were again on the way to Jerusalem after leaving Ephraim, walking along the borders of Samaria and Galilee.

At the edge of a village, there was a group of ten men who had the disease of leprosy; the lepers made sure that they kept their distance.

When they knew it was Jesus approaching the village, all of them started shouting in loud voices, "Jesus, Master, have mercy on us!" They called out, though they did not directly ask to be healed.

They called the Lord, 'Master,' the lesser title of honor, as if uncertain of his credential. However, they would have heard that he had indeed healed other lepers.

This was on account of the Leaders' failure to do their part in officially giving witness and announcing Jesus' arrival as the long-awaited King (from the line of David), Lord, and Messiah.

Jesus took note of them, "Go to the priests and show yourselves." He instructed them as an act of their faith.

This was to be done when the person with leprosy had recovered.

Before Jesus' time, it had only ever occurred one time with Miriam Moses sister; and another with Naaman (Hebrew: נַעֲמָן, "pleasantness") the Aramean general from Syria, and only through the grace and mercy of God.

All the people knew that only the Messiah of Israel could do such a miracle. Lepers, shunned as the outcast of the society, were doubly sure of this.

Knowing enough to appreciate Jesus healed the sick, including other lepers, they should be in no doubt of whom he is.

Jesus could have handled them and healed them, but he instructed them to go to activate some faith and trust in him.

So as they exercised some much-needed faith and moved off to do what Jesus instructed them, it turns out that they were cleared of the disease.

One of them, a Samaritan, who was considered a non-Jew; when he realized that his skin was clear, turning around, he came back, and with a loud voice, was praising and thanking God.

He went down with his face to the ground at Jesus' feet, worshiping him and giving him thanks. This Samaritan knew and acknowledged that here was the Lord; this was the Messiah.

"Were not all the ten cleansed? Except where are the other nine? Jesus asks.

Was there not one other found, apart from this stranger who returned to give the glory to God?"

Jesus spoke to the Samaritan, "Stand up and go on your way. Your faith has restored you and saved you."

This now intensely interested the Pharisees, who were out to show that Jesus was not, in fact, the Messiah. Even despite all the incredible miracles never seen since the creation of the world.

The Pharisees from then on kept asking Jesus when the Kingdom of God would arrive.

"The Kingdom of God will not be known to you or arrive through any observation; nor will you find it if you are told, 'Look, here!' or, 'Look, there!' However consider, the Kingdom of God is within you." He told them.

Then turning and addressing his disciples directly, "There will come the days when you will desire to see just one of the days of the Son of Man, and you will not see it." Jesus told them.

"Some people will insist, 'Look, here!' or 'Look, there!' Do not go anyplace or follow them. Because just as the lightning, when it flashes out from one part under the sky, shines across to the other part; just so will the Son of Man be in his day.

However, he must first suffer many things and be rejected by this generation.

Repeating what occurred in the time of Noah, it will also be the same in the days of the Son of Man.

Just as they ate, they drank, married, and were given in marriage. Until the day Noah entered the ship. Then the flood arrived, destroying them all.

Similarly, the same as had happened in the days of Lot, they ate, drank, bought, sold, planted, and built. However, on the day Lot went out from Sodom, it rained fire and sulfur from the sky, destroying them all.

It will be just the same way on that day that the Son of Man is revealed.

On that day, anyone outside the house, having goods in the house, should be sure not to return to retrieve them.

And whoever is in the field, likewise do not turn back.

Remember Lot's wife!

The one who is looking to save his life loses it. However, the one who loses his life preserves it.

I tell you, on that night, even from the bedroom, there will be one that is taken, and the other will be left.

As with two women working making bread, one will be taken, and the other will be left.

Of two men working in the field, the one will be taken, and the other left." He concluded.

"Where, Lord?" The disciples asked.

"Wherever the remains are, there the eagles will be gathered together." He replied with finality.

Jesus also told a parable. To illustrate to them why they must always pray and not give up.

"In a city, was a judge who did not fear God, and he also did not esteem man.

A widow lived in that City, often approaching him, saying, 'defend me from my opponent!'

He would not for some time, however afterward, he said to himself, 'Although I neither fear God nor esteem man, yet because this widow troubles me. I will defend her, In case she will wear me out by her continual persistence.'"

"Listen to the unrighteous judge what he said," Jesus extolled in conclusion.

"Will God not also do justice for his chosen ones, who are crying out to him day and night, yet despite that, he exercises patience with them?

I tell you, at the appointed time, he will avenge them; however, when the Son of Man returns, will he find faith on the Earth," He asked firmly?

To another group of very self-confident people who despised all others and were confident of their own uprightness, Jesus gave them this illustration.

"Two men, one a Pharisee, and also a tax collector went up into the Temple to pray.

This Pharisee stood praying to himself like this. 'God, I thank you for I am not like the rest of men, extortionist, unrighteous, adulterers, or even this tax collector, I fast two times a week. I give one-tenth of all that I get.'

However, the tax collector standing far away would not even lift his eyes to Heaven but acted in remorse. 'Be merciful to me, O God, I am a sinner!' He cried.

This man, I tell you, of the two went back to his house justified. Because all those acclaiming themselves will be brought down, yet the humble one he will be acclaimed." Jesus told his delighted audience, who were well acquainted with the actions of the Pharisees, and this was an accurate parody of their play-acting at being religious.

As part of the daily prayer sequence, three praises were to be uttered every day for the Jewish faith:

"Praised (be to the Lord) that He did not make me a heathen. For all the heathen are as nothing before Him.

Praised be unto Him, for He did not make me a woman, as women are not under obligation to fulfill the law.

Praised be unto Him, for He did not make me an uneducated man. For the ignorant man, he is not cautious to avoid sins."

Sometime later, people were bringing their little children and infants to Jesus. To lay hands on them, pray for and bless them, the disciples were scolding the people who were taking the children to him.

However, when Jesus noticed, he was moved with righteous anger, "Allow these little children to approach me since it is the little one just like these that will have the Kingdom of God. So never forbid them.

I tell you most positively; the one who is not like a little child in accepting the Kingdom of God will in no way enter it." He told them.

Then taking the children up in his arms, he blessed them, laying his hands on their heads in the ancient style of the blessing.

After this, he was traveling to another town; a young man ran to Jesus on the journey and knelt before him, "Good Teacher," he called, "what actions shall I do to enable me to have eternal life?" The young man asked.

"Why are you calling me good?" asked Jesus, "There is no one good, apart from one, only God. However, for you to enter into life, you must keep the commandments." Jesus instructed him.

"Which ones," the young man inquired?

'You must do no murder.' 'You must not commit any adultery.' 'Do not steal.' 'You must not ever offer any false testimony.'

'Always give honor to your father and mother.' Jesus replied, quoting from the great law, only the five of the six commandments relating to human interactions.

"Teacher," those that you quoted, I have observed all of them from my youth. What else is still missing?" He asked Jesus eagerly.

Jesus looks at him lovingly and with an appreciation for his determination, "One other thing then you will require, for you to be complete." He told the young man.

"Go on your way, and sell all your possessions, then give money to the poor, this will ensure that you have treasures in heaven, after the return, then take up the cross and follow me. He instructed.

However, when the young man had heard this, he left, going away very sad since he had a significant number of assets.

[This young man made a declaration, followed by a question that was both superfluous and futile.

"Good teacher," he asked, "what actions must I do to inherit eternal life?"

It's a question based on a moot point; the simple answer is nothing.

Jesus told Nicodemus that God so loved the world; he gave his only begotten son to ransom the world. Hence to inherit eternal life is God's gift.

Therefore, good works or keeping of the law is not within the remit of the gift from God.

Good works are as far from eternal life as no works;
And the gift of God is Jesus the Messiah, who is Lord (Adoni).

The totality of the law hangs on two pillars, four outline our dealings with God, and six outline our dealings with each other.

But not knowing God is to not know he is completely good. A lack of relationship with God also leads to not knowing that one cannot do anything to gain eternal life.

Hence the question Jesus posed to him, why call me good?

His great need is first to know God and have a relationship with him. But as it was apparent, this was not yet so. Jesus dealt with five of the commandments that pertain to our interactions with each other, those that this young ruler would have known and worked hard to keep.

Namely;
- 'Do not commit adultery
- do not murder
- do not steal
- do not give false testimony
- honor your father and mother.

And the young man was proud to say he had kept all of those. Jesus was pleased, 'he loved him.'

Now he desired to offer him a chance to get to know God, the only one who is good.

It is a simple invitation, go sell your possessions and give, or 'tithe' to the poor, and come, follow me!

Yet his reaction showed he neglected the first and greatest commandment, 'to love the Lord your God, with all your heart, your soul, and mind!'

His possessions and wealth occupied that spot in his heart and life.

He did not even get to, 'love your neighbor as yourself.' which incorporates all the above.

Proverbs 19:17 (EXB) **Being kind [gracious; generous] to the poor is like lending to the Lord; he will reward you for what you have done [fully repay you]**.

Isaiah 58:7: (NKJV) **Is it not to share your bread with the hungry, And that you bring to your house the poor who are cast out;**

When you see the naked, that you cover him, And not hide yourself from your own flesh?]

His actions saddened Jesus, who looked around at his disciples. "Those who have riches, how formidable it is for them to find how to enter the Kingdom of God?" Jesus asks rhetorically, with more than a bit of wonder.

"I tell you; it is with great difficulty that a rich man will enter the Kingdom of Heaven." He said what he was saying shocked the disciples. However, Jesus repeated, "Children, it is especially hard to enter the Kingdom of God, for those who have their confidence in riches! I tell you again; it is far easier for a camel to pass through the little eye of the needle than a rich man to go through into the Kingdom of God!"

The disciples were extremely shocked, "Well, who can ever be saved then?" They asked, having been taught all of their lives that riches were a sure sign of God's blessings.

Jesus looked intently at them; "This is impossible with men, although not so with God because all things are possible with God." He told them.

Peter spoke up for the stunned group, "See, we left everything and have followed you. Then what will we have?" He asked.

"I tell you most certainly, you that have followed me; when in the new birth the Son of Man will be sitting on the throne of his glory, you will also sit on twelve thrones, where you will rule the twelve tribes of Israel.

Every person after leaving houses, brothers, sisters, father, mother, wife, children, or lands. Because they carry my name and because of the work of the Good News, will receive one hundred times of houses, brothers, sisters, mothers, children, and land in this age, with persecutions.

They will also inherit eternal life in the age to come, although many who are first will be last, as many who are last will be first." Jesus told them.

He continued with an illustration to make the point regarding the kingdom. "We can compare the Kingdom of Heaven to a man being the master of an estate who went early in the morning to find hired laborers for his crop of grapes.

After agreeing on a full silver coin wage per day's work to the workers, he sent them to work the crops.

The master again returned to the market about nine in the morning and noted others standing idle.

To them, he said, 'You also go and work with my crops. I will give to you whatever is right.' So they went and joined the first.

The master again returns about noon and three in the afternoon, each time doing the same.

At about five in the afternoon returned yet again, found others also standing idle. 'Why do you stand here idle all day?' He enquired.

"'Because no one has hired us,' they replied."

"'You go and work in the vineyard, and you will receive whatever is right.' He told them"

When the evening arrived, the estate's lord told his manager, 'Call the laborers and settle their wages, starting from the last one to the first.'

"When the men hired at about five pm arrived, they each received a silver coin. When they also came, the first assumed they would receive more, yet equally, each received a silver coin.

After they received it, they grumbled against the master of the estate,

'These last have spent only the last hour, yet you have made them equal to us, who have tolerated the burden and the scorching heat of the day!' they were saying.

"However, the master replied to one of them, 'Friend, I am not doing you any wrong. You agreed with me for a silver coin, did you not?

Take what is yours and depart; it's my wish to give this last just as much as you.

It is lawful for me to do what I want, with things I own! Or because I am good, is your eye evil?'

So the last will indeed be first, and the first will be last, since many are called, but few are chosen."

Jesus again resumed the journey towards Jerusalem. Now, there was a marked difference as he purposefully led the way, not allowing himself to be slowed by the crowds and people they met with. Which amazed his followers; some were even afraid, though not entirely certain why, yet the pace and intensely affected them all.

He was now careful to separate the twelve chosen and prepare and explain clearly; about what would happen to him in the City.

"We are coming to the fulfillment of all that the prophets wrote about the Son of Man. As it was written, in Jerusalem, the Son of Man will be betrayed then brought to the Chief Priests and Scribes, who after condemning him to death, will hand him over to the Gentiles to mock and spit on, to whip and kill Him," Jesus told them.

The disciples did not comprehend any of what Jesus was telling them.

Their minds were not taking it in, so they did not understand the things that were said.

One primary reason they were not getting the message of what Jesus was teaching them was through prolonged and deeply held ideas of the Messiah as the ruling King, who would re-establish Israel. So as they realized that the pace of Jesus towards Jerusalem became more and more intense, with him always leading from the front. The excitement among the followers grew; there were high expectations and even divisions and factions.

At one point, while they all rested, one woman that traveled with and helped them came to Jesus and, kneeling, she requested on behalf of her two sons.

She was Salome, the mother of the disciples James and John, called the sons of thunder, by Jesus.

Her twin sons also came with her.

"What is it you would want for me to do for you?" Jesus asks her.

"That you command, these my two sons would be approved in your coming Kingdom, one sitting on your right hand, with the other on your left hand," Salome replied.

"You do not know what it is you are asking. Do you imagine you can drink the cup I am about to drink and be baptized with the baptism that I am to be baptized?" Jesus asked the two disciples.

The brothers spoke up, "Yes, we are capable." They replied.

Jesus replied. "Certainly the cup that I will drink, you will also drink, as you also will enter the baptism that I am baptized with. However, my Father decides and has prepared who sit on my right hand and my left hand. It is neither for you nor is it for me to grant," he told them.

When they heard all this, the other ten disciples were incensed and irritated with the brothers.

Jesus called them all together, speaking to them about this. "You know how those who are recognized as rulers over the nations. Lord it over their people, and the ones the people call their great ones. Exercise influence and power over them?" He asked them.

"It will not be like that between you, any of you who desire to become great among you all; should be prepared to be the servant of all.

Because the Son of Man, even he came to serve not to be served, he is here to give his life as a ransom for many.

So the one who wants to be first among you he will be your unpaid servant." Jesus soundly notified all his followers.

The relentless pace towards Jerusalem continued. As they walked on, they came to one of the two cities with the name of Jericho.

The time spent there was short; however, a large crowd followed Jesus.

At the edge of the City on the road, two blind men were sitting by the road begging Bartimaeus, the son of Timaeus, and his companion.

As they heard the passing crowd's commotion, Bartimaeus asked what the meaning of the noise was.

People in the crowd told him that it was Jesus of Nazareth that was passing.

On hearing this news, they started shouting at the top of their voices, "Lord Jesus, O Son of David. Have mercy on us!"

They not only addressed Jesus as Lord but also used the clear Messianic title of Son of David.

Some people in the crowd showed displeasure at this, telling them they should be quiet, yet they cried out the louder, "Have mercy on us, O Lord, Son of David!" Then Jesus stood still and said, "Call them."

They called the blind men, telling them, "Be happy! Come on, get up. He is calling for you!"

Straight away, they did not hesitate to throw away their garments used for begging and springing up and heading towards Jesus. (*This was an act of faith, as the garments would not be needed anymore.*)

"What would you want me to do for you?" Jesus asked.

"Lord, that our eyes may be opened." They answered promptly.

Jesus, being moved with compassion, touched their eyes and told them, "Go your way. Receive back your sight; your faith has made you well." Their sight was returned to them immediately! Following Jesus along the way, they gave praise and glory to God. All the people, after seeing this, also praised God.

ON HIS WAY TO JERUSALEM, JESUS ENTERED AND PASSED THROUGH JERICHO.

Jericho sat a few miles from the Jordan, spreading out into a plain on the valley's western edge. The City lies amid lush greenness and broad areas amongst the substantive and lavish abundance of beauty. Settings of limestone hills and wild uninhabited barren ravines, with its palm trees and luxurious gardens watered by living springs, the place, gleaming like an emerald, would punctuate the landscape between Jerusalem and the City of the plain.

John the Baptizer had preached at the Jordan only a few miles from Jericho, where the call to repentance had been heard. Along with John's instruction to the publicans, 'Exact only that which is appointed you.'

Jericho was one of the ancient cities set apart for the priests, and large numbers of priests had their elegant residence there.

Although the City also had a population from a widely varied character since it was a great center of traffic.

Roman officials, along with soldiers and strangers from various quarters, were all found there. At the same time, the collection of customs made it the home of many publicans.

There in the City was a rich man, one of the chief tax collectors, by the name of Zacchaeus. (זכי, *Meaning: pure, innocent*).

The collection of customs at Jericho was profitable for officials in a city grown rich as it produced and exported a considerable quantity of balsam. The Balsam tree of Jericho is renowned for its therapeutic and highly agreeable aromatic qualities.

Balsam oil - a precious commodity produced at Jericho and traditionally used to anoint Israel's rightful kings.

The heady aroma was one method said to have been used by 'sinful daughters of Zion' to entice lovers. 'She would place the balsam between her heel and her shoe when she saw a band of young men; she pressed upon it so that the perfume seeped among them like snake poison,' was the saying.

(The rabbis also taught that the righteous will, 'bathe in thirteen rivers of balsam' in Messianic times).

This tax collector Zacchaeus desperately wanted to see who Jesus was. Though he tried, he could not because of the crowd's size and his being a man tiny of stature.

Zacchaeus ran on up ahead, where he found a sycamore tree and climbed up to get a better view since Jesus was to pass that way.

From συκῆ, fig tree, and μόρον, the mulberry, (the Sycamore tree in Israel (Ficus sycomorus), a large tree with a thick trunk and leathery leaves. The fig-mulberry, resembling the fig in its fruit and the mulberry in its leaves, represents regeneration because the sycamore tree has a notable ability to regenerate.

The Sycomore's, in Hebrew - shikma - is drawn from the root sh.k.m. To restore, regenerate, re-establish).

When he arrived at the tree, Jesus stopped, looked up, and watched Zacchaeus, and then he told him, "Zacchaeus, hurry and come on down since today I will stay at your house."

Zacchaeus hurriedly descended from the sycamore tree and was a very thrilled and happy host.

When they saw this, people began muttering and grumbling, "He has gone to be the guest of a man who is a sinner." They said.

The tax collectors worked on behalf of the Romans; they were called "publicani" because the person granted the contract paid an agreed amount to the Roman treasury 'in publicum.'

And because it was a franchise, they collected more than was required and pocketed the extra. This made tax collectors not only wealthy but also extremely detested regarded not only as traitors. But they were ceremonially unclean by intention, through their regular personal contact with the Gentiles and friends of the occupying Romans oppressors. People also saw them as the worst sinners, barred from the Synagogues and not accepted in regular Jewish life.

In the house in front of all the people, Zacchaeus stood and exclaimed to the Lord. "Lord, see, one-half of my goods I will give to the poor. Also, if I wrongfully demanded anything of anyone, I will now restore four times as much."
This fulfilled the legal requirement.

Exodus 22:1 (NET) *If a man steals an ox or a sheep and kills it or sells it, he must pay back five head of cattle for the ox, and four sheep for the one sheep.*

Leviticus 6:5 (NET) *Or anything about which he swears falsely. He must restore it in full and add one-fifth to it; he must give it to its owner when he is found guilty.*

Numbers 5:7 (NET) *Then he must confess his sin that he has committed and must make full reparation, add one-fifth to it, and give it to whomever he wronged.*

2 Samuel 12:6 (RSV) *And he shall restore the lamb fourfold, because he did this thing, and because he had no pity.*

"Today has salvation come to this house," Jesus announced, "because he is also a son of Abraham.

Since the Son of Man is here to search for and to save that which was lost."

As the crowd listened, he continued with a parable to illustrate the Kingdom; because he was near Jerusalem. They supposed and expected that the Kingdom of God would be unveiled immediately.

This is what he told them, "A particular notable Lord traveled into a distant country to secure a kingdom for himself, and to return.

Before he was to set off, he called ten of his servants, giving each of them a portion of funds, and told them, 'Conduct business until I come.'

Except his citizens hated him and sent a messenger after him, 'We do not want this man to reign over us.' They had the messenger relay.

When he returned after securing the Kingdom, He commanded that these servants, to whom had given the money, were summoned to recount what they had gained by conducting business.

The first that appeared to stand before him said, 'Lord, your money has gained an extra ten shares more.'

'Well done,' his lord replied, 'you excellent servant! Since you are faithful with very little, you will have the rulership over ten cities.'

When the second appeared, He said, 'Your money, Lord, has gained five shares extra.'

'And you are to rule over five cities.' The lord told him.

Another who appeared to stand before him said, 'lord, see, your money, which I had kept stored away in hiding since I feared you because you are a demanding man, hard to deal with. Appropriating things you did not put down and reaping what you did not sow.'

The Lord replied, 'Out of your own mouth will I judge you, you wicked servant! You knew I am a demanding man, taking up what I did not lay down and reaping what I did not plant.

In that case, why did you not deposit my money in the bank, and at my return, I may have earned interest on it?'

The lord instructed those who stood by, 'Take that money away from him, and give it to him who has the ten shares.'

They replied, 'Lord, he already has ten shares!'

'I tell you, this is because more will be given to everyone who has. However, anyone who does not have, even the little he has, will be taken away.

Bring those my enemies who did not want me to reign over them and execute them before me." Jesus pronounced, as a conclusion of the parable for the people. Showing the apparent need for diligence where the Kingdom is concerned.

Once he had told the people all of this, he continued on the journey, leading the way heading to Jerusalem.

As it was near the Feast of Passover, people came from throughout the country to Jerusalem, purifying themselves before the start of the Feast.

The people looked all over for Jesus; all the talk was about him as they stood in the Temple, asking one another. "What do you think; perhaps he's not coming to the feast at all?"

The Chief Priests and the Pharisees earlier issued orders that if anyone knew where he was, he should report it, that they might seize and arrest him.

Then six days before the Feast of Passover, Jesus arrived at the town of Bethany, journeying there from Jericho. Bethany was the town where Lazarus lived, the friend of Jesus who had been dead, whom he raised from the dead.

Swiftly news had spread that Jesus was there, and as people learned of it, they came, not only because of Jesus but also so that they might see Lazarus, whom he had raised from the dead.

This caused the Chief Priests to conspire to kill Lazarus as well. Since on his account, many of the people firmly believed Jesus was the Messiah.

As they approached the outskirts of Jerusalem and came to Bethphage and Bethany, at the Mount of Olives, Jesus selected two of the disciples and gave instruction.

"Go into that village opposite you, and immediately as you enter the town, you will find a donkey tied there, with her a colt. Untie them, and bring them to me.

Should anyone ask you, 'Why are you untying them?' you will reply, 'The Lord is in need o them,' and immediately he will send them."

The two disciples left and did just as Jesus instructed them; they found things just as he had told them.

Just as they were untying the donkey and colt, its owners arrived, "Why are you untying the donkey and colt?" He asked them.

"The Lord needs it." They replied.

So the disciples could go with the Animals.

All of this was the fulfillment of the words that was given through the Prophet, Zechariah, who said, "Rejoice greatly and Do not be afraid tell the daughters of Zion, take a look, raise a shout, your King is here triumphant, yet he humbly rides a donkey, a colt, the foal of a donkey.'"

Jerusalem was now crowded with the people who had come to the Feast of Passover. Then as word spread that Jesus was on his way to the City, the people took the branches of palm trees and went to the outskirts of the City to meet him; as they did, others from the crowd spread their clothes on the road. They cut more and more branches from the trees and lay on the road.

The entire group, along with Jesus, was now close to the City, having progressed to the base of the Mount of Olives. The disciples who traveled in front of him and many people who followed started celebrating and praising God with great shouts, exclaiming all the extraordinary miracles they had witnessed.

The people shouted, "Hosanna to this the son of David! Blessed is this our King who comes in the name of the Lord! Hosanna in the highest! Peace in Heaven, glory in the highest!"

Blessed in the Lord's name is the Kingdom of Our Father David that is here now! Hosanna in the highest!"

They greeted Jesus with words from the Messianic Psalms. With this cry, Hosanna! Which is "save now," the crowd recognized Jesus' arrival as the triumphant Messiah, despite the leader's lack of official recognition. This was their King, who comes in the name of the Lord.

Shouting, "save now," they had in mind political salvation from oppression. However, by riding a donkey fulfilling Zechariah's prophecy, he showed that his purpose was peace.

When Jesus was close enough to see the City, he started to weep over it. He said, "If you Jerusalem, even you, had recognized this day the things which belong to your peace, except, now they are hidden and veiled from your eyes.

For this reason, the days will come on you, when your enemies will put up a barricade against you, surrounding you by siege, hemming you in on every side. They will throw you and your children within you to the ground. They will not leave within you even one stone standing on another since you did not know the time of your visitation."

CHAPTER SEVENTEEN

THE KING ARRIVES: THE CITY IS ECSTATIC.

The City was in an enormous uproar on Jesus' arrival in Jerusalem.

"Who is this?" Some of the people were asking.

The crowd in front of him shouted, "This is 'The Prophet,' this is Jesus, from Nazareth in Galilee."

Jesus entered the Temple where the blind and the lame flocked to him, and he healed them.

However, the Chief Priests and Scribes, seeing the astonishing things he did, also with many children playing and shouting, in the Temple, "Hosanna to the son of David!" The children sang. This was too much for those leaders.

So, some of the Pharisees who had mingled in with the crowd approached and challenged Jesus. "Teacher, reprimand your disciples!"

"Do you hear what even these children are now saying?" They demanded with irritation.

"Surely, have you never read in the scripture, 'Out of the mouth of infants and nursing babies have you perfected praise?" Jesus asked, quoting Psalm 8:2, putting them to silence.

"And I tell you that if these were silent, the very stones would at once cry out!" Jesus declared. Reminding them of what Joshua had said. Joshua 24:27, *See, this stone will be a witness against us; because it has heard all the words of Jehovah which he spoke to us: it will be then a witness against you, in case you reject your God.*

(Habakkuk 2:10-12, *You have created a disgrace to your house by killing many people and have sinned against your soul. Since the stone will cry out of the wall, and the beam out of the timber will answer it. Shameful despair to him that builds a town with blood, and create a city by iniquity!*)

[At Passover on The tenth day of Nisan (Aviv), each year, the High Priest went out of the City of Jerusalem in a grand procession to the fields to select the perfect lamb.

(The scriptures say in Exodus 12:6: *the lamb is to be killed at dusk on the fourteenth of the month after four days of inspections leading to the slaughter*).

After The High Priest chooses the perfect yearling Passover lamb, he returns carrying the lamb back up to the Temple; he does not let it walk because it might stumble, receiving a blemish. They examined this lamb daily over the next four days. To ensure it is flawless and fit for sacrifice].

Worshippers packed Jerusalem, coming into the City for the Feast, lining the road. Ready to begin the shouting of praises for the lamb, selected for Passover by the High Priest.

This year being a Sabbatical year, was exceptional, a year for which the entire land had to rest. Many widespread rumors ran throughout Israel that the Messiah would appear on the Shabbat of years. This was not only a Sabbatical year. But it was a Sabbatical Passover. The Highest Passover occurs only every seventh year, bringing the dispersed Jews and foreign converts from every nation to Jerusalem to worship.

This was the time of the highest excitement and expectations.

The people did not know this ritual was about to be fulfilled perfectly by Jesus, the Lamb of God. Who is the true Davidic King, Israel's Messiah, proclaimed such by John the Baptizer.

The disciples of Jesus did not appreciate the meanings of all these things at first. However, after Jesus had taken on trans-dimensional body and power after his resurrection. They finally realized that all the things done to him had been written through prophecies in the scriptures about him.

Jesus, with the disciples, went out of the City, leaving the people and the Temple behind, went back to Bethany, and stayed there for the evening.

The crowds of people that were with him when he summoned Lazarus to come out of the tomb, raising him from the dead: were giving evidence about it widely to everyone and confirming the fact.

Because of this declaration, many people from the City and surrounding towns went and met him, having heard that he had done this great miracle.

This prompted The Pharisees to complain among themselves; they said to each other, "Can you perceive, you are now accomplishing nothing at all. Look, the world has gone after him."

The following morning as Jesus returned with the disciples to the City, having left Bethany and were traveling on the way, Jesus was hungry.

Noticing a fig tree in the distance having already produced leaves, Jesus left the road and went over to see if he possibly might find anything on it.

He found that the tree had nothing but the leaves since it was not the season for figs when he approached it.

Jesus then spoke to it, "From this day, let no fruit come from you forever, so none will ever eat fruit from you again!"

The disciples who were still on the road had by this time passed the point where the tree was. They all heard the words that Jesus spoke to the tree.

The Scriptures say,

(Psalm 90:6, **That which springs up blooms and flourishes gloriously looks so fresh in the morning, by evening it is dry, withered and cut down without a second thought!**).

The presence of a vibrant, fruitful fig tree was deemed a symbol of blessing and prosperity for the nation of Israel.

The fruit of the fig tree, in general, appears before the leaves; then, because of the green fruit, it blends in with the leaves until it is almost ripe. 'As the young leaves appear in the springtime, every flowering fig tree will have on it some young fruit called taksh. However, should a tree with leaves have no fruit, it will be barren for the entire season.'

From a distance, it would be expected that a tree with leaves also has fruit on it even if it is early in the season; a leafy fig tree would be bearing taksh.

Jeremiah 24:2 (RSV) *'One basket had very good figs, like first-ripe figs, but the other basket had very bad figs, so bad that they could not be eaten.'*

THE LEADERS ARE UNHAPPY BUT PROVE INEPT AT STOPPING JESUS.

They later arrived in Jerusalem going into the Temple of God. Jesus immediately commenced expelling sellers and buyers from within the Temple precinct, overturning the moneychangers' tables and seats of the people selling the doves.

After that, he would not allow any person to carry any vessels or containers through the Temple.

"It is written, 'my house it shall be called a house of prayer for all the nations, yet you have made it into a den of robbers!'" Jesus exclaimed, forcefully speaking with the words spoken through the Prophet Jeremiah.

Isaiah 56:6, Isaiah 1:10-17, Jeremiah 7:1-16.

(*The process of bringing an animal to the Temple for a sin offering was not meant to be a simple or a convenient act.*

God had intended to demonstrate both the price and cost of temporally covering sin, more so removing it altogether.

We see in Exodus 12:6: How families were to 'Take exceptional care of the chosen animal, right up to the evening of the fourteenth day.'

Often, the animal would become a family pet, so it was not easy to see that pet destroyed and offered as a sacrifice. And that was the whole point. It was important for people to understand, even from childhood, that sin was costly and deadly.

Even more impoverished people who carried only doves to the Temple had to take good care of the bird on the often long trip. A bird that was not perfect was not accepted.

What the money people had managed to do was to make a mockery of the whole process for the sake of convenience. Just come to the Temple and change your money to the local money for a fee. Then go buy the animal that you need and take it to the Priest. Everyone wins, and some get rich).

This action of Jesus stung and shook the Chief Priests, Lawyers, and leaders who profited the most from all the trade taking place in the court of the Gentiles. They did not approach him directly because they were fearful of him; instead, they went to meet together, seeking how to find a method to defeat and kill him. Determined as they were, they carefully intended to avoid the days of the Feast to launch any confrontation since all the massive crowds were overwhelmed and thrilled at his teaching.

Jesus continued teaching each day in the Temple; this frustrated the Chief Priests, Lawyers, and other leaders. They could find no way to stop or destroy him.

The people came gladly to hear him and clung dearly to every word that he spoke. This became a matter of great apprehension and jealousy among the leaders.

As Jesus was in the Temple teaching, some men there were Greek converts who also came to Jerusalem to obsessive the Feast and worship at the Temple.

These men approached Philip, knowing that he was also from their area of Bethsaida of Galilee. The name Bethsaida is of Aramaic origin, meaning the "fishing house" or "the house of fishing." This town was located east of the Jordan River, on the north shore of the Sea of Galilee.

The Greeks asked Philip, "Sir, we would like to see Jesus."

So Philip went to find Andrew and told him, and then, both Andrew and Philip approached Jesus with the request.

"The time is here for the Son of Man to be glorified," Jesus replied.

"I tell you absolutely, a grain of wheat unless it falls into the Earth and dies; it remains alone, as it were by itself. However, if that grain dies, it bears a great deal of fruit.

Whomever it is that loves his life will lose it; the one hating his life in this world will keep it into eternal life.

Any person serving me will follow me, and the Father will honor that one. Wherever I am, my servants will be there as well.

"Now, my soul is troubled. And what then will I say, 'Father, save me from this time?' Yet it is for this cause why I am here at this time.

Father, glorify your name!"

They heard at that moment a voice from out of the sky; the voice said, "I have glorified it. And will glorify it again."

Some of the crowd, standing there and hearing the voice, said that 'it had thundered.'

"An Angel has spoken to him." Some of them said.

"It was not for my benefit, but yours, that this voice has come," Jesus replied.

"Here is now the judgment of this world. And now the prince of this world will be thrown out, and I after I am 'lifted up' from the Earth, I will draw all to myself."

Jesus here was using this to indicate the type of death he must die.

Some people from the crowd asked him, "From the law, we have heard that the Messiah continues without end. How do you then say, 'The Son of Man must be 'lifted up'?' Who then is this Son of Man?"

"The light has been with you a little while until now. Walk within that light while you have it, so the darkness does not overtake you. Any person who walks in the dark will not know where they are going.

While you still have the light, believe in the light, so that by believing you can become children of light." Jesus told them.

Jesus, after he had finished speaking, departed, having concealed himself from their sights.

Even after doing all the miracles witnessed by the leaders and the people, yet they still did not believe who he was.

So in this, the word of the Prophet Isaiah became exact; he said, "My Lord, who has believed our message that we heard, and to whom has the arm of the Lord, the Lord's great power been revealed?"

They would not believe, given that Isaiah also had said this. "He blinded their eyes and has dulled their understanding, that they might not see with their eyes, grasp with their perception, and turn to me, that I might heal them."

This Isaiah spoke of him when he saw his glory.

From among the rulers, many believed that Jesus was the Messiah. Yet, they were so intimidated by the hostile stance of the Pharisees; they did not dare to admit it openly.

They were carefully avoiding the threat of being put out of the synagogues since their love was for the praise of men more than the praise of God.

The majority of the leaders of the people had adapted themselves so that a state of unbelief would, for them, become inherently natural.

Jesus' voice rang out 'loud and clear' in the Temple, as he announced, "The one believing in me, also believes in him who sent me, not only in me.

Anyone who sees me sees him who has sent me.

I am here as light to the world; as a result, those who believe in me will not remain in the darkness.

If anyone listens to my words and does not believe, I do not judge him because I am not here to judge the world, but instead, I am here to save the world.

He who has rejected me, and does not receive my words, has one who judges him. These very words that I have spoken will judge him on the last day.

Because my words are not from myself, they are from the Father who sent me; he gave me a commandment of what I should say and all the things I should speak.

I know that his instructions are eternal life. These are the things which I speak, just as the Father has said to me, then so I speak."

Jesus remained in the Temple teaching day after day, and each night he would leave there for the mountain called Olivet, where he would spend the night. This area was situated a short distance outside the City and across from the Kidron valley.

When he returned to the Temple in the mornings, all the people would gather early to listen to him.

On the second morning, as they were re-entering the City and passing the site of the fig tree Jesus had encountered on the previous morning, the disciples saw the fig tree. It had died drying up from the roots.

The fig tree visibly had immediately withered away the day before when Jesus spoke to it.

(*Joel 1:12. The vines have become dry, and the fig tree is dying.
All the trees in the field!
The pomegranate, the palm, and the apple! Have withered. And
happiness among the people has died*).

Peter recalling what he said the previous day, spoke elatedly of it, "Rabbi, see! The fig tree you had cursed has withered away.

How did the tree wither away so soon?" He asked.

"Have faith in God," Jesus affirmed distinctly.

"I tell you positively, if you have faith in God, and do not doubt. You will do what I did to the fig tree and even if you told this mountain 'to be picked up and hurled into the sea,' it would be done." Jesus replied, not only to Peter but addressed all the disciples.

"I tell you absolutely. Whoever will tell this mountain, 'Be removed from here and heave into the sea' without doubting in the heart; but believes what he has said is happening; he will have whatever he says.

Therefore, I say to you formerly. All the things that you ask for in prayer with belief, you will receive.

Believe you have received them because you will have them. (*Jesus is guaranteeing his faith is operating, bringing to pass what his followers ask.*)

At whatever time you are standing to pray. Forgive anyone you find have done anything against you; as a result, your Father who is in Heaven will also forgive you your offenses."

Early in the morning, Jesus and the disciples once again arrived in Jerusalem. Not long after, he started teaching in the Temple. A delegation of the Chief Priests and the elders of the people approached Jesus. "By what law do you do these things? Who gave you this authority?" They demanded with pomposity.

(What they are speaking of here is S'mikhah. Commissioning involving laying on of hands, receiving his authorization by them.

The leaders had failed in the formal declaration of all their findings that Jesus was indeed the Messiah, and as long as he was there. Jesus did not allow the usual trade within the court of the Gentiles. He was severely hurting the pockets of the leaders).

"I will also ask a question," Jesus replied, "Then if you tell me, similarly will I tell you of the authority for me doing these things.

Regarding John's baptism, where was it from?

Was it from heaven or men? Answer me." He demanded.

They started debating and reasoned among themselves, "Should we reply, 'From heaven,' he will then ask us, 'Why did you not believe him?'

Although if we say, 'From men,' we fear the crowds, all the people will stone us as they are convinced John was a Prophet."

Eventually, their answer was, "We do not know."

"Then, said Jesus, neither will I tell you by what authority I do these things.

Although what do you think? A man who had two sons went and told the first, 'Son, go work in my vineyard today.'

The son answered, 'I will not,' except afterward he went having changed his mind.

He went and said the same thing to the second son. This son answered, 'I go, sir,' however, he did not go.

Which one of the sons performed the will of his father?" Jesus asked.

"The first," They replied.

"I tell you most emphatically, tax collectors and prostitutes, they are entering the Kingdom of God ahead of you.

John, he came to you in the way of righteousness; you did not believe him, yet tax collectors and the prostitutes believed him," he said with emphasis. "You, after seeing it, did not even repent afterward so you could believe him."

"Hear now another parable. A man was the master of a household. He planted a vineyard, placed a hedge around it, dug a wine vat, and built on the land a tower. Then leased it out to farmers and went off for a long time to live in another country.

As the fruit season drew near. He dispatched one of his servants to the farmers to collect his share of the fruit from the vineyard.

The farmers took the servant, beat him, and sent him away empty.

Again, he sent them another servant; they threw stones at him, wounded him in the head, and sent him away disgracefully treated.

Again he sent another, who they killed, and many others, beating some and killing some.

The vineyards lord said, 'what will I do? I will send my beloved son. Maybe having seen him, they will respect him.' So, he sent them his son, 'They will at least respect my son.' He said.

However, when the farmers saw the son, they said to each other, 'this is the heir. Come let us kill him, seizing his inheritance.'

So they grabbed him, throwing him out of the vineyard, and killed him." Jesus told them, concluding the story, taking this parable from the well-used Jewish scriptures from Isaiah 5.

(Isaiah 5, Is the song of praise that was sung by the people of Israel, with a chorus and responses, used on important occasions, and was a thanksgiving song for God's eternal Goodness, in protecting and returning the people to the land).

"As a result, when the lord of the vineyard appears, what will he do to those farmers?" He asked the Chief Priests directly.

"He will sadly destroy those miserable men leasing the vineyard to other farmers, who will give him the fruit in its season." They replied readily, knowing that in the law, the issue is about ownership. If the land-lord cannot collect anything for a certain period, he forfeits his rights over the land. This is why in the story, he kept sending representatives.

"Have you never read in the Scriptures," asked Jesus," 'the stone the builders rejected, they made the same head of the corner, the chief cornerstone: This was from the Lord. It is marvelous in our eyes?'

"Accordingly, I tell you, the Kingdom of God will be taken away from you and given to a nation bringing forth its fruit.

Whoever falls onto this stone will be smashed into pieces; on the other hand, the one on whom it will fall, it will scatter him as dust."

The elders and Chief Priests were aware of the quote; from Psalm 118 that it referred directly to the Messiah.

After they had heard his parables, they realized he spoke, drawing a direct parallel with them.

They wanted to seize him as soon as they could, except they feared the people who considered him to be a Prophet. The people knew and were delighted that he had spoken this parable against them. As a result, they left him, going off very humiliated.

As they left, Jesus turned his focus back to the people, explaining the Kingdom.

"We could compare the Kingdom of Heaven to a particular king. After making a marriage feast for his son, he sent out his servants to call those who were invited to the festivity; however, they would not come.

Again he sent out other servants, with instructions, 'Tell those who are invited, "Consider, I have prepared my dinner. My cattle and fatted creatures are killed, and all things are ready. Come to the marriage feast!"' He said to them.

They, however, making slight of it, went their own ways, one to his own farm and another to his merchandise. The rest grabbed his servants, treating them unmercifully, killing them.

Having heard of it, the King was angry and sent his armies, destroying those murderers, and burned their city.

"Then he gave commands to his servants, 'the wedding is ready, but those who were invited were not worthy.

Go, Therefore, to the highway intersections, and as many as you can find, invite to the marriage feast.'

Those servants departed to the highways, gathering as many as they found, both bad and good, filling the wedding with guests.

However, having entered to see the guests, the King noted a man not dressed in the correct wedding clothing. The King addressed the man, 'Friend, how did you come in here not wearing wedding clothing?' he asks him.

The man was speechless.

The King then instructed his servants, 'Bind his hand and his foot, then take him away throwing him into the outer darkness; there is where the weeping and grinding of teeth will be.' Jesus concluded.

Because many are called, yet only a few chosen," he exclaimed.

(Isaiah 5:1-7 (CEB) *Let me sing for my loved one a love song for his vineyard.*
My loved one had a vineyard on a fertile hillside.
He dug it, cleared away its stones, planted it with excellent vines, built a tower inside it, and dug out a wine vat in it.
He expected it to grow good grapes— but it grew rotten grapes.
So now, you who live in Jerusalem, you people of Judah, judge between me and my vineyard:
What more was there to do for my vineyard that I haven't done for it?
When I expected it to grow good grapes, why did it grow rotten grapes?
Now let me tell you what I'm doing to my vineyard.
I'm removing its hedge, so it will be destroyed.
I'm breaking down its walls, so it will be trampled.
I'll turn it into a ruin; it won't be pruned or hoed, and thorns and thistles will grow up.
I will command the clouds not to rain on it.
The vineyard of the Lord of heavenly forces is the house of Israel, and the people of Judah are the plantings in which God delighted.
God expected justice, but there was bloodshed; righteousness, but there was a cry of distress!).

(Psalm 44:2: *How you did drive out the Gentile nations with your hand and planted them; how you did make the people suffer, and throw them out*).

The Chief Priests and the elders, having left, closely monitored Jesus. The idea of the plan was to try trapping him in something he said, something that would bring him in direct opposition to the power and authority of the Roman governor. They chose to send out spies, who would pretend to be honest.

The Pharisees took the lead and met to formalize the plan of action. How they might entrap him in something that he said.

So the Pharisees (*Shammaiites*) joined forces with the Herodians. (Who were their literal enemy) to give them some political backup, sending some of their followers to confront Jesus with their newly devised plan.

They approached Jesus, "Teacher, we know you are honest, and you teach the way of God in truth, regardless of whom you teach, since you truly teach the way of God and are not biased to anyone." They said, oozing compliments, these angry men with hardened hearts.

(Psalm 55:21. *The words spoken were as smooth as butter, yet war is in his heart, silky words softer than oil, but with hidden drawn swords*).

In that case, will you tell us, is it lawful or not, for us to pay taxes to Caesar. What do you think?

Should we pay, or shall we not pay?" They asked as pious as possible.

(In addition to property taxes, the Romans required annual payments of one Denarius, a day's wage, per adult male. The Jerusalem Sanhedrin itself had the responsibility for collecting this particular head tax.

And there was previously one, Judas the Galilean, who had refused to pay the tax and started a revolt, which resulted in him being executed by the Romans. This was as much a political trap as an attempt to discredit Jesus).

Yet, Jesus perceived their wickedness, "Why do you try to test me, you hypocrites?" He queried.

"Show to me one of the tax money."

They brought him a Denarius.

"Whose is this image and inscription on it?" He asked them as they held it up.

"Caesar's," They replied.

Then Jesus told them, "Give to Caesar then, the things that are Caesar's and to God the things that are God's." It amazed them when they heard this; silence fell on them all. It greatly frustrated them as their big plan could not trap him in his words in front of the people. So they silently slipped away and left him there.

Later that day, some Sadducees, the group that alleged there is no resurrection or an afterlife, arrived to try Jesus with their brand of reasoning. The Sadducees were the Jewish elite. They believed that the soul ceased at the time of death. And held that there was no reality of a spiritual world or Angels and was concerned with politics over religion, yet incongruously, strongly believed in the Torah (*the Books of Moses*).

They approached Jesus. "Teacher, in the law Moses wrote, 'If a man dies, leaving a wife behind without children; His brother shall raise up seed for the first brother's inheritance by marrying the widow.'

Now consider, there were with us seven brothers. The first took a wife and later died with no children.

The second brother then took her as a wife, and he died with no children.

The third married her, and likewise to the seventh. All the seven died, leaving no children.

And in the end, the woman also died.

"As a result, when they arise in the resurrection, whose wife of the seven will she be? Since all the seven had her as a wife." They concluded, sure that they had found the perfect trap.

"You are in error, not knowing the Scriptures, or of the power of God," Jesus replied.

"The children belonging to this age marry and are given to be married.

However, those who are regarded as suitable to reach that age, into the resurrection from the dead,

Will not marry, nor are they given to be married; instead, they are similar to the Angels of God in Heaven.

Because they cannot die anymore, since being like the Angels, they will be the children of God, comprising children of the resurrection.

Nevertheless, regarding the resurrection of the dead, have you not read the account in the book of Moses? That which God spoke in the burning bush when he said, 'I AM, the God of Abraham, Isaac, and the God of Jacob'?

God is the God only of the living, not the God of the dead, since they are all alive to him. As a result, you are badly mistaken."

The crowds, when they heard this, were amazed at his teaching.

Having heard about Jesus silencing the Sadducees, all the Pharisees met together to formalize their plan.

One Scribe a teacher of the law, on hearing the exchange between Jesus and the Sadducees. Observing how well he had answered them, he approached and spoke to him. "Teacher, you speak well." He said.

"Teacher in the law, which one is the greatest and most important of the commandments?" he asked, testing him with a question.

"The greatest of all the commandments is this, 'Hear, O Israel. The Lord, our God, is the only Lord, the Lord is one: You will love the Lord your God with all your heart, your soul, your entire mind, and with all your strength.'

This is the first and great commandment." Jesus replied.

He continued. "A second similarly is this, 'You shall love your neighbor in the same way as you love yourself.' No other commandments are more significant than these.

On these two commandments, the entire written law and all the Prophets depend."

"Truly, teacher, you have spoken well, saying that, 'God is the only Lord.'" the Scribe replied, "Also, there is no other but him, and loving him with all the heart, the understanding, the soul, all the strength and loving his neighbor as equal to himself.

These are more essential commands than the entirety of burnt offerings and animal sacrifices."

"You, indeed, are close to the Kingdom of God," Jesus told him, welcoming the wise answer of the Scribe.

All the various groups and factions among the rulers did not dare to ask him any more questions.

The Pharisees arrived back, massing together in one group in the Temple court.

Jesus addressed them with a question, "Concerning the Messiah, what do you think? Whose son is he?" Jesus asked them.

"Messiah is the son of David." They replied.

Jesus continued. "In the writings of the Psalms: How is it then that David in the Spirit calls him Lord, when he said, 'The Lord said to my

Lord, sit you down on my right hand until I make your enemies a foot-stool for your feet?'

"If David calls the Messiah his Lord (Adonai), then how is he his son," Jesus asks firmly.

They were silent; none of them could answer him a word (As only God Himself could be David's Lord).

From that day, none of the groups dare risk asking him any more questions.

Jesus addressed his disciples, as well as the crowds, "The Scribes and the Pharisees, sit on Moses' seat." He said.

"As a result, all the things in whatever they tell you to study, that study and do, but do not follow and do their actions; since they say it, and yet do not do it.

Watch out for the Scribes because they bind heavy burdens too harsh to tolerate and place them on the shoulders of men, except they themselves will not lift a finger to help them.

However, every action they perform is so that men can see them; they like to walk in long flowing robes, broadening their phylacteries and enlarging their garments' borders.
(*Note: Texts from the Hebrew Scriptures contained in either of two small leather cases, 'known collectively as Tefillin,' traditionally worn 'on the forehead and the left arm' by Jewish men during Morning Prayer).

The place of honor at feasts, also the best seats in the synagogues they love, recognition in the marketplaces, plus being called 'Rabbi, Rabbi,' and 'Great one,' by men, they love.

Nevertheless, you do not allow yourself to be called 'Rabbi,' since only the Messiah is your teacher. You all being brothers, having only one Father, he who is in Heaven. Then no man on Earth should you call father.

Neither be called masters because one is your master, the Messiah. However, the greatest among you will be your servant.

The one who acclaims himself will be humbled, and the one who humbles himself will be praised.

Watch out! To you, Scribes and Pharisees, you hypocrites! Who devour widows' houses, and as a pretense, you make long prayers. As a result, your condemnation will be greater.

To you, Scribes and Pharisees, insincere play-actors! Watch out! Shutting the Kingdom of Heaven from men, you do not enter yourselves. Neither do you allow access to those who are entering.

To you, Scribes and Pharisees, you hypocrites! Watch out! Since to make one proselyte, you will travel around by sea and land, later having them converted, making each twice as much of a son of Gehenna as yourselves.

Watch out! To those who teach. 'It is nothing to swear by the Temple; however, to swear by the gold of the Temple makes an obligation.'

You blind fools! Since which one is the greater, the gold, or the Temple that sanctifies the gold?

You say, 'The one who swears by the altar, it is nothing; yet, swearing by the gift placed on the altar, he is obligated!'

How blind are you? Is it the gift or the altar that sanctified the gift? Which is more significant?

Any promise then made by the altar is valid for everything on it.

Any oath then made by the Temple is valid for the Temple and him who was living in it.

Making any oath by Heaven is an oath by God's throne. And therefore by him who is sovereign reigning from that throne.

Watch out to you, Scribes and Pharisees; you are hypocrites, going out of your way, paying tithes of little herbs of mint, dill, and cumin, having left undone the law's authority for the more substantial matters of justice, mercy, and faith.

These, however, you should have done, leaving the other undone.

You blind guides; filtering out a small fly, yet swallow a camel" (In Aramaic, eliminating a gnat 'Kalma' swallowing a camel 'Gamla'). Jesus used the humor of the quest for ritual purity, of the person who does not know he is blind. And so is fussing to get a tiny unclean 'gnat' from his drink, yet missing the equally unclean camel. Leviticus 11:4... The camel, because he chewed the cud but parted not the hoof, he is unclean unto you.

This parody from Jesus was a stinging picture of the zealous Pharisees as being picky about trivialities while ignoring their more severe wrongdoings.

"Watch out! To you, Scribes and Pharisees, insincere play-actors! Cleaning only the outside of the cup and the dish, yet inside, they are full of extortion and unrighteousness.

You, Pharisee, are blind; first, clean the inside of the cup and the dish so that its outside may also become clean.

To you, Scribes and Pharisees, hypocrites! Watch out! Because you are like tombs whitened and whitewashed, which outwardly appear beautiful, yet inwardly full of dead men's bones and all uncleanness.

Just the same, you also outwardly appear righteous to men, but inwardly you are full of hypocrisy and iniquity.

Watch out, to you, Scribes and Pharisees, play-actors, because you build the Prophet's tombs. Also, decorate the monuments of the righteous. And say, 'had we lived in our father's days, we would have not been partakers in the blood of the Prophets.'

You, therefore, testify about yourselves that you are children of those who killed the Prophets.

Fill up the tombs then, with the same methods as your fathers.

You serpents, you offspring of vipers, how will you escape the judgment of Hell?

Consider as a consequence. How I am sending to you prophets, wise men, and Scribes.

Some of them you will kill some crucify. And some you will beat and lash in your synagogues, persecuting from City to City. Hence on you may come all the righteous blood, shed on the Earth, from the spilled blood of righteous Abel, even to the blood of Zachariah, son of Barachiah, whom you killed between the sanctuary and the altar.

> (Zechariah 1 (CSB) *In the eighth month, in the second year of Darius, the word of the Lord came to the Prophet Zechariah, son of Berechiah, son of Iddo*).

I tell you absolutely; all these things will come upon this generation.

Jerusalem, Jerusalem, you who has killed the prophets and have stoned those who are sent to her! How I would have often gathered your children together, as a hen gathers her chicks under her wings, and you would not!

Take note then, from now your house is to be left uninhabited to you.

And so I declare, you will not see me from now on, until you say, 'Blessed is he the one appearing in the name of the Lord!" Jesus proclaimed, quoting Psalm 118:26, pronouncing judicial blindness on the nation. With the prophecy from (Hosea 5:15, *'I will return again to my place, awaiting on the people acknowledging their guilt, then turn back looking for me.*

Yes, in their trouble, they will intently search to find me').

(Jeremiah 7:25 ERV *'From the day that your ancestors left Egypt to this day, I have sent my servants to you. My servants are the prophets. I sent them to you again and again.'*)

After he finished speaking and teaching, having stood in the Temple from early in the morning, with challengers coming all day, Jesus went and sat down to rest opposite the treasury in the court of women.

He is deeply aware of Israel's sinful rebellion and unbelief, its leaders, and people, having just pronounced the seven curses on the leaders.

After seeing their inability through outward zealousness and inward evil, of recognizing the Messiah, for their flawed use of the Scriptures, their primary failure to resolve the genuine spirit of Scripture, as well as being the descendant of the very ones who failed to identify yet killed the prophets.

All of this caused Jesus' ultimate pronouncement of judicial blindness on the nation. Knowing what it would mean for the Temple, the people, and the country. Knowing how many would be the people lost without receiving him, the only light of the world, knowing that this state of blindness would remain until he returns.

Jesus sat there looking down, in this grand Temple which these corrupt men had made into a den for robbers, having forgotten the commandment of the Lord their God; to take care of widows and orphans. Making a corrupt system instead of true worship; they were the blind, and they taught the people their brand of blindness.

They taught that the poor were under God's judgment and was deserving of their condition because of their own sin. They taught that people, because of their own neglect in a previous life, had caused them to return, reborn in a state of sickness or poverty. They assumed that by exploiting the poor.

They were doing God's will and furthering His divine purpose. The poor lowliest, and helpless were their merciless prey.

After sitting and resting there, he looked up, looking across at the treasury; he observed how the rich people put their gifts into the chests.

Thirteen chests shaped like trumpets, with a narrow mouth and wide at the bottom, were set in the large open square.

They mark all with a sign on the bottom to designate precisely the purpose for the money given. Nine were for the acceptance of what was to be offered by worshippers in the law. Another four were set aside for voluntary gifts. All were constructed so that people would publicly put their giving on display.

Decreed offerings were 1-2 The Half-shekel tribute, 3 Turtledove offering, 4 Pigeon offering, 5 Wood, 6 Incense, 7 Golden Vessels.

After sacrifices, money remaining would be given as offerings in 8 Sin-offering, 9 Trespass offerings.

Voluntary Offerings were 10 Offerings of birds, 11 Nazarite offerings, 12 Cleansed Leper, 13 is General voluntary offerings.

A poor widow approach, she cast in two small brass coins ('*lepton*'), which equals a Quadrans coin (*Tiny*).

Jesus called his disciples to gather closer and then told them. "I tell you the truth. This poor widow put in more with her gift than all the money the others are giving into the treasury because they all gave out of their sufficient riches.

She, however, out of her poverty, put in all that she had to live on."

(Proverbs 15:25, *The LORD will destroy tearing down the house of the proud, yet He will protect the boundary of the widow's property*).

(Malachi 3:5, "*At that time I will bring you to justice. I will draw near to be a swift witness and testify about the evil things people do, against the sorcerers and the adulterers and against those who swear falsely, who make false promises and cheat their workers the wage earner in his wages.*
I will testify against those who do not help only deprive strangers, the widow. The orphan, and those who turn aside the foreigners and do not fear or respect Me," Says the LORD of hosts).

Upon the observation of the awful tragedy of the religious system, taking a widow from being merely poor into extreme poverty, Jesus went his way.

Then, as Jesus left the Temple courts and walked out, heading to the Mount of Olives to spend the night, his disciples approached to point out the Temple's buildings. How splendid the Temple was, adorned with the beautiful stones used in its construction and all the gifts dedicated to God that had been placed in it.

Jesus asked, "Do you see all these great buildings? I tell you in truth, they will leave not even one stone on another. Every stone will be pulled and torn down."

CHAPTER EIGHTEEN

THE OLIVET DISCOURSE: ANSWERING THREE IMPORTANT QUESTIONS.

Later, when Jesus was sitting down on the Mount of Olives, several disciples, namely, Peter, James, John, and Andrew, came and asked Him three questions privately. Relating to what Jesus had taught previously, about his return at the end of the age, also what he had said about the destruction of the Temple. "Tell us," they asked, "when will all this happen?

What will be the signal for your return?

And what sign will there be for the end of the world?"

Jesus answered the questions this way. "Do not allow anyone to deceive you," he said, "because many people will come using my name, claiming, 'I am the Messiah. By this, they will mislead many.'

At that time, you will hear of wars and threats of wars, but don't be fearful. Indeed, these things must first take place, yet that won't bring the end right away. First nations will go to war against nations and kingdoms against other kingdoms.

People will starve through famines, and many places throughout the world will experience earthquakes.

Yet all those things are only the start of the birth pains.

Then you will be persecuted because you are my followers, arrested, even killed, as well as hated by people from all nations throughout the world. This will cause many to turn away from me, giving up, betraying, and hating each other.

It will be an evil time where rampant sin will spread universally, causing many people to stop loving and grow cold. Also, many false prophets will emerge and will mislead many people. Even so, those who endure faithfully to the end will be saved.

And whenever the Good News about the Kingdom has been preached throughout the entire world to all nations, then the end will come.

There is a time coming when you will see what Daniel the Prophet spoke about, the blasphemous object of desolation set-up in the Holy Place." (Whoever reads this must understand!), "Then any in Judea must flee to the hills. A person out on the roof deck should not go down into the house for clothes.

As for pregnant women and nursing mothers in those days, sadly, it will be horrifying. Anyone out in the field should not return, not even for their coat! So pray that your escape won't take place in the winter or even the Sabbath, for since the world began, there won't have been any more enormous suffering than at that time. Nor will it ever be so great again.

In reality, unless that disastrous time is shortened, no flesh would be saved.

Yet, for the sake of God's selected ones, it will be reduced.

Subsequently, should anyone inform you, 'Look, the Messiah is here,' or 'there he is,' do not accept it!

For false messiahs and false prophets will emerge doing such grand signs and wonders that, if possible, would deceive even those selected of God. Notice, I have warned you about this in advance.

Therefore, if someone informs you, 'Come see, the Messiah is out in the desert,' do not trouble yourself to go out to see. Or 'Look, he is in this hiding place,' do not believe it!

The Son of Man's arrival will be unmistakable, just like the lightning when it flashes in the east is seen shining in the west.

Wherever the remains of a dead body are, there the vultures will gather. Likewise, these signs indicate the close proximity to the end.

Directly following the tribulation of those days will the sun be darkened, with no light from the moon; also the stars will fall from the sky, as the powers in the heavens are shaken.

And finally, appearing in the sky will be the sign of the Son of Man. Intense mourning will break out from the peoples of the Earth as they see the Son of Man approaching on the clouds of heaven with power and great glory. As he sends his Angels out with the mighty blast of a trumpet so that they can gather his chosen ones from over the entire world, even the farthest ends under all heaven.

Now, learn lessons from the fig tree. Its branches, when they bud, and its leaves begin to sprout; you know that summer is near.

Likewise, when you witness these things, you can be sure the Son of Man's return is very near, almost at the door.

I tell you truthfully, this generation will not pass from the scene until all these things occur.

Heaven and Earth must dissolve and pass away. Still, my words will never depart, though; the day and hour when these things will happen; knows none, not the Angels in heaven or the Son himself. Only the Father knows.

When the Son of Man comes back, the world will be just like it was in the time of Noah, in the days before the flood. The people were feasting, partying, and getting married right up to the moment Noah entered his boat.

People did not appreciate what was going to happen until the flood came and swept them all away. That's just the way it will be when the Son of Man appears.

Two men will be together working in the field; one will be taken, and one left. Two women will be milling flour; one will be taken, and one left.

Hence you also must keep watching, not knowing what day your Lord is returning.

Be aware of this; if an owner knew precisely when the burglar was coming, he would keep watching, not permitting his house to be broken into. You must also be ready all the time for the arrival of the Son of Man will be when least expected.

Who is a faithful, prudent, and loyal servant whom the master can give the responsibility of managing and providing for his other household servants? If the master finds that the servant had done an excellent job upon returning, he will receive a suitable reward.

I tell you truthfully; the master will promote that servant to manage all he owns.

Just suppose the servant instead to be a corrupt person who thinks. 'My master will not be back for a long time.' So he commenced beating the other servants while partying and getting drunk? The master's return will be without warning and unexpected; he will cut to pieces that servant consigning him to a position with the hypocrites.

In that place, people will weep and grind their teeth with pain.

"Consequently, the Kingdom of heaven will be like ten young bridesmaids, who took lamps going out waiting to meet the soon-approaching bridegroom.

Five of the ten were foolish; the other five sensible and prudent girls. The five foolish bridesmaids took their lamps but did not take the extra oil needed for the lamps to burn. The wise girls prudently took lamps but also extra oil in containers.

Then since the bridegroom was delayed and late, they became tired with the wait and went to sleep.

"Suddenly at midnight, someone shouted, 'Look, the bridegroom is approaching, come and meet him!' Subsequently, all the bridesmaids woke up trimmed their lamps, getting them ready, except the foolish girls had to ask the wise. 'Give some of your oil to us since our lamps are going out.'

The wise girls answered, 'No, the oil we have might not be enough for us and you. Go and buy some for yourselves from the people who sell oil.'

And so, while the five foolish girls went off to buy oil, the bridegroom arrived. The ready bridesmaids went into the wedding feast with the bridegroom. After that, the door was closed and locked.

Later, the others came back, saying, 'Lord, Lord open the door to let us in.'

However, the bridegroom went and answered, 'I tell you in truth, I do not know you.'

Therefore, always be ready, keeping watch, since you don't know the day or the hour the Son of Man will arrive."

A FURTHER PARABLE REFERENCING THREE SERVANTS.

"Because understanding the Kingdom of heaven, it could be compared to a master with a financial empire who on leaving on a distant trip. Arranged a meeting of his managers and assigned to them his assets.

He divided all his money into eight parts, distributing the assets between them all. Giving five shares to the first, two shares to the second, and one share to the third, selecting each of them on the merit of their competence. After this, he departed for an extended journey.

The first two wasted no time in putting their management skills to use; the one with five shares traded them and increased the total by another five.

The one who received the two shares did the same and increased the total by another two.

However, the manager with the one share did nothing except hide the money.

It was quite a long time before the lord of those managers returned, calling for an audit of all the accounts.

The first with the five shares arrived showing the increase of another five, 'lord, you allocated to me five shares. I have made an increase of five more shares.' He said.

'You did very well; you are a faithful manager and a good person.' His lord told him, 'Because you have shown that you are reliable with even a few things, I will promote you to be in charge over many things. You will share in celebrating my success.'

"The second manager with the two shares arrived showing the increase of another two, 'Lord, you allocated to me two shares. I have made an increase of two additional shares.' He said.

'You did very well; you are a faithful manager and a good person.' His lord told him.

'Because you have shown that you are reliable with even a few things, I will promote you to be in charge of many things. You will share in celebrating my success.'

The third manager with the one share arrived, 'Lord, you are a tough boss, and I know it, you gain profit with ease, from areas where you did not even invest.'

I lost my nerve and thought it best to play it safe, not risking your money. Look, here is your share intact.'

'You are lazy and immoral, though knowing that I gain profit easily from areas I did not even invest.' His lord replied.

'The least you should have done is deposited it in the bank; that way, it would have at least given me nominal interest.'

As of now, all your authority is removed. The share is taken from you and will be given to the manager with ten shares.

Since everyone who performs shows they have, extra will be given to them, for a surplus. However, anyone who shows a lack by doing nothing, what little they have will be taken away.

Throw this futile manager out into the wilderness, where there will be sorrow and anguish."

When the Son of Man arrives in majesty with all the holy Angels, he will sit on his throne of splendor.

Every nation will be assembled in front of the glorious throne. Like a shepherd who separates the sheep from the goats, all the nations will be divided, positioning the sheep on his right hand, with the goats on the left.

The King will offer to those on the right hand, an invitation of inheritance, to my Fathers Kingdom, which had been prepared for you, from the world's establishment.

Since I was once hungry, and you provided food for me to eat. And gave me a drink when I was thirsty, taking me into your home, even though I was a stranger, clothing me when I was naked. Visiting me when I was sick and when I was in prison.'

'Lord, at what time did we ever see you hungry and feed you, or thirsty, and give you a drink?' The righteous will ask.

When did we ever take you in after seeing you as a stranger, clothe you when naked?

Whenever did we see you sick, or in prison, and visited you?'

'I tell you most certainly; you did it to me by performing it to anyone of even the least of my brothers.' The King will answer.

Then to those on the left hand, ' get away from me, into the eternal fire prepared for the devil and his Angels you who are cursed: because you did not give me food to eat though I was hungry, and no drink when thirsty.

You found me a stranger and did not take me in, naked, and did not clothe me; sick, imprisoned, and you did not visit me.' He will say.

'Lord, whenever did we see you hungry, thirsty, a stranger, naked, sick, or in prison, and did not help you?' they will ask.

'I tell you most certainly, by not performing this to even the least of my brothers, you did not do so for me.' He will reply.

These will depart into perpetual punishment. However, the righteous will go into eternal life."

Jesus concluded in clarifying for them the details of the destruction of the Temple, including many events leading up to and beyond his return; he then started to tell his friends of the events immediately upon them. "The Passover will start in only two days, as you know. It is also the time of The Feast of Unleavened Bread. And this is when the Son of Man will be arrested and handed over and surrendered to be crucified." Jesus stated, reminding them of his previous forewarning.

During the daytime, Jesus was in the Temple area teaching the people. Each evening, he went out of the city to spend the night on or beyond the Mount of Olives. Every morning all the people came early to Jesus in the Temple to listen and hear him teach.

At that very time, Caiaphas the High Priest had the Chief Priests and the lawyers; also the leaders of the people assembled at his palace.

The purpose of the meeting was to work out a way to seize and kill Jesus by trickery. They were resolute on when it should and should not happen. "Because we fear the people may riot because of any incident, it cannot be at any period during the feast time." They said.

At the same time, Jesus and the disciples returned to Bethany, which is set east of Jerusalem set on the other side of the Mount of Olive from the city.

A man in the town known as Simon, the leper invited Jesus and his followers to dinner at his house (*Jesus had earlier healed this Simon of his sickness; he was possibly the father of Judas, the disciple*).

Lazarus and his two sisters Martha and Mary, friends of the disciples from the same town, were also there. Lazarus, his friend, was one of the guests at the table, one of the sisters, Martha, was helping with serving the food.

The other sister Mary entered the dining room; she bought some very costly ointment contained in an Alabaster Jar. (*Jars of white alabaster stone were hand-carved, slight, and relatively transparent.*)

This lotion was exceedingly precious, weighing about a pound, of (*Genuine Nard from the Himalayas in India.*)

After breaking the jar, Mary poured it on Jesus' head as he sat at the table. She poured some on his feet, and after loosening her hair, Mary proceeded to wipe his feet with her hair.

The warm, beautifully delicate fragrance of the ointment filled the entire house.

Then one of the disciples, Judas Iscariot, Simon's son, (*The dinner was held at his father's house*).

Who would later betray him, saw this, and was incensed: "All this waste, why? What is the purpose of this," He asked. "Why did we not sell this ointment for three hundred Denarii's and given to the poor?" (*A year's earnings for a typical worker*) He remonstrated, protesting against her action.

Judas was not so much concerned over the plight of the poor, but because he was the treasurer and kept the funds. He was stealing parts of the money.

Judas was from Kerioth, a city close to Hebron, south of Jerusalem, in Judea. Judas was a local Judean; the 'Iscariot' after Judas' name stands for Kerioth. Ishkeriyyoth, in Hebrew, means man of the village of Keriyyoth (Judas being the only one of the twelve disciples not from Galilee in the northern part of Israel).

"Why harass her," Jesus asked? "Leave the woman alone since, on my behalf, she has done this good work. In the act of her pouring this ointment on my body, she has done what she could because she did it in preparation for my burial. She, in reality, kept this for the day of my burial. Therefore, she has anointed my body ahead of time.

So let her be; because you have the poor always with you, and you can do good things for them whenever you want to. However, you will not always have me.

I tell you absolutely, wherever in the whole world this Good News is preached, what has been done by this woman will also be told as her memorial."

At that moment, Judas, called Iscariot, went away in a rage and allowed Satan to enter into him. Judas hurried back to Jerusalem in the dark of the night. Finding the Chief Priests and elders; meeting there. He discussed what he could do to bring Jesus into their hands.

When the group of schemers heard it, they were delighted, pledging to reward Judas.

"For me bringing him to you, what are you prepared to give to me?" He asked.

The Chief Priests and elders gladly weighed out thirty pieces of silver for him (*The nominal price for a slave! Zechariah 11.*) *In the thirteenth verse, it declares this. 'The Lord said to me, "Throw it to the potter," that magnificent princely price that they valued for my worth. Therefore, I took the thirty pieces of silver and threw them to the potter in the house of the Lord.'*

All the men involved in this act became guilty of breaking the law at this moment. This constituted a serious crime, as written in *Exodus 23:1-8. You should not raise a false report: put not your hand with the wicked to be an unrighteous witness.*

(Verse eight)... And you should take no gift: because the gift blinds the wise, and pervert's the words of the righteous.

Judas approved this. The plan was that he would search for any prospect of handing Jesus over to them (they were careful to get assurance that it would not take place in the holiday period.) It was to be in the absence of the crowds and away from the eyes of the Roman soldiers.

Their fear was of the Romans' swift and severe reaction to any disturbance during the feast period, being the time when the occupying soldiers were on high alert; and because they had prohibited the Jews from carrying out any capital punishment or executions, all was to be done at a time that suited the leaders and in secret.

CHAPTER NINETEEN

THE PASSOVER IS CELEBRATED WITH A NEW COVENANT INSTITUTED.

The time had arrived for the 'Feast of Unleavened Bread,' which begins formally in the Passover, which lasted through seven days. It would be the celebration of Israel's deliverance from bondage.

As it was the first day of unleavened bread, during the time the sacrifice of the Passover animal would take place, some disciples approached Jesus. They questioned. "Which place shall we get arranged so that you can eat the Passover meal?"

Jesus gave instructions to Peter and John; "You go and get the Passover ready for us, so we will eat together." He told them.

"Where do you want us to organize it all," they enquired?

"Go into the city and take note as you are entering the city; a man carrying a pitcher of water will meet you. Just follow him into the house that he enters." He directed in reply. (*This was unusual and served as a suitable signal since it was usually the women, not men, who would carry pitchers of water*).

State to the house's owner, 'The Teacher says to tell you, "My time is at hand, and asks, where is the guest room in which my disciples and I will eat the Passover meal?"'

He will show you a large room in the upper part of the house, furnished for the purpose. Make all arrangements for the meal there."

The two of them went and did as Jesus had instructed, finding arrangements precisely as he had said, so they prepared the place for the Passover.

Later that evening, the small party of people arrived at the house. When Jesus eventually was reclining at the table with the twelve disciples, he lovingly addressed them all. "I have sincerely desired to eat this Passover meal with you before I suffer. Because I tell you, I will no longer by any means eat again of it until its fulfillment in the Kingdom of God." He expressed.

Then, in an unusual move, Jesus took first the cup before the bread; he gave thanks for it. He then handed it to one of the disciples, "Take this cup, and share it between all of you, since I tell you, I will not drink the fruit of the vine again until the Kingdom of God comes." He told them.

Because Jesus spoke about the Kingdom of God, the disciples started an intense argument over which of them was regarded as top or best in the Kingdom?

"The kings of the nation's rule over them and the ones having power over the people are called 'patron.'" Jesus informed them.

"However, with you, it will not be so. On the contrary, the one who is to be the greater of you must permit himself to be as the youngest. The one who is leading must permit himself to be the servant of the others.

Think of this, which person is greater? Is it the one who sits at the table, or is it the one who serves those at the table?

It is the one, who sits at the table, is it not?

However, here I am amongst you as a servant to you.

Nevertheless, you are the ones who have continually been with me through all my adversities.

I then award you a kingdom, even as my Father granted to me; therefore, you will join the banquet at my table in my kingdom. Sitting on thrones, you will be judges reigning over the twelve tribes of Israel."

Jesus, now fully aware the time for him to leave this world to return to the Father, approached. However, he was leaving his followers and disciples in the world. They were his own; his love was perfect towards them all, to the end.

The feast of the Passover was still ahead. Still, at some point during dinner, Judas Iscariot, the son of Simon, having already allowed the devil to influence him, determined in his heart to hand over Jesus to the people conspiring to put him to death.

Jesus, knowing he was going to God, having emerged from God, and knowing that the Father had allotted all things into his control. Got up from dinner and put down to one side his outer clothing (*himatia*). This would be his mantle and his tunic; a linen shirt (*chaluq*) was worn underneath the tunic.

He took a towel, wrapping it around his waist. Then having poured water into the basin, proceeded to wash the feet of the disciples. Then he used the towel wrapped around him to dry them in the manner of a servant. Each disciple's feet were washed; when it was the turn of Simon Peter, he spoke up, "Lord, are you likewise going to wash my feet?" He asked, protesting.

"You do not recognize what I am doing now, although you will understand it later," Jesus affirmed.

"You will certainly not wash my feet!" Peter stated, even though he had just called him Lord (Adonai).

"If I do not wash your feet, you will have no place with me," Jesus responded with tenderness.

"Lord, not only just my feet but my hands and head also!" Peter exclaimed.

"Having already bathed, a person then will only need to have his feet washed, to be completely clean. You then are clean, except it is not all of you." Jesus told him, and indicating all the others.

Jesus knew exactly who would hand him over, and that is why he stated it.

Having finished the washing of their feet, he put on back his outer garment. After sitting down again in his place, he spoke to the group collectively, "You address me as your 'Teacher' and as 'Lord.' This is correct and true since I am.

Do you appreciate what I have done in teaching you this?

As your Lord and your Teacher, if I have washed your feet, you, therefore, should also wash each other's feet.

Because I have given this to you as an example to encourage you to do as I have done.

I tell you, the servant is not superior to his lord, or the one who is sent, ever superior to who sent him.

Once you have grasped these things, and you, by also doing them, will be blessed.

I know all those I have chosen, so I do not speak this relating to everyone. Even though the Scripture will become true, *'The one who eats bread with Me has lifted up his heel against me.'* (Psalm 41:9).

I tell you from now before it occurs so that you will believe that I am the Messiah when it does.

I tell you unquestionably, by accepting the one I send. They will accept me, and he who receives me is accepting my Father who sent me."

Then in the middle of the dinner, Jesus took some bread, blessed it, giving thanks for the bread. Then broke it, giving the pieces to the disciples, "Take this bread, and eat of it; this bread is representing my body which is broken and is given for you. In the future, when you do this, you do it to remember me." He said.

Jesus then took the cup, and having blessed it by giving thanks for the cup, he gave it to them, "This cup represents the new covenant in my blood, which is poured out for you. Drink it each of you because this is a new covenant in my blood, poured out on behalf of many for the forgiveness and pardon of sins. And repeatedly as you drink this cup, do it to remember me." He told them.

Because you are proclaiming the death of your Lord each time you eat this bread and drink this cup, do it often until I return.

However, I tell you I will not any more drink of this fruit of the vine, in anticipation of that day in the Kingdom of my Father, when I drink it with you once more."

(They used four cups *for the meal of the Passover. Exodus 6:6, 7 The cup of the Bringing Out, The cup of the Delivery, The cup of Redemption or Blessing, The cup of Taking Out.*

During this meal, the first three cups were drunk, and then the fourth and last cup was not taken; as a result, all stopped after the cup of blessing, leaving 'The cup of Taking Out.' And as Jesus said, they would conclude the fourth and last cup in the Kingdom to come).

Jesus became sorrowful in spirit as they were still eating the meal. So he gave the others confirmation of what was approaching, "I declare to you, one of you eating with me will hand me over.

See, on the table with me is the hand of the one who betrays me.

Without a doubt, the Son of Man departs, exactly as written about him. However, watch out to that man by who the Son of Man is betrayed!

It would have been better if that man had not been born!" Announced Jesus, this caused all the disciples to become very distressed.

Each one looked at the others, confused as regards to which of them he meant.

They queried between each other, which out of them all would do this thing.

At the table, one of his disciples, John, was the one leaning back against his chest, being the youngest, and took the position traditionally taken by the youngest son.

Simon Peter gestured to him, "Ask him of whom of us he speaks, and then tell us who it is." He told him.

As he was close enough to be heard, he posed Peter's question, "Lord, which one of us is it," Asked John?

As soon as that was spoken, each of the disciples pleaded with him, "Not me, Lord? Certainly, it is not I?" They each asked, in turn.

"The one who betrays me; he dipped his hand into the dish with me.

Once I have dipped this piece of bread, it is the one to whom I will give it." Jesus answered, giving Judas a last opportunity for repentance.

Then dipping the piece of bread, he offered it to Judas Iscariot, the son of Simon.

"Rabbi, surely it is not me, is it?" Judas asked, knowing positively that his plot was no longer a secret.

"You have said it," Jesus replied.

Then after eating the piece of bread, Satan entered and took control of Judas.

Then Jesus instructed him, "What you are going to do, go swiftly and do." He said solemnly, seeing he did not take the opportunity to turn from his intent.

The others at the table did not know why he was told this by Jesus since Judas was the keeper of money for the group. Some had the notion that Jesus said to him, 'Go buy the things that we will need for the feast,' or even that he should, as was traditional at feast time, give a portion to the poor, as it was their standard practice.

Because of receiving that piece of bread, Judas left at once. It was now nighttime. Judas hands were now forced; his skillfully concealed plan was made known. Even though The Chief Priests and Leaders had tried to ensure that nothing would happen during the Feast time. All arrangements had to be hurriedly made, as the plans were now in the open.

> Psalm 55:12-13 (ESV) **Now it is not an enemy who insults me otherwise I could bear it; it is not a foe who rises up against me otherwise I could hide from him.**
> **But it is you, a man who is my peer, my companion, and good friend!**

As soon as Judas had left the premises, Jesus spoke to the rest of his followers. "At this moment, the Son of Man has been elevated, and in him, God has been lifted up.

And through him, God has been honored; God will also honor him in himself, and immediately.

My little children, I will be with you for just a little time longer. Even though you will search for me, as I said to The Chief Priests and Leaders, 'Where it is that I am going, you cannot follow,' so I also tell it to you now.

This is a new commandment that I give to you, that you will love one another, just as I have loved you.

Through that love, you have one for another; by this, all will know that you are my disciples." Jesus spoke tenderly with such fondness and so much love; it was clear it was a farewell of sorts.

"Lord, where is it you are going?" Simon Peter asked him earnestly.

"Children where I am going, you cannot follow, for now, although you will follow afterward," Jesus answered reassuringly.

"Lord, why can I not follow you now? I will lay down my very life for you." Peter told him unreservedly, with his customary boldness.

"Will you, Peter, will you really lay down your life for me? Jesus asked him, challenging the statement knowingly yet not pressing the issue.

"This very night, all of you will have reason to stumble because of me since the scriptures predict, 'I will strike the shepherd, and scatter the sheep of the flock.'

However, I will be going ahead of you. You are to follow me into Galilee after I am raised up," Jesus expressed, including them all, turning the focus away from Peter.

"Even if all will have cause to stumble because of you, I, however, will never be made to stumble," Peter stated resolutely.

"Simon, Simon," Jesus tenderly spoke to him. "Consider this, Satan repeatedly asked to take you so that he may separate and sieve you as wheat. However, I have prayed for you to be strengthened and your faith would endure and not fail.

So then, once you have been transformed, build up and strengthen your brothers." Jesus told him to encourage him.

Simon yet persisted, "Lord, I am prepared to go with you to prison and even to death!" He said.

"I tell you definitely that before the end of the night, even before the rooster crows twice. Three times, you will have denied that you know me," Jesus replied firmly, without offense.

Simon would not let it go, "If I should have to die with you, I still will not deny you." He said. Then the other disciples also spoke up, saying the same.

"Did you find you lacked anything when I had sent you out without purse, wallet, or shoes?" Jesus asked the group, again shifting the focus away from Peter.

"No, we lacked for nothing." They answered eagerly, knowing he was about to teach something.

"Although in the time that is soon-approaching, the one who has a purse let him take it, and likewise a wallet.

And in those days, the one with no sword; he will even need to sell his cloak to purchase one.

'They reckoned him along with the transgressors.' Jesus told them, quoting the Scripture written in the fifty-third chapter of the book of Isaiah.

I tell you, this will be the fulfillment of what they wrote about me in Scripture. Since all that concerns me must have its conclusion."

"Lord, look, here we have two swords between us!" Some of them exclaimed, missing the point of the lesson. (*These swords the disciples had were not primarily fighting weapons, which were prohibited from being carried openly; instead, tools to be used for daily activities such as fishing and making camp overnight*).

"That is enough of that," Jesus stated dismissively, knowing that they failed to grasp the spiritual meaning of his words. Namely, they, to that point, had been under his divine protection. In the future, the times will become difficult for them.

JESUS' PRESENTS A PROFOUND PROMISE AS OBLIGING AS A LEGALLY BINDING KETUBAH.

"Do not permit your heart to be anxious just as you believe in God. Then also believe in me.

Many are the dwellings in my Father's house. I would have told you if it was otherwise. I am departing to arrange a place for you there.

If I leave and arrange for you a place, I will return, and I will gather you to return with me; then you will be where I am as well.

You know where it is I go, as you also know the way." Jesus explained reassuringly, letting them know that through all troubles, he was with them.

"Lord, we don't know where it is you are going, so how can we possibly know the way?" asked Thomas, voicing the confusion of the entire group.

"I AM, The way! The truth! And the life; except it is through me, no one can come by any other way to the Father," Jesus replied.

"You, because of knowing me, should also recognize my Father. As of this time, you know him and have seen him." Jesus reminded them how often they had witnessed so much of his splendor and glory.

"Lord, if you now show to us the Father, that will be enough for us," said Philip, being the spiritual seeker of the group. Jesus had said of him he would see the fulfillment of Jacob's dream.

"Have I been with you for such a very long time, Philip, yet you still do not know me? Those who have seen me have seen the Father. How then do you say, 'Show to us the Father?' Jesus asked tenderly, slightly amazed.

"Don't you believe I am in the Father and the Father in me? All the words that I say to you are not from myself; instead, it is the Father who lives in me that is doing his works." Jesus explained, again reminding them, knowing it is essential that they finally grasp this before the events to come.

"Accept as true I am in the Father, and the Father is in me; if not, believe me then for the evidence of the very miracles.

I tell you, any person believing in me will also do the miracles that I do, and greater miracles than these, they will do, since I am leaving to go to my Father.

You will ask for anything in my name; I will do it! So in the Son, the Father will be honored.

So then, should you ask anything in my name, I will do it.

If you love me, then you will keep my commandments.

I will pray and ask the Father, and he will give you the helper who is another Counsellor so that he will stay with you forever. He is the Spirit of truth, he the world cannot accept; since it neither sees him nor knows him.

You will know him since he lives with you and will be within you.

I will not leave you as orphans. I will return to you.

However, the world will not see me anymore in a little while, though you will see me. And because I live, you will live as well.

You will appreciate that I am in my Father, and you will be within me; on that day. And I will be within you.

Everyone who has and keeps my commandments, that person is the one who loves me. My Father will love all those loving me, and I will love and will make myself known to them." Jesus spoke reassuringly to them, explaining the soon-to-come change of the relationship between them and the father.

"Lord, what is it that happened that you are about to make known yourself to us, yet not to the world?" One disciple asked, startled, having gotten the revelation. This was Lebbaeus Thaddaeus, also known as Judas.

"If a man loves me, through keeping my words will he show it, and he will be loved by my Father, then we will appear to him and make our home with him." Jesus continued, wanting them to focus and understand all he was saying.

"Those who do not keep my words show they do not love me.

The words that you are hearing are not mine; instead, they are from the Father who sent me." Jesus emphasized.

"I have expressed these things to you while I am still living among you.

However, the Counsellor, the Holy Spirit, whom the Father will send in my name, he will teach you, and all things that I have said to you, he will remind you.

I leave with you, peace! I give to you my peace, which is not as the world gives. Never allow your heart to be anxious, or ever let it be fearful.

When I told you, 'I go away, and I return to you.' You heard it, and since you love me, you should have been delighted because I said 'I am going to my Father;' since my Father is greater than I.

I have told you now previous to it happening so you may believe when it takes place.

No more will I speak much with you because now the prince of this world approaches, even though there is not one thing in me that he can have any part of.

However, I do exactly as the Father instructed me, so the world will know that I love the Father. Let us get up and leave from here."

An ancient Jewish marriage starts with an agreed betrothal by the father (ketubah) or a wedding contract concerning terms of conditions, price, and payment for a bridal match.

This ketubah becomes a legally binding document, listing the husband's obligations to his wife, usually a young woman chosen by the bridegroom's father. Mostly, the bride would not see the prospected husband, only received details about him through an intermediary.

The groom's family made a financial settlement, called a (mohar) a bride price, to the bride's family as part of the engagement contract.

The groom would give his bride wedding presents (mattan), beginning with the betrothal or engagement.

The Hebrew word for betrothal is erusin. Another word, kidushin, was also used to describe this step in the marriage process; Kidushin bears the meaning sanctification or holiness being set apart, taken from the Hebrew word for holy, Kadosh.

The word for the betrothed woman was m'kudeshet, also related to the word holy.

They presented the completed ketubah to the father of the bride.

Jesus is leaving the bride (the Ekklisia, Church) to go and prepare a wedding chamber in his father's house for her. He promised to return for her and to take her with him.

A bride in ancient times would not know the day or hour her bridegroom would return to take her to the wedding chamber.

The groom also did not know. Only his father knew the date and was the one to decide when all was suitable for the wedding, in due time once the groom completed the bridal chamber.

Jeremiah 33:11 (NKJV) *the voice of joy and the voice of gladness, the voice of the bridegroom and the voice of the bride, the voice of those who will say:*
"Praise the Lord of hosts,
For the Lord is good,
For His mercy endures forever."
And of those who will bring the sacrifice of praise into the house of the Lord. For I will cause the captives of the land to return as at the first,' says the Lord.

The group sang a hymn and left the other followers, supporters, and those of the household who had taken part in the meal. As was their recent practice of the past few days, Jesus and his disciples departed for the Mount of Olives.

Once they had arrived at the Mount of Olives. Jesus continued giving the Apostles necessary instructions. "I am the true fertile and life-giving vine, and the cultivator is my Father.

He takes away each branch in me that produces no fruit. He shears every branch that bears fruit to sustain it in bearing more fruit.

(*Ezekiel 36:25 (AMP) Then I will sprinkle clean water on you, and you will be clean; I will cleanse you from all your uncleanness and from all your idols.*)

Through the word I have already spoken to you, you are pruned clean.

Then remain in me, and I will remain in you, since the branch unless it remains in the vine, can bear no fruit by itself; because of that, neither can you unless you remain in me.

I am the true vine. You are the branches on the vine. The one remaining in me, as I remain in him! The same produce much fruit, since separated from me, you can do nothing.

Any not enduring but is detached from me are cast out withering as a branch. Those branches are gathered, thrown into the fire, and burned.

(Psalm 80:8 (NKJV) you removed us and brought out of Egypt, your special vine from Egypt; you forced out the pagan nations from this land and planted it.

Psalm 80:15 (NKJV) the vineyard, which your right hand has planted, and the branch (the Son) that you made strong for yourself.

When you keep my words and remain in me, whatever you will desire, you will ask, and I will do it for you.

It honors my Father immensely when you bear significant fruit; therefore, you will be my disciples.

I have loved you unwaveringly as the Father has loved me; continue in my love.

You will continue in my love by keeping my commandments, just as I have kept my Father's commandments and remained in his love.

These things I have declared to you so that my joy may remain in you, giving you the fullness of joy.

This then is my commandment to you; love each other, just as I have loved you.

Greater love no one has, more than someone laying down his life for his friends.

You are my friends if you do all that I command.

I will no longer call you servants since the servant does not know the actions of his Lord.

However, I have called you my friends; because to you, I have declared everything that I heard from my Father.

You did not choose me; instead, I select and appointed you so you will go producing fruit and your fruit should endure; plus in my name, anything you will ask from the Father, he will give to you.

"I give these commands to you, so you will love one another.

Be aware that the world, if it hates you, has hated me previous to hating you.

Had you yet belonged to the world, then the world would love you as its own. However, since you are not of the world for I selected you out of the world; as a result, the world hates you.

Keep the word I spoke to you in mind: 'no servant is greater than his lord.' If they mistreated me, they will also persecute you; if they kept my word, they will also keep yours.

Although all these things they will do to you because you carry my name, since they do not know him who sent me.

Had I not appeared and spoken to them, their sin would not have been revealed, so now they have not any cover for their sin.

Whoever hates me also hates my Father.

Had I not done the miracles in the middle of them, which no one else did, they would not have had sin. However, they have now seen and hated both my Father and me.

This happened so that it may fulfill the word, which was written in their law, 'They hated me without a cause.'

After the Counsellor arrives, the Spirit of truth, who I will send to you from the Father, he will give evidence about me.

You will also be a witness since, from the beginning, you have constantly been with me.

I have spoken these things to you; as a result, be strong, and then you will not be made to stumble.

They will drive you out of their synagogues. Yes, the day is near where they will think that they offer service to God by killing you.

It is because they have not known of the Father or me they do these things.

However, I tell you in advance, so remember I had told you about them when the time comes.

Since I was constantly with you from the beginning, there was no need for me to tell you these things.

However, I am now going to him who sent me, though none of you have asked me, 'Where are you going?'

Except now, your heart is filled with sorrow since I have told you these things.

Yet I tell you: it is to your advantage if I leave.

I cannot send you the helper if I do not leave; however, I will send him if I go.

Then on his arrival, He will declare and pronounce the world guilty regarding its sin, righteousness, and judgment.

Of its sin, since they do not believe in me. Righteousness, because I now depart to my Father, hence you will not see me anymore; judgment, because already judged, is the prince of this world.

"I still have many more things to tell you; however, you cannot accept them now.

Yet when he, the Spirit of truth, arrives, He will guide you into all truth since he is only speaking whatever he hears. He will proclaim to you future things that are approaching.

He will give me honor since he will take from that which is mine, proclaiming it to you.

All things that the Father has belonged to me; that's why I said that he receives from that which is mine and will declare it to you.

In just a short time, you will not see me. Then another short time, and you will see me."

Some of his disciples quietly asked each other, "What is he telling us, 'in just a short time, you will not see me. Then another short time and you will see me;' and, 'since I depart to the Father?'"

"What does he mean by the saying, 'in a short time?' we do not know." They said, confused.

Jesus perceived their questions, "Do you inquire between you relating to this, that I said, 'in just a short time, you will not see me. Then another short time, and you will see me?'

I tell you most positively that while you weep and grieve, the world will celebrate. You will be distressed, but your sorrow will be turned into happiness.

A woman has grief when she gives birth because her time has come. However, having delivered the child, she no more remembers the distress since she sees the joy of a human born into the world.

Likewise, you have sorrow now, although I will see you again, and your heart will rejoice, and that joy cannot be removed from you.

"On that day, you won't question me. I tell you absolutely; the Father will give you anything you will ask for in my name.

Until now, you have never asked for anything in my name. Ask, and you will receive, then you will have complete happiness.

All these things I have spoken to you in metaphors and figurative language. However, the time is coming when I will tell you plainly about the father. Then I will no longer speak to you in figurative language.

During that time, all that you ask will be in my name.

Since you have loved me, believing that I came out from God. The Father himself loves you, so I do not need to tell you. I will pray on your behalf to the Father.

Yes, I came into the world from the Father. Once more, I leave the world and return to the Father." Jesus explained with patience, knowing that they would need time to understand all the implications.

"We now recognize that you are speaking plainly, and not speaking figuratively.

We now see all things are known to you, having no need that anyone questions you. Therefore, we believe you came out from God!" His disciples said, seeing some part of what was being imparted.

"Do you now believe?" Jesus asks with incredible tenderness.

"Watch and be alert; there is a time, yes, it is here now, all of you will be dispersed, each to his own home, leaving me on my own, though I am not alone since I have the Father with me.

These things I am telling you so in me you will have peace. There is only distress for you in the world, yet be happy, as I have triumphed over the world." He warned them so that their confidence would remain during all events.

THE LORDS PRIESTLY PRAYER.

Jesus spoke all of this and then lifted his eyes to heaven, continuing with a prayer of thanks. "Father, the time has now arrived. Honor yourself in your Son, that in you, your Son also will be honored.

Having given him authority over all flesh, he will provide never-ending life to all those whom you have given to him.

This is the everlasting life they can have by knowing you, the only true God, and your son, whom you sent, Jesus their Messiah.

The work you had given me to do, I have finished. I have honored you on the Earth.

Father, adorn me now with your own self. Glorifying me with the exalted majesty I had with you, previous to the world's existence.

The people selected out of the world you gave to me were all yours, and you have given them to me. I had made your name known to them, and they have kept your word.

I have given them the words you have given to me, and they have received them.

Now they know for sure that I came out from you, believing that you sent me. And all things you have given me are from you.

I do not pray for the world; my prayer is for the ones you have given to me since they are yours.

All the things I have are yours. As yours are all mine, and in having care of them, I am honored.

I am not in the world any longer, yet these will remain in the world as I return to you.

Keep them protected by the power of your Name Holy Father, the name that you gave to me, and even as we are together as one, they will also be united as one.

Whilst with them in the world, I kept them protected by the power in your name.

I have kept all of those you gave to me. And that it would be the fulfillment of Scripture; I lost none of them apart from the son of destruction.

Although I now return to you, I speak of these things in the world so that they will have my complete joy.

After I have given your word to them, they are no longer of the world, just as I am not of this world; as a result, the world hated them.

I do not pray for you to take them from the world, only for you to keep them from the evil one.

They are now no longer of the world, just as I am not of the world.

Set them apart in your truth. Your word is the only truth.

You sent me into the world, and to their advantage, I set myself apart, that the truth will also set them apart.

Now, in the same way, I have sent them into the world.

I pray not only for these. But also for all those who will believe in me through their word.

So they will all be one, just as you are in me, Father, and I am in you. Then they also will be one in us, and the world will believe that you sent me.

I have given them the honor you have provided to me so they may be as we are, together as one in unison.

I in them, you in me, then all will be perfected into one. Then the world will know you had sent me, and you loved them, just as you loved me.

Father, I also desire that they will be with me where I am. And see the glory you gave me because you loved me prior to establishing the world.

Though the world has not known you righteous Father, I knew you, and these select ones recognized you sent me.

I have made your name known and will make it known to them; so that the love you loved me will be in them. And I will be in them."

After Jesus finished his priestly prayer for his disciples, he led them over the brook Kidron into a garden situated there (*Garden of Gethsemane, the place of the winepress*).

CHAPTER TWENTY

JESUS' PRAYER OF INTIMACY TO HIS FATHER IN THE GARDEN.

In the garden called Gethsemane, Jesus instructed his disciples, "You sit down here, as I go on further over there and pray."

Jesus selected Peter, James, and John to go with him; he became grief-stricken, severely concerned, and troubled as he went on.

Jesus spoke to the three disciples with him, "My soul is extremely sorrowful, even to death. Stay here, and watch with me."

"Pray in order that you will not enter into temptation." He told them.

Leaving them, Jesus moved on a short distance and fell to the ground on his face asking in prayer if it was possible, even the hour could pass away from him.

"Father, Abba, to you, all things are possible. Providing that you are willing, My Father, if expedient, allow this cup to depart from me.

Please remove this cup from me. Though, not what I desire, however, what you want." He prayed.

At that very moment, an Angel from heaven became visible to strengthen him.

Jesus' agony was so extreme he prayed more intently.

As he continued in prayer, His perspiration became like great drops of blood dripping from his face, falling on the ground.

Jesus got back up and returned to where the disciples were; they were asleep, "Simon, are you sleeping? What, could you not stay alert for one hour with me?" He asked.

"Stay alert, praying, so you will not go through temptation; the Spirit is in fact truly willing, though the flesh is weak," Jesus told him.

Once more, Jesus went a short distance to pray, "My Father, this cup, if it cannot depart from me except I drink it, then may your desire be done." He said.

Returning to the three he had asked to watch; they had fallen asleep again; they got up but were drowsy and did not know what to say.

A third time Jesus left them, went and repeated his prayer.

When he returned to where his disciples were, he spoke to them, "Continue to sleep and take your rest now. I have prayed enough. Jesus told them.

The disciples were wide awake now, and Jesus continued, "Look, here is the time; now the Son of Man is delivered into the control of sinners.

Stand up now; we will leave; notice that the one who hands me over is near."

THE ARRESTING PARTY ARRIVES WITH JUDAS.

The betrayer Judas knew the place since Jesus and his disciples regularly met there. Judas, however, not being sure if they were still in the upper room where the dinner was eaten, so after going there to find Jesus, this garden was the likely location.

Judas arrived there with a detachment of soldiers and officers from the Chief Priests and other conspirators carrying lanterns, torches, and weapons.

So at the same time as Jesus was speaking, Judas approached with many hurriedly assembled men from the Temple guards, the High Priest's men, and some Roman soldiers.

Jesus, who was in control of the timing and events, stepped forward of his disciples, "who are you looking for?" He asks them, commanding an instant silence.

"Jesus of Nazareth," They answered.

"I AM, he," Jesus declared.

Judas was standing with them. But when Jesus told them, "I AM, he," they all went backward sharply, falling to the ground, stumbling over each other.

Jesus waited when they had collected themselves; then, he repeated his question, "Who are you looking for?"

"Jesus of Nazareth," They replied.

"I have told you I Am. So then, if you are seeking me, allow these others to go on their way," Jesus commanded them, fulfilling the words of his earlier prayer. "I lost none of those that you gave me."

Jesus waited while they gained some courage and composure; they had a previously arranged signal, given by Judas, where he had told them. "I will kiss the one who you are to detain. Grab him, and then lead him away safely."

Although Jesus had already identified himself and in doing so secured the safety of his followers.

The band of men charged with arresting him was paralyzed with fear. Judas stepping forward, approached Jesus, "Greetings, Rabbi!" He said and kissed him as identification. Though the signal was now worthless, and Jesus had protected him also, giving him still yet another chance of a way out.

"What is your purpose here, Judas? Do you think to deceive the Son of Man with a kiss?" Jesus asks him.

Psalm 55:20, *He has put out his hands against such as be at peace with him: he has broken his covenant.*

The others of the arresting party gained some courage from Judas's action then approached Jesus to grab him.

The disciples, who were all surrounding Jesus, saw the men move forward, called out, "Lord, shall we strike with the sword?"

This shout galvanized Simon Peter into action. He snatched the sword being carried, taking the opportunity against the stunned arresting party, and slashed at the head servant of the High Priest, cutting off his right ear. The servant's name was Malchus.

Jesus turned his attention to him, "Put back your sword into its place since all those who take the sword will also die by the sword." Jesus commanded, warning Peter, telling him this action would bring him certain death.

"Or do you somehow imagine that even now, I cannot ask my Father, and he would immediately send to me above twelve legions of Angels?

Then how would it fulfill Scriptures that say it must be so?

The cup given to me by my Father, Shall I indeed not drink it?" Jesus inquired, letting them know he was still in complete control of all that was happening.

Jesus turned his attention to the arresting party, "I will at least do this," he told them, then, touching Malchus' ear, Jesus healed him.

Jesus spoke sharply to the leaders lurking in the relative safety back of the enormous band of men. "Have you arrived to seize me as you would against a common bandit, bringing swords and sticks?

I sat daily there in the Temple teaching openly, yet you did not arrest me. (*Common bandit; would be 'robbers,' the term the Romans used for insurrections. While the 'sticks' were fighting staffs used by the temple Guards. The swords would have belonged to the Roman soldiers, the only ones who were permitted to bear arms.*)

However, this hour is yours, in accord with the power of darkness." He said, berating them for their barefaced cowardice.

These things all fulfilled the Scriptures written by the Prophets. Then the disciples all ran off and left him. (*Zechariah 13:7: "Awake, O sword, against my shepherd, also against the man that Man, My Associate, the Lord of hosts says: Smite the shepherd, and scattered the sheep: and I will also turn my hand upon the little ones."*)

As the disciples all escaped in various directions, a young man had been following the guards and others in the arresting party from the house where the dinner was held, after they had arrived at the home as the obvious first place to find Jesus.

The hope was to warn Jesus or the disciples. And not having time to dress, he threw a linen cloth around himself, which was his only clothing.

Some men in the party tried to grab hold of him; he left the linen cloth as they held on to it, escaping from them naked.

So this armed unit comprised the Roman officer and the officers of the Chief Priests and Leaders, seized and after securely binding Jesus, led him first to the palace of Annas, Caiaphas father-in-law. However, Caiaphas was the actual High Priest.

The entire family had wielded significant power through their wealth for some sixty years, and Annas was at the top of the Empire. *(The Romans had appointed Caiaphas to the position, but Annas maintained all the power and influence.)*

Caiaphas had earlier advised the leaders that it was practical that one man should die for the people.

The High Priest questioned Jesus relating to his disciples and his teaching.

"I spoke to all openly. I was always teaching in synagogues and in the Temple where The Chief Priests and Leaders met, where I said nothing in secret.

Why are you asking me? Ask those here who have heard me what I have said to them. See, these here know the things which I said." Jesus told him, correcting him on the point of law, as it did not require him to give evidence against himself.

After saying this, an officer standing near hit Jesus with his hand in a flagrant illegal move, "Is that how you answer the High Priest?" He spoke with a castigating snarled.

Jesus addressed him, "Have I said something evil, then give evidence of the evil; however, if I speak well, why then do you strike me?" He queried.

They sent Jesus bound from Annas to Caiaphas, the High Priest. Annas shared the High Priest's palace with Caiaphas, the two residences separated merely by a courtyard.

His captors led him to the High Priest Caiaphas, where some Scribes and the elders assembled and waited. This was not all the Sanhedrin (*the Great Court*).

Being an illegal night trial, only a select number could hurriedly be convened for this, those with particular vested interests of their money and power. However, present among them were followers of Jesus.

Of his disciples, Simon Peter quietly followed Jesus, albeit somewhat of a distance, as did Joseph but more boldly, continuing right into the High Priest's palace. Joseph could enter the residence through his well-known connections; he sat with the officers to see the outcome.

The Chief Priests, along with all the elders, including the gathered council, had a massive problem of evidence because the events had been sudden, and they had not expected to have the opportunity so soon.

To have the outward show of any semblance of a trial, they looked for any testimony, regardless of how false, because they needed and wanted him dead.

They could find none. Even though many false witnesses spoke up, unfortunately for the conspirators, no two could agree. (*From the Scriptures in Deuteronomy 17:6, there is always a requirement of two or three witnesses to establish any matter*).

Eventually, two men spoke, saying, "We remember hearing this man say, 'I can destroy the Temple of God which was made by hands. And in just three days, I will build another Temple made without hands.'" They both gave a variation of this allegation.

However, each of the witnesses did not entirely agree with the other.

Caiaphas, the High Priest, getting impatient and frustrated with the lack of progress, stood up and spoke, "Have you no answer to this? What are all these things that they testify against you?" He asks Jesus directly.

However, Jesus remained perfectly calm and answered nothing.

This infuriated Caiaphas, frustrating him more. "I adjure you by the name of the living God, that you tell us whether you are the Messiah, the Son of God, The Son of the Blessed?" The High Priest asks Jesus, resorting to using God as an oath.

(*He is cleverly invoking a law from Leviticus 5:1 (KJV) 'And if a soul sin, and hear the voice of swearing, and is a witness, whether he have seen or known of it. If he does not utter it, then he will bear his iniquity.'*

Requiring a person to speak up after an oath charges them if the person then remains silent, they are then by default judged to be guilty).

"You have already said it. Even so, I AM, and tell you, after this, you will see the Son of Man sitting down at the right hand of power (*the Almighty God*), and coming on the clouds of the heavens." Jesus replied, quoting two separate 'momentous' Messianic Scriptures, one from the Prophet Daniel, where he wrote his picture of Israel's Messiah in the seventh chapter.

And importantly for the status of the High Priest, the prophecy of the Messiah from the hundred and tenth Psalm of King David, which says several essential things pertinent to the situation: the first two verses, "The Lord said unto my Lord, Sit you at my right hand, until I make your enemies your footstool.

The Lord will send out 'the rod of your strength' out of Zion: rule, you in the middle of your enemies." Then importantly, it continues with,

"The Lord has sworn, and will not repent, you are a priest forever after the order of Melchizedek."

Then, in what was a brazenly illegal move, the High Priest tore his clothing (*Completely and expressly forbidden for Priests: in Leviticus 21:10*). This was a calculated attempt to impress the others with the gravity of the situation. Yet, in reality, he displayed his case's weakness.

And this act was severe enough to bring a death sentence upon his head.

> (*Leviticus 10:6. And Moses said unto Aaron, and unto Eleazar and unto Ithamar, his sons. Uncover not your heads; neither rend your clothes lest you die and lest wrath come upon all the people*).

"He has spoken this blasphemy! Why then do we need any more witnesses? Consider this evidence, now that you have heard his blasphemy. What do you think?" He asked, knowing he dared not risk letting any more witnesses speak.

Caiaphas was knowingly taking an enormous gamble (*In the tearing of his priestly garment. This effectively ended his role as High Priest and permanently and mortally damaged the office, which is the implication of the Psalm that Jesus quoted.*

The office of High Priest was by this time not much more than a political tool of the Romans, rather than being taken hereditarily from Aaron's lineage as was the requirement in Israel.

By tearing the High Priest garment, the office ended that very moment, passing from the Aaronic line to the Messiah. Who being from the order of Melchizedek is therefore eternal!

Caiaphas instinctively knew how much more he had to fear from this one man standing before him than any of the others).

*Note: In less than a generation פנחס בן שמואל Pinhas ben Shmuel became the last High Priest to serve in this the Second Temple in Jerusalem. They had reduced the office to being chosen by Lots.

"Yes, he is worthy of death!" They rejoined.

Then they spat on him even in his face, also beating him, slapping him with their hands and fists.

They used a blindfold to cover his face and then struck him on his face. "Prophesy then, who is it that struck you?" They said, mocking him.

They spoke many other vile and insulting things against Jesus.

While this was happening inside, outside was Simon Peter, who followed the bound Jesus at a distance, standing at the door to the house.

Joseph, a disciple who was known to the High Priest household and had entered with the arresting party to the inner grounds of the residence, Joseph went back outside and spoke to the young woman who was the doorkeeper enabling him to bring Peter inside.

This servant girl of the household of the High Priest, who was the doorkeeper, carefully stared at and studied Peter, and then she spoke, "You were also with Jesus, the Galilean! You are one of this man's disciples also, are you not?" She demanded firmly. Using the term 'Galilean' by her intimated that trouble was expected.

Many people were crowding around within the courtyard; Peter denied what she said, "No, I am not. And I do not know what you are talking about." Peter replied, simply intending to brush her off, and then walking away, went out to stand on the porch. At that moment, the rooster crowed.

Though people were intensely interested in all the tumultuous events and waited excitedly for the news, they eventually tired. They made there a coal fire in the middle of the courtyard.

Having stood a considerable length of time, the servants and officers sat down together around the fire to keep warm as the dawn was approaching, and it was now quite cold.

They were all there warming themselves.

Simon Peter, who had been standing, eventually went over and sat down with them, warming himself.

Another servant girl could see him in the fire's light as he sat there, and she spoke as she stared at him, "You, are you not also one of his disciples? You are!"

"This is one of them." She stated.

This time Peter was more forceful with her; he denied it using an oath to strengthen his words, "woman, I am not. I do not know the man!" He exclaimed.

This succeeded in quietening things down for about an hour.

Then one of the High Priest's servants, this time it was a relative of Malchus whose ear Peter had cut off earlier.

He assertively questioned, "Did I not see you with him in the garden? Of course, you are also one of them because of your dialect; we do know that you are a Galilean!" The servant stated adamantly.

Peter then began to curse and swear, as he remembered and reverted to his fisherman roots, "Man, I know not what you are talking about! I do not even know the man!" He managed to say in ordinary words between the swearing bouts.

And then instantly, while he was still speaking, a rooster crowed for the second time.

At this moment, they were leading Jesus out to take him over to the hurriedly assembled leaders. So the Lord turned and looked directly at Peter.

Peter remembered what Jesus had told him. "Before the rooster even crows twice, you will have denied me three times."

Peter left and went out of the residence, and he wept with bitter remorse.

A little while earlier before this, as the day was dawning, after arranging for a majority of the Sanhedrin to assemble in the Temple quarters. The people with Caiaphas had to wait until they received the message that they were now all together.

Rome had removed all consent for capital punishment from the council. Plus, lacking the full backing of the Sanhedrin, no High Priest had any power to order a person's death. Caiaphas's only alternative was to strive to transfer the entire affair to Pilate, Rome's representative.

The Chief Priests had joined with the lawyers. They now desperately needed to find a way to kill Jesus and would satisfy the Romans. Still, they had a big problem with this since their charge of blasphemy was meaningless to the Romans.

So with a new plan set in motion, they took him to the waiting members of the council seeking how to make a case out of Jesus' claim as Messiah, which could be considered a king. (*That would challenge Rome's authority and rule*).

They began questioning Jesus, who had now been awake for twenty-four hours and beaten by their officers, "If you are the Christ, tell us." They ask repeatedly.

"You will not accept, even if I were to tell you. And you will in no way answer me should I also ask you questions, neither will you be releasing me.

From this time onward, the Son of Man will be seated at the right hand of the power of God." Jesus told them, predicting their course of action and the outcome.

"Are you then the Son of God?" They asked, now with added interest.

"It is because I AM why you are saying it." He answered plainly.

"Why do we need the evidence of any more witnesses? Since we for ourselves have heard it from his own mouth!" They said.

Now quite satisfied with themselves, they all stood and had Jesus taken to the Roman Governor Pontius Pilate.

JUDAS ATTEMPTS TO RETURN THE MONEY TO HIS CO-CONSPIRATORS.

Judas, who was watching in the background, realizing that these men condemned Jesus without just cause, felt remorse and returned to the Chief Priests and elders with the thirty pieces of silver. "I have sinned and wronged an innocent man, handing him over to you to be killed," Judas told them. And in doing so, he was unknowingly the first to pronounce Jesus innocent.

"What do we care about that? That problem is your affair." They answered.

Judas hurled down the pieces of silver in the sanctuary and departed. He went away, and later it was eventually reported that he killed himself.

"Since this money is the price of blood, it is therefore not legal for us to put them back in the treasury." The Chief Priests said, taking up the pieces of silver.

After hurried consultation among themselves, they purchased a piece of land with the money. Much later, they secured a plot known as the potter's field. Which purpose was to be used for the burial of strangers!

This was the realization of the words of the Prophet Jeremiah, "The people of Israel took silver coins in all thirty pieces. That was the value of him, the price they chose to pay for his life. Giving them in exchange for the potter's field, as the Lord directed."

On the other hand, Judas also purchased a field with the money he had taken while he was in charge of the funds. Here then, is an overall summary of the occurrences that happened to him after this time.

He acquired a field, which became known to everyone who lived in Jerusalem. In their language, that field was called, 'Akeldama,' that is, 'the field of blood,' to this day.

Later Judas took his own life in the same field that he had purchased.

THE PLOT TO USE PILATE TO CARRY OUT THEIR PLAN.

In the early morning, they took Jesus from the place where the council gathered to the Praetorium for a trial before the Governor, Pontius Pilate.

The Chief Priests would not themselves enter the Praetorium. Considered the home of a Gentile, it would cause them to be defiled, therefore not taking part in the Passover.

As a result, this forced Pilate to go out to speak with them, "What allegations do you have against this man to bring him here?" He asked with rising disapproval.

"This man, if he were not an evildoer, we would not have handed him over to you." They answered with frustration, forgetting not to revert to religious terminology.

"You take him and have him judged following your laws," Pilate said dismissively.

"We cannot lawfully put anyone to death," They said with deepening frustration, stipulating the sentence before the trial.

This vindicated the prophetic words of Jesus, showing the type of death he would die. (*The punishment for the death penalty not deemed lawful under Israel's covenant, which consisted of hanging or stoning, instead a Roman execution would be one of torture*).

The frustration boiled over at this point; they started shouting various allegations against Jesus. "We have discovered this man corrupting the nation; he was even forbidding the paying of taxes to Caesar and declaring he is the Messiah, a king." They lied, trying to regain the initiative, with something that was against Roman rule. (*The act of turning over the money tables and not allowing any trade in the Temple hurt the leader's pocket, as they were using it to gain vast fortunes. However, paying taxes was still their responsibility, and the Governor frankly knew if 'taxes' were being paid or not*).

Because of them saying Jesus claimed himself a King, Pilate, now having something to investigate, returned to the Praetorium and then instructed for Jesus to be bought.

When Jesus was led in and was standing in front of the Governor, he wanted clarification, "Then are you, in fact, the king of the Jews?" Pilate asked him.

"It is as you are saying." Jesus replied, "Are you saying this by yourself, or was it that others have told you about me?"

"I am not a Jew, now am I," Pilate asked?

"Your own nation and the Chief Priests are the ones that brought you to me. Hence tell me, what is it you have done?"

Jesus dealt with the only part of the allegations that were near the truth, "My kingdom is not any kingdom of this world." Jesus answered, "If indeed my kingdom were of this world, in that case, my servants would fight so that I would not be placed under the power of the Chief Priest. Except at present, my kingdom is not from here."

"So then, you are, in reality, a king?" Pilate then asked tentatively, more of a statement than a question, clearly understanding that there were no solid grounds for the allegations.

"You are saying I am a king!" Jesus answered, "This is the reason that I have been born and is the reason I came into the world, so I should give evidence of the truth. Each person who belongs to the truth listens to my voice." He added, ensuring that Pilate had to face the truth about himself and his actions.

"Truth, what then is truth?" Pilate asked rhetorically been embarrassed by Jesus' statement, confirming now what he suspected, that this is more a religious than a political issue.

After this exclamation, he went back out and addressed the Chief Priests, the lawyers, and the others making up the crowds. "I can find no foundation for any charge against him." He pronounced.

This made them all the more desperate, so they began shouting many accusations of many things about Jesus (*although during all of that time, Jesus remained silent*).

Then Pilate again returned to question him, "Do you not have an answer to any of this? Do you not hear just how many things they are saying against you?" He asks Jesus with mounting frustration, knowing he was not making any real progress.

Jesus simply remained silent. Saying nothing extra to what he had already said, he had answered to the only actual allegation and did not need to say anything further. This much surprised Pilate, the Roman Governor; he was amazed.

Meanwhile, the Chief Priests and the elders along with Temple guards continued to shout, "He has been stirring up all the people, teaching right the way through all Judea. Beginning from Galilee continuing even here in Jerusalem," They shouted, among other things. Knowing the Galileans were branded as rebels and troublemakers. They were hoping to find something that would be emotive for Pilate.

Although only the mention of Galilee caught Pilate's attention, he then inquired if the man was a Galilean.

Then having discovered that Jesus was under the jurisdiction of Herod, and as this was primarily about Jesus being accused of being King of the Jews, Pilate sent him over to Herod. So that Herod could look him over and send back and report of his opinion. The father of Herod had been placed on the throne by Roman patronage. And their entire family, who were not Jews but Idumaean by race, had been vicious in the ruthless removal of potential rivals and opponents.

It was habitual for Herod to be in Jerusalem for safety reasons and to be residing in the city during the main days of the feast (*Due to the strength of the numbers of troops that would be stationed in the capital*).

He was delighted when Jesus arrived at his palace. He had heard about all the things that had been done by Jesus.

He wanted to see him with the idea that he would finally be able to see a miracle from Jesus, so while the Chief Priests and the Scribes stood there and was heatedly and intensely condemning him.

Herod tried unsuccessfully to question Jesus himself with much talking; during all of this. Jesus simply remained silent.

This gave courage to Herod, along with his soldiers. So they eventually resorted to beating him. And then, in the act of mockery, they draped on him a purple robe to signify royalty, a cloak for a king. After this, they sent him back to Pilate the Governor.

Herod and Pilate, who had been adversaries before and up to this point, developed into friends with each other over this incident from that day.

With Jesus' arrival back to the Praetorium, Pilate stood before the Chief Priests, the rulers, and the people, addressing them. "You have brought here to me this man that you consider someone who leads the people astray. As you can see, I have examined him and can see no basis for a charge against this man regarding those things which you are accusing him.

And neither has Herod because, as you see, I had sent him to Herod to examine him.

He was returned to me; it is clear he has done nothing worthy of death."

"So given that, I will then have him whipped then released." He announced.

Pilate could easily discern and know that it was only because of envy they had brought these charges, as a man of politics.

Pilate had a message delivered to him at this time. This message came from his wife, presently as he was sitting on the judgment seat. The news having an urgent tone, said, "That man is righteous. Have nothing to do with him. Since I have endured and suffered through many diverse things in a dream this day, on account of him."

So Pilate then consented to Jesus being beaten by the soldiers. This was the most severe of three beatings that he had now endured in the one night and two days that he had been awake, arrested, and mistreated.

The soldiers, now released from constraint, twisted thorns into a crown, placing it on his head, and dressed him in a purple garment. "Hail, to the King of the Jews!" They continuously chanted, as they also slapped him repeatedly.

Then Pilate went out again to address the waiting mob, "See, I bring him out to you, that you may know I find no basis for a charge against him." He said, hoping to get the upper hand finally.

Jesus then walked out, wearing the crown of thorns on his head and the purple garment over his shoulders. (*Zechariah 3:8: 'because they are men wondered at since, see, I will bring into view my servant the BRANCH'*).

"Behold, the man!" Pilate exclaimed with surprise when Jesus walked out unaided and with natural regal dignity. "Take a look at your King!" He called out to the crowd, not realizing that he had just used the very title given to the Messiah in Prophecy.

(Zechariah 6:12 (AMP) *Then say to Joshua, 'Thus says the Lord of hosts, "Behold (look, keep in sight, watch), a Man (Messiah) whose name is Branch, for He shall branch out from His place*

***(Israel, the Davidic line); and He shall build the [ultimate] Temple of the Lord.*)**

This shocked the Chief Priests and the officers, and when they saw him emerge, they started shouting the prearranged words, "Crucify! Crucify! Away with him! Away with him! Crucify him!"

Pilate spoke over their raised voices, "Then shall I crucify your King?" He asked, "You take him yourselves, and you crucify him since I can find no basis for a charge against him."

By this, to the Chief Priests and Leaders, it appeared that Pilate was seeking to release him there and then. So they shouted out. "If you were to release this man, you are not a friend to Caesar! Any man making himself a king speaks against Caesar." They called to the Governor, knowing politically this was substantial leverage to use.

"We do not have any king but Caesar!" They shouted outrageously, not only claiming a foreign king in desperation but as a solemn pledge to be subjected to the authority of Pilate from then on.

[The Emperor had given both Herod and then much later Pilate the title of high esteem 'Friend of Caesar.' (*Amicus Caesaris)*

He certainly knew that it was the end of his career when Augustus stripped this title from Herod.

Herod the Great had been a powerful and respected eastern ally of Rome's growing Empire for many decades.

He built and named an ambitious new city to honor his patron Octavian Caesar Augustus to enhance this alliance. Herod shrewdly had a grand opening of his newly built port of Caesarea. So that trade of luxury goods from the east, destined for Rome, would have to pass through the port, enhancing its status.

Political intrigue and the changing power structure in Rome; caused Herod to be tricked into an ill-advised military campaign across the Jordan region. In this failure, he had made some miscalculations that did not go well with Rome.

His title, 'Friend of Caesar,' had then been stripped from Herod, losing the last of the independence for the Jews, having won this at a high cost and courage against the Greeks by the Maccabien's nearly two hundred years before.

Rome then changed the policy and appointed Governors to collect taxes from the people towards the upkeep of the relatively small occupying Roman army.

Pilate came to Jerusalem with the backing of his army friend Marcus Agrippa before he died. Marcus was at one point the commander of the Praetorian Guard for Caesar.

However, it was through Sejanus that Pilates's position was confirmed.

Tiberius had granted considerable authority to Sejanus concerning such matters, including any provincial governorship.

Sejanus proved to be an exceptional administrator for almost a decade; by 29-30, his hands were firmly on the levers of power in Rome. Rising and becoming the second most powerful man in the Empire, even marrying Caesar's daughter.

Sejanus, Pilate's sponsor, and protector had been executed in the year 31 AD. Just over a year or two previous, Caesar had discovered details of a plot to overthrow him. He eventually narrowed the suspects, executing Sejanus as its leader, then purging any friends or supporters connected to power in and around Rome.

In Pilate's position, any immediate report to Rome stating that he was not 'Caesar's friend' would carry considerable risk, regardless of his particular opinion of Jesus].

There was a practice of the Romans, the releasing of some prisoners, which had its roots in their Saturnalia celebration. They had introduced this as an act of concession to the Jewish people during feast times. This had started sometime before, long enough to have become a tradition.

Then Pilate, in an unusual move, reminded them of it. "According to your custom, I should discharge someone to you at the time of Passover. So then for the discharge, this year, do you want me to release to you the King of the Jews?" He asked, still seeking a way out of this.

The Chief Priests and the elders had been busy with the crowd persuading the people to ask for a known criminal named Barabbas and to have Jesus killed.

Then they all shouted again, "No, not this man, Away with this man! Give to us instead, Barabbas!" They yelled.

"Of the two, which do you want me to release to you?" Pilate again asked. "What then shall I do with Jesus, whom you call Messiah, the King of the Jews?"

"Let him be crucified! Crucify him!" The crowd all shouted repeatedly.

When he heard all of this, Pilate brought Jesus further out to a place called "The Pavement" (Gabbatha in Hebrew), and then Pilate sat down on the judgment seat that was there.

He could see that nothing had been gained by his efforts. Instead, this was likely to start a disturbance, as more people were gathering.

Pilate took water, and in a symbolic move, which was borrowed from the rituals of the Pharisees! Washed his hands in the view of the crowd, "I am totally innocent of the blood of this righteous person," Pilate said, remembering his wife's note; "Go yourself, and you see to it!" He pronounced, thoroughly disgusted by having his efforts blocked, by these angry men.

The people all responded with, "May his blood be on all of us, also on our children!" They said, knowing that they had won.

They thought with hardened hearts. They were under no risk in saying this, thinking they would be rid of an undesirable and doing a noble thing. Yet God's mercy had provided for them and their children.

(Deuteronomy 24:16 (ESV) *Fathers shall not be put to death because of their children, nor shall children be put to death because of their fathers. Each one shall be put to death for his own sin*.)

[Every part of the arrest and trial of Jesus was illegal!
The following are some points that catalog some key factors.
The law was clear stating, no person's life, liberty, or reputation, could be endangered by the malice of any who has admitted himself a criminal.

By taking a bribe from the ones who were the judges in the trial was evidence showing Judas to be guilty of a criminal offense.

Any sort of bribery from a member among the judges disqualifies that member from partaking in the court.

Those involved in Jesus' arrest comprised the priests and elders, his judges, and the very ones who bribed Judas.

As an accomplice of Jesus, any testimony of Judas was not permitted; consequently, he could not accuse or be a witness against him. (Which is why after the betrayal, he was not bought to the assembled Synhedrion).

Moreover, the arrest of Jesus was secretly by night; and not on the formal charge of any crime. No actual charges were presented; they showed no permits for his arrest, no statement of what He had done. They just simply bound Him (which was not legal to do) and led Him away.

Only during the daytime can criminal cases be acted upon by the various courts; the first is from the ending of the morning service till noon by the Lesser Synhedrion, then by the Great Synhedrion till evening.

A private individual, Annas (Caiaphas' father-in-law and the former high priest), could not question the accused.

Only during daylight did the law allow such an investigation; night meetings were strictly not permitted. Charges were to be offered by witnesses, yet the Sanhedrin illegally brought charges and produced false witnesses.

They did not allow courts of justice in Israel to hold sessions on the Sabbath or any of the seven Biblical holidays.

So in capital crime cases, no trial could continue on the Sabbath or holiday and could not begin on Friday or the day before any holiday. It was unlawful to adjourn such cases longer than overnight or continue on Sabbaths or holidays.

It was unlawful to bind a prisoner before the sentence. Capital trials had to last over several days to allow for ample consideration on the judge's part.

The accused must have an "advocate in court" to defend him. Jesus had none. Also, any person charged must have sufficient time to defend himself from any accusations.

When Caiaphas accused Jesus of blasphemy, he illegally ripped his clothes.

When deciding on a capital crime, if the decision is unanimous against the accused, they should actually throw out the case. The Judges did not invite any members of the Sanhedrin who may have defended Jesus to this court session. As the court found unanimously against Jesus, He then should have been set free.

Instead of the trial being held at the proper court, they first gathered at Caiaphas' palace. Early the following day, part of the Sanhedrin convened at the correct place to make things look legal.

The judges may not assault the accused. (Or permit such).

The court did not prove Jesus' testimony to be blasphemous.

Witnesses had to be the ones who cast the first stones at the criminal. With two or three of the witnesses agreeing, they would receive the same punishment if they were untruthful.

When the Sanhedrin took Jesus before Pilate hoping for a death sentence to be carried out according to Roman law, they changed the charges from blasphemy to treason, illegal under the Law of Moses.]

So then, in a desire to please the crowd, Pilate decreed that what they asked for should be done.

He released to them Barabbas (*Whose name means son of the father, from Bar, for son and Abba, for father*). They had thrown him into prison for the double charge of revolt against the Romans and murder.

Barabbas, whom they had asked for, was released; Jesus, however, was handed over to their will. Jesus had been flogged, and now he was handed over to be executed by the torture of Crucifixion.

Consequently, they led Jesus away.

(Ezekiel 12:11, *Say, I am your sign: like as I have done, so shall it be done unto them: they will remove and go into captivity*).

They led Jesus out, carrying the heavy Crosspiece (*patibulum*), going through Jerusalem over to the Joppa Gate.

And as they exited the gate, the soldiers found a man, a stranger coming into the city to take part in the Passover celebration.

This was Simon from the community of dispersed Jews in the city of Cyrenaica in Northern Africa. Simon was the father of Alexander, later known to the followers of Jesus. (*Cyrene, with a sizeable Jewish population, dispersed and was a flourishing city in the north of Africa since the time of Pharaoh Ptolemy I. The Cyrenians had synagogues in Jerusalem*).

The soldiers conscripted Simon to assist in carrying the Crosspiece, from that point outside the gate, going with them to Calvary. Both men had to take the heavy Crosspiece, with Jesus at the front, as they slowly walked up the hill.

In this slow procession, they were followed by growing numbers of people who had gotten news of what was happening to Jesus. There were groups of women following as they wept and grieved for him.

At this moment, Jesus, with pure compassion, turned to them as he walked and addressed them. "You Daughters of Jerusalem, weep not on my behalf, though you should cry on behalf of yourselves and your children.

Because there are days coming where it will be said that those women who are childless and cannot have babies are certainly fortunate. The wombs that have not produced a child and the breasts that have never nursed is a blessing.'

People will plead with the mountains, 'Fall on us,' and, 'Cover us.' they will say to the hills.

Since they can do these things when the tree is alive and green, what will be done to the dry one?" Jesus told them as a warning of dire things to come within their generation.

> Hosea 10:8: (KJ21) **The high places also of Aven, the sin of Israel, shall be destroyed. The thorn and the thistle shall come up on their altars; and they shall say to the mountains, "Cover us!" and to the hills, "Fall on us!"**

> Isaiah 32:13-14 *unto the land of my people, will come up thorns and weeds; yes, unto all the houses of joy in the joyous city: Because the palaces will be abandoned; the crowds of the city will be missing; the forts and towers will be for dens for ever, a joy of wild donkeys, a pasture of animals...*

CHAPTER TWENTY ONE

COMPLETE AND PERFECT FULFILLMENT: AS WELL AS ALL DEBTS PAID.

They arrived at a place on the hill called Calvary (*Golgotha in Hebrew*); this was "The place of a skull." They also led there two criminals to be executed with him.

The soldiers attempted to give Jesus some sour wine mixed with bitter gall or Myrrh to drink. However, the instant he tasted it, he refused and did not drink any.

It was mid-morning, at nine o'clock, when they nailed Jesus to the cross and tortured him by Crucifixion.

Jesus' death fulfilled the Scripture, which he had quoted from the Prophet Isaiah; the previous evening, the Scripture predicted, "He was counted with transgressors."

When they crucified him, they placed him in the middle of two robbers, placing one on his right hand and the other on the left.

As the people were in the act of doing this, He prayed for them with amazing love and genuine tenderness. "Father, forgive them," Jesus pleaded, "Because they do not know what they are doing."

After those soldiers took the clothing of Jesus, each of the four soldiers received one item, but when they came to the coat, it was woven in one piece and without a seam (*The Greek, 'chiton,' Hebrew, 'kethoneth,' chiton is the standard word for the undergarment of a priest.*) "Let us not tear it, but decide by casting lots which of us will own it," Said the soldiers to each other.

This was the fulfillment of the Scriptures from the Psalms. Where the Prophet said, "*My garments were parted among them because of my coat; they cast lots*" (Psalm 22).

As a result, the soldiers did these things, and they sat there watching him.

Up over the head of Jesus, a title was written by Pilate, which was placed on the cross. 'THIS IS JESUS OF NAZARETH, THE KING OF THE JEWS.'

HaYehudim v Melech HaNazarel Jesus, this comprised the accusation made against him.

They reached the acrostic meaning through (*Spelling out a word, or phrase, using the first or last letters*). Of which the Jews love so much. This is what it read, (י "Y" Yodh ה "H" He ו Waw ה He). From the right to the left as it was read, spells, YHWH. (I AM).

And because the place where Jesus was crucified was near the City, as a result, many Jews read this title; Pilate wrote it in Hebrew, Latin, and Greek.

The Chief Priests of the Jews, as a result, went complaining to Pilate and said. "Do not write, 'The King of the Jews,' but instead, 'he said that I am the King of the Jews'" (*Knowing that if he did that, it would remove the acrostic meaning, which all could see.*)

"What it is I have written, I have written, and it will forever remain written," Pilate answered, with purposeful finality. Letting them know that the subject is closed.

[He may have lost the battle of will with the neat political trap these men had set for him.

Pilate was smart enough to understand. Political underlings could cunningly outmaneuver all rulers and authority figures. Who always gambled on the fact that they had less to lose! This was accomplished by placing those above them on the horns of a dilemma. While at the same time, the subordinates would promise unending loyalty.

Pilate was vindictive enough to ensure that by knowingly writing this with his own hand, he accordingly guaranteed that he would have the last word].

MANY OF THE PEOPLE OF JERUSALEM STOOD WATCHING.

Some of those passing by were cursing him, and wagging their heads, as they hurled insults, "Ha! You who could destroy the Temple, rebuilding it again in three days, now save yourself! If you in truth are the Son of God, then come down from the cross!" They said, among many things.

Similarly, the Chief Priests, along with the Scribes, Pharisees, and the elders, also mocked. "He could save others, yet he cannot save himself. Let see him now come down from the cross; if he is the King of Israel, then we will believe in him.

He trusts in God, so if God desires him, let him set him free now, since he stated, 'I am the Son of God.

Let him save himself as he saved others. If this is God's chosen one, the Messiah!" They gloated. Not realizing that they were 'inducing on themselves,' the prophecy of *Psalm 22:8*. They jeered, "He trusted on the LORD that he would deliver him: let him deliver him, seeing that he has delighted in him."

(Psalm 91:14 (NKJV) *Because he has set his love upon me, therefore will I deliver him: I will set him on high because he has known my name*).

The soldiers mocked him also, coming to him and offering him vinegar, "Save yourself then if you are the King of the Jews!" They jeered.

Psalm 22:6 (CEB) *But I'm just a worm, less than human; insulted by one person, despised by another*. (The word used for worm here is Tola'ath, meaning 'Crimson worm' / 'Scarlet worm.')

Isaiah 1:18 (NKJV) *"Come now, and let us reason together,"* *Says the Lord, "Though your sins are like scarlet, They shall be as white as snow;* *Though they are red like crimson, They shall be as wool.*

Tola'at Shani (Heb. שָׁנִי תּוֹלַעַת), i.e., worm yielding a dye, called Shani, tola, Karmil, zehorit, obtained from the body of the "crimson worm" (carmine), or kermes dye.

The Hebrew word 'Tola' carries the meaning, worm, also scarlet, a color. They used the scarlet dye from this worm for the curtains of the Tabernacle.

A gloriously beautiful, fast red dye which is used in dyeing the curtains of the Tabernacle and the high priests' garments (Exodus 26:1.)

They would make Royal robes in scarlet, also, for purification rites of a leper (Leviticus 14:4–6).

This worm has a unique life cycle that allows a rebirth, going from crimson to white in three days.

Genesis 38:28 (EXB) *While she was giving birth [in labor], one baby put his hand out. The nurse [midwife] tied a red [crimson] string on his hand and said, "This baby came out first."* (*The Lineage of Judah.*)

The robbers also crucified with him had their say. As one cast on him the same insults and rebuked him, this criminal hanging on the cross insulted him with, "If you are the Messiah, then save yourself and us!" He mocked.

On the other hand, the other of the two cautioned him, "Do you not even fear God, seeing you are under the same conviction? He challenged.

And we without a doubt rightly, since we receive the appropriate reward for our deeds, however, this man has done nothing wrong."

"Lord, when you receive your Kingdom, remember me." He called to Jesus.

"I declare to you, without a doubt, you will be with me in Paradise today," Jesus replied to him.

Standing there by the cross at that moment was the mother of Jesus and two other women; one was Mary Magdalene, and the sister of his mother, Mary, the wife of Clopas.

Then Jesus, when he saw his mother, and John his disciple and a near relation, whom he loved standing there, he spoke to his mother, "Woman, see your son!"

Then to John, "See, your mother," He said, indicating that John should care for her.

So John took her away from the horrific scene to his own home from that hour.

As Jesus suffered all the agony of the cross from noon to three in the afternoon, there was 'a total darkness' covering the entire land for the complete three hours.

(Amos 8:9: (ASV) *And it shall come to pass in that day, saith the Lord Jehovah, that I will cause the sun to go down at noon, and I will darken the earth in the clear day*.)

At three o'clock during the afternoon, Jesus cried with a loud voice, "Eloi, Eloi, lama sabachthani?" He asked his father.

These words are Amharic and mean, "My God, my God, why have you forsaken me?"

Some people standing near the cross heard it and said, "This man is calling for Elijah."

At this point, Jesus, realizing that all things were now finished, spoke the words of the Psalm so it would fulfill the Scriptures, "I am thirsty." He said.

There was a pot of vinegar nearby, which prompted one of them to run to get a sponge, soaked it in the vinegar, placed it on a reed of hyssop, giving him to drink by holding it to his mouth.

Other people said. "Leave him, let him be. We will see if Elijah will come to save him and take him down."

After Jesus had taken some of the vinegar, he called out once more with a loud voice, "It is finished." Was the phrase he shouted (*Tetelestai*). Meaning 'Paid in full.'

It is a term a builder uses when he hands over the keys to a new building and says. 'Tetelestai, it is finished; I have done everything according to the plan; it is complete.' ('Tetelestai, it is finished; ultimately, I cannot add anything more to it. It is complete.'

The word Tetelestai was also written on official business documents or receipts in the Greek / Roman world of those times, showing that they had paid a bill in total).

In Hebrew, 'ka'lal' has the meaning to complete, perfect, make complete.

Then Jesus, shouting in a loud voice, "Father, into your hands, I commit my spirit!" He said, having said this, and bowing his head, yield up his Spirit, and breathed his last breath. (*Psalm 31:5 Into your hand, I commit my spirit: you have redeemed me, O Lord God of truth*).

(*On this day at 3 pm, they blew the Shofar from the Temple to sound the last sacrifice of the great day. All the people would stop for a few moments to reflect on the nature of sin and its need for atonement; at this precise moment, Jesus cried out, "It is finished!"*

He had kept the promise made long ago. He had paid the price for all sins in full.

God's promise to Abraham, which had been sealed with a covenant involving five animals, the blood of which He passed through in the form of a flame to make that unbreakable covenant.

Using the blood of a sheep, goat, cow, dove and a pigeon on that occasion set the pattern for the people of Israel to follow. They had followed the pattern for near two Millennia, sacrificing them as the perfect rehearsal.

Since the time of the First Temple built by Solomon, they sacrificed these animals daily at 9 am and would end at 3 pm. And on this day, they saw the total fulfillment of these rehearsals and would hence no longer be of necessity).

The sun was darkened, with the darkness spreading over the whole land.

At that moment, the earth quaked with such force that even some of the rocks were split.

In the Temple, the heavy veil separating the Holy of Holies was torn in two, with the tear starting from the top down to the bottom.

[Jeremiah 31:31 (CSB) **"Look, the days are coming"—this is the Lord's declaration—"when I will make a new covenant with the house of Israel and with the house of Judah."**]

(The Temple Veils was woven of seventy-two cords, each cord comprising twenty-four strands. This curtain was called the sacred curtain or 'Peroketh.'

Its length was 60 feet by 30 feet in width.

The thickness of it was many inches. Made of 72 squares sewn together, each one made of fine-twined linen into which twisted blue, purple, and scarlet threads were interwoven.

The remarkable figures of the cherubim and angelic beings were artful images of the highest order elegantly woven into the veil).

[The Shekinah Glory (*Shiloh*.) It was only present when the Ark of the Covenant was in the Holy of Holies, its correct place.

Previously, each time the Ark was not in the Temple, Ichabod was used.

The moment the veil was torn, it became evident to all who stood in the Holy Place or at the Incense Altar that the Most Holy Place was empty. The Ark of the Covenant or the Glory of God was not there. Ichabod was written upon the Temple for all the priests to see].

EVENTS SURROUNDING THE MOMENT OF DEATH: THEN THE BURIAL.

When the earth quaked so violently, splitting and opening many tombs, many of the saints who had died through the ages were raised bodily from the dead (*The Omer of the first fruits from the barley harvest, Leviticus 23:9-14*).

Then, after the resurrection of Jesus, they exited from the tombs, entered into the Holy City, appearing to many people there.

> (*Haggai 2:6 (CSB)* **For the Lord of Armies says this: "Once more, in a little while, I am going to shake the heavens and the earth, the sea and the dry land**.)

> (*Joel 3:16 (CSB)* **The Lord will roar from Zion and make his voice heard from Jerusalem; heaven and earth will shake.**
> **But the Lord will be a refuge for his people, a stronghold for the Israelites**.)

> (*Ezekiel 37:12-14* (CEB) **So now, prophesy and say to them, The Lord God proclaims: I'm opening your graves! I will raise you up from your graves, my people, and I will bring you to Israel's fertile land.**
> **You will know that I am the Lord, when I open your graves and raise you up from your graves, my people.**
> **I will put my breath in you, and you will live. I will plant you on your fertile land, and you will know that I am the Lord. I've spoken, and I will do it. This is what the Lord says.**")

At the time of Jesus' death, the soldiers assigned to watch and guard the ones executed, along with the centurion in charge, having witnessed how Jesus cried out loudly to his Father, then he breathed his final breath.

After witnessing the earthquake and all the other events surrounding his last hours, they became terrified. The centurion spoke of it.

This man was indeed the Son of God. This was, without doubt, a righteous man!" He exclaimed. (*In effect, his words gave God the glory*).

After witnessing all of what transpired, the crowds of people who watched the Crucifixion also went away mourning, with sadness and regret.

However, many of the people associated with Jesus, including the women who had followed from Galilee, ministering to him. All stood at a distance as they witnessed all these events.

Among the women who traveled up to the City with him. Were, the mother of James and John the sons of Zebedee. Mary of Magdalene, and Mary, the mother of James the less, Joses, and Salome, were among many other women who were present.

Because it was the Preparation Day, the Chief Priests and Leaders had already gone to Pilate, asking if the soldiers could break the legs of the executed men to hurry their deaths and also that they might be taken away before nightfall.

This was to prevent the bodies from remaining on the cross during the Sabbath (*Because it was one of two special Sabbaths, being the 'Feast of Uneven Bread,' and was the day that followed that Passover*).

Then the soldiers went to break the legs of those executed to increase the torture and hurry the death. So the legs of one criminal were broken and then the other; however, because Jesus was already dead when they stood below him by his cross, they did not break his legs.

However, one soldier pierced his side with his spear, seeing blood and water instantly running out of the deep wound.

(This evidence is from the testimony of John, who was an eyewitness to this event. He has given the actual facts so that others may know and believe what happened).

Because these things are all the fulfillment of Scriptures that predicted, "Psalm 34:20, All his bones will be kept intact, without a single one being broken."

Again another Scripture prophesied.

Zechariah 12:10 (NKJV) *And I will pour on the house of David and on the inhabitants of Jerusalem the Spirit of grace and supplication; then they will look on Me whom they pierced. Yes, they will mourn for Him as one mourns for his only son, and grieve for Him as one grieves for a firstborn.*

Joseph of Arimathaea was a wealthy and important member of the High Council, a good and righteous man who was a disciple of Jesus. He was longing and waiting for the Kingdom of God. Joseph was wary of The Chief Priests and other council Leaders and did not approve of their actions or methods.

Joseph went boldly to Pilate and requested the body of Jesus.

Because death by Crucifixion was a method of torture, which could last for several days! Pilate questioned whether Jesus had already died. And to be sure, he sends for the centurion, asking him how long he had been dead.

After getting all the facts of the death, Pilate decreed the body to be given over to Joseph.

Joseph took him down, wrapping him in a new linen cloth, with the help of Nicodemus, the other Council member who had visited Jesus under cover of the night several years before.

Nicodemus brought with him about seventy-five pounds weight of a mixture of Myrrh and Aloes to embalm the body.

(*Myrrh was many times more valuable than Gold or even the Spikenard that Jesus had previously been anointed with, as a King. One pound of Spikenard was about three hundred pence, and Myrrh was about ten times more expensive*).

The two men received the body of Jesus, wrapping it in wide strips of the clean new linen cloth soaked with the spices, as was the custom of the Jews concerning burial.

Jesus was put to death at the place of the skull near a garden; there was in this garden a new tomb belonging to Joseph, which he had cut out in the rock, and had never been used.

The first of two Sabbaths was drawing near; this was the High Sabbath. Women usually did the work these two men from the Jewish high council were undertaken; with far more expertise and competence. Moreover, they also needed to hurry because it was almost the National Preparation Day of Israel.

Because of this, they laid Him in Joseph's own new tomb. Then they rolled a great stone to the door of the tomb and left, having done what they could.

The idea of wrapping the body in this manner was to allow the cloth, spice of Myrrh, and aloes to harden over time; this was the King's burial by a Priest. But it was quick and was not done in the exacting style and manner that the women who followed Jesus would have completed the task.

Of the many women faithfully following Jesus, often ministering to him and the other followers out of their finances, some went along but did not interfere with the procedure. Though they carefully observed it all, including how the body was laid out in the tomb.

They sat opposite the tomb to see it all; these included Mary, the mother of Joses, and 'the Mary' of Magdalene.

The women eventually left the garden (*having noted how all things were set*), returning home. To prepare spices and ointments to adequately cover the body, yet rested on the Sabbath to comply with the law. Purchasing all they needed after the Sabbath ended.

The Chief Priests and the Pharisees went with a delegation to Pilate. This was the following day, which was the day after the Preparation Day. "Sir, we remember something that was said by that deceiver while he was still alive, namely that, 'I will rise again, after three days.'" They said, "Because of that. Issue an order that the tomb will be sealed and made secure until after the third day.

In case his disciples might arrive at night and steal him away, then tell the people, 'He has risen again from the dead.' making the last deception so much worse than the first." They pleaded, clearly worried because of all the amazing things that happened contiguous to the death of Jesus.

"You go ahead making it as secure as you can; you already have a guard detail given to you," Pilate replied, somewhat uncommitted.

So these desperate men went with their guards and made the tomb secure by sealing the stone. Then they left the Roman soldiers as guards there to watch the place.

CHAPTER TWENTY TWO

THE GOOD NEWS: AND THE WOMEN'S AMAZING LOVE AND FAITH.

The two Sabbaths had now passed, just before dawn on the morning of the first day (Sunday). The two Marys, Magdalene and Mary, the wife of Cleopas, along with Salome, left with the spices so as to arrive at the tomb at first light to anoint the body of the Lord.

While the two Marys were on their way from Bethany, there was a great earthquake. And those soldiers who were guarding the tomb saw the Angel of the Lord descending out of the sky, the Angel, whose appearance was like lightning, with dazzling white clothing: Rolled away the great stone from the tomb's entrance and then remained sitting on the rock. Frightened and panicking, the soldiers passed out.

The women, on their way, knew the difficulties they would face, "The boulder is too large for us to manage; who will roll that stone away from the door of the tomb for us?" They asked each other.

The two Mary's met up with Salome and other women.

As they climbed the hill while it was still dark and was yet a long way from the tomb. As they walked up the hill and looked in the distance, it was clear the stone had already been removed.

Mary Magdalene concluded the authorities must have opened the tomb and moved the body. She turns around, running back to Jerusalem in panic and grief to find Peter and John. "They took the Lord out of the tomb, and we do not know where they have laid him!" She cried in grief; Mary had left the other women and had not yet experienced the Angel who was waiting inside the tomb.

As a result, Peter and John went out, and they went toward the tomb.

They both ran together, with Mary following. Mary, the mother of James, joined her on the journey.

When the guards came round, they discovered the tomb was empty; all of them fled in terror, as they were now guilty of a capital offense under Roman law.

Their only hope now was in hurrying back to the Jewish authorities to tell of their experience.

Having gained advice on the matter, the leaders agreed to use their influence on behalf of the soldiers. If they will spread a story, saying that the disciples had come in the night and stolen the body of Jesus. They gave a sizeable amount of silver to the soldiers of the guard detail to seal the deal.

"If this comes to the ears of the governor, be confident that we will convincingly satisfy him and keep you free of any trouble." They disclosed to the soldiers.

As a result, the soldiers took the money doing as they had been told.

The authorities used this story, and it was widely circulated and continues to be so among the Jews.

At the same instance, the soldiers were running away from the frightening events at the tomb, the rest of the women were on their way to the grave!

By this time, the sun had risen, and a further two joined the two women who had remained there.

As they finally went into the garden, the Angels were already waiting inside the tomb.

When the perplexed women arrived, they immediately entered the tomb and did not find the body of the Lord Jesus.

The Angels were there in the tomb.

They first saw a young man dressed in a white robe sitting on the right side upon entering the tomb. It astounded them when suddenly, two men stood by them also in dazzling clothing.

Becoming terrified, the women bowed their faces down to the earth as they asked each other what it all meant.

"Why are you seeking the living in around the dead? The Angels ask them.

"Do not be afraid, since I know you are seeking Jesus, who had been killed by Crucifixion.

He is not here since precisely as he told you would happen; he has risen. Come and have a look at the very place where the Lord had been lying.

He is raised now alive and so is not here, however. Do you remember what he had made clear to you when he was still in Galilee? He stated how the Son of Man must be handed over to sinful men, and die by being crucified and after three days take back his life again?" They asked with prescience.

The memory of what Jesus had said about this came rushing back to the women.

"Quickly go tell his disciples the news, and also tell Peter, 'Jesus has returned from the dead, and take note he will be going to Galilee, so go back and meet him there.' And now Note; I have told you."

Hosea 6:1-2, (KJV) **Come and let us return unto the LORD: for he has torn, and he will heal us; he hath smitten, and he will bind us up.**

After two days, will he revive us: in the third day, he will raise us up, and we will live in his sight.

Briskly the women headed off, away from the tomb really excited. Also, with a mixture of astonishment and great joy, they were trembling with amazement.

Because they were so afraid, they did not speak to anyone, although they ran to bring his disciples the message.

And as this was happening, Peter and John race back to the tomb, managing to miss the other four women who were now returning from the grave, conveying the message given to them by the Angels.

John, being younger, outran Peter and arrived first at the tomb. He did not enter; instead, he stooped to look inside. He could distinctly see the linen cloths lying there.

Following him, Simon Peter arrived.

Hence upon their arrival at the tomb, Peter and John could see that the tomb was empty, complete with the grave clothes; however, they saw neither the Angels nor the body of Jesus.

Peter, anyway, did not hesitate to enter the tomb. Seeing how the linen cloths were lying, likewise, the material that had been on his head, how it was rolled up, not with the rest of the linen cloths. But separated and in a place by itself.

John also entered in, and seeing this indisputable evidence of the hardened remains of the bandages intact, he believed the extraordinary news.

They, as yet, still did not identify the Scriptures, which say that Jesus must rise from the dead.

Therefore, the disciples left, wondering what had happened — returning to join the others back in Jerusalem.

Peter and John departed the garden making their way back to the others in Jerusalem, leaving Mary Magdalene standing near the tomb, weeping.

Eventually, she went to the tomb. But unlike Peter and John, when she stooped and looked inside the tomb, she saw the two Angels in white. One sat at the head of where his body would have been, the other at the feet. At this point, she still did not recognize them as Angels.

"Woman, why is it you are weeping?" One Angel asked her.

"Because they have removed my Lord from this place, and I do not know the place where they have laid him." She answered, sobbing.

Just as she spoke, she turned around and saw Jesus standing there; Mary did not know that it was Jesus.

"Woman, why is it you weep? Who do you look for?" Jesus asked her.

"Sir, if you have transferred him from here, please tell me where you have placed him, and I will remove him." She replied, supposing that he was the gardener.

"Mary," Jesus uttered, calling her name softly.

"Rabboni" (*Teacher*!), she exclaimed, with surprise as she turned around fully to see him.

The two women approached Jesus, grasping his feet worshipping him.

"Do not cling to me," Jesus implored. "Seeing, I have not yet ascended to my Father. However, go back and inform my brothers. 'I am ascending up to my Father and your Father, and to my God and your God.'"

In the meantime, the four other women had arrived back in Jerusalem, at the residence where John was staying, and told all their news of having seen the Angels. Who had given them a message to give to the disciples and expressly included something addressed to Peter.

So as Peter and John had earlier run off to go to the tomb, the women simply remained there and waited for their return.

After the return of Peter and John back to the house, from their visit to the tomb, the women gave them the information, and hurried away crossing the Mount of Olives over to the village of Bethany, to relay the amazing news to the other eight disciples there.

Then, as Mary Magdalene finally returned from her meeting with the resurrected Jesus, Cleopas and his friend set out on a trip to the town of Emmaus, just a little way from Jerusalem.

Salome and Mary, the wife of Cleopas, were two of the women hurrying to the other disciples with the wonderful news.

Also, they were doing this to complete the task given to them by the Angels.

As the women hurriedly made their way along the road to Bethany, an encounter with Jesus occurred.

He simply said, "Rejoice!"

The women approached him and took hold of his feet, worshipping him.

"Do not be afraid." He reassures them.

"Go to my brothers and tell them they should go back to Galilee, and there they will see me," Jesus instructed them.

Mary Magdalene arrived back at the house and told the disciples, who at the time were still expressing a great deal of grief and were weeping. She told them the details of how she had seen the Lord; however, they did not believe her.

As the morning wore on, the news had come from Mary Magdalene and Joanna and Mary, the mother of James.

Also, the other women with them; who told the apostles of these things, assuring them it was true.

They did not believe the women. They took their account of events to be idle stories and discounted their testimony.

THE RESURRECTED JESUS GIVES A UNIQUE BIBLE STUDY ON THE ROAD TO EMMAUS.

A little later that day, the two disciples who had left earlier before the return from the tomb of the larger group of women, and was traveling to a village named Emmaus, situated about seven miles outside of Jerusalem, were deep in conversation about all of these things that had occurred in the recent past.

And as they were discussing these matters, Jesus joined them as they were leaving the city, catching up with them as they walked along, and continued with them. At this point, they were unable to identify that it was Jesus; he looked like a foreigner to them.

He joined the discussion and asked them a question, "What is the topic of your conversation that is causing such a gloomy outlook as you journey?" Jesus enquired of them.

Cleopas (who was related to Jesus through marriage, he was married to the sister of Mary, Jesus' mother) queried his knowledge of events "in the whole of Jerusalem. Are you the only one of the pilgrims and such a stranger who is not familiar with all the many events of the past few days?" He questioned.

"What events," asked Jesus?

"Events regarding the Prophet Jesus the Nazarene; mighty in words and deeds in the sight of God and among all the people; and how our leading men also the Chief Priests handed him over to the Romans condemning him to death by Crucifixion!" They both explained with quiet excitement.

"Yet we had hoped before his death that he was the one, destined to rescue and restore Israel.

And now there is also, even more of a twist to this. All these events took place three days ago, and we were startled by some women that were among us because they arrived early at the Prophet's Tomb this morning. They did not find the body but hurried back to the group, reporting they had observed visions of Angels, who told them he was now alive again.

Some of the group went to investigate. Finding things in the tomb as the women had said. However, they did not see our Prophet," continued Cleopas, replacing the initial enthusiasm with a level of grave concern.

"O how foolish you men are," Jesus exclaimed, "with hearts so slow to believe in the words of the prophecy given by the prophets.

The Messiah, was he not supposed to endure the very same things and receive his crowning glory?" He asked them rhetorically.

Then Jesus began explaining the meanings of all the Scriptures, beginning from Moses and going through all the Prophets, showing them the things relating to him written in them.

When the three travelers arrived in the vicinity of the village of Emmaus, Jesus appeared to be traveling on without stopping.

The two disciples pleaded with him to rest with them. "As it is almost the start of the evening. (Any time after the passing of noon was considered the beginning of evening). And it is not long before the day is over; remain here with us!" They requested.

Jesus agreed and went to remain there with them.

Then at mealtime, when he sat with the two disciples at the table, Jesus took the bread, giving thanks for it. After breaking it, he then gave the bread to them.

Finally, they recognize him, as they had their eyes open suddenly; Jesus then vanished from their presence.

*(The disciple could not recognize Jesus until they saw the nail scars in his wrists as he broke the bread and held it up to bless it.

His appearance was vastly different, not only because his body was now glorified, but also he was without his previous beard after suffering all the extraordinary abuse he endured before the cross.

Isaiah 50:6 (NKJV) *I gave My back to those who struck Me, And My cheeks to those who plucked out the beard; I did not hide My face from shame and spitting*.)

Psalm 22:6 (NKJV) *But I am a worm, and no man; A reproach of men, and despised by the people*.

Isaiah 52:14 (ESV) *As many were astonished at you; his appearance was so marred, beyond human semblance, and his form beyond that of the children of mankind*.)

JESUS CONSOLES AND COMFORTS THE FRIGHTENED FOLLOWERS.

Now with proof of the truth of what they had not dared believe, evidence of the very resurrection, to which the women had given testimony. They spoke excitedly to each other. "Did we not find that our hearts were burning within us along the road and while He opened and expounded to us the Scriptures?" They asked each other.

They decided to return and share the wonderful news with the others in Jerusalem, and having made the trip back, found the apostles together and many other followers with them.

There was great excitement among the followers. Who told the two travelers of more news. Adding to the excitement of the morning's event, "We have significant news of the Lord, who is in fact raised and has had a meeting with Simon!" The others told them.

The two who returned from the country, Cleopas and companion, relayed their experience, what Jesus had taught them on the journey. And the extraordinary way they were given sight to recognize him as he came to the moment of the breaking of bread!

Many of them still found it hard to accept; therefore, they were not believed by all.

It was still late in the day on this first day of the week. While, they were all discussing these things with the whole company, who were secluded together in the house. With the doors firmly locked because of the threat against any followers of Jesus, from The Chief Priests and Leaders among the Jewish people.

As the eleven apostles with disciples and followers were sitting there together having dinner (except for Thomas), abruptly, there was Jesus in the middle of them. "Peace! Be with you," he announced reassuringly, with a heavenly greeting customarily given to the children of Israel (Daniel 10:19).

Nevertheless, they were frightened and thought that they were witnessing a ghostly apparition. Jesus reprimanded them on account of their hardness of heart and lack of belief because they did not accept the witness of all those who had already seen him since his resurrection.

"Why are you so disturbed? Why are there doubts taking place in your hearts?" He asked them all, promptly showing them his hands and his side and inviting them to touch. "Here, see, this is my hands and my feet. Touch me and see that it is truly me. Because no spirit has flesh and bones, as you can see I have." Jesus insisted that they all witness his hands and his feet.

And yet, they still did not believe for the sheer delight and pure wonder.

"Do you have here with you anything to eat," Jesus asked?

They offered him a piece of fish that had been broiled along with some honeycomb.

Jesus took the portions and ate them so that they all could see.

The disciples and all the others all relaxed when they saw this; they all knew for sure that it was the Lord.

"Peace! Be to you." Jesus repeated to comfort them, "In the same way that the Father has sent me, then I also send you." He told them.

After telling them this, Jesus breathed on them, "Receive the Holy Spirit!" He said as he did this.

"The one whose sin you forgive, they are forgiven them. The one whose sin you retain, they have been retained." He said to them, giving them authority for a special commission.

Thomas, one of the disciples, one of the chosen twelve and who was selected as an apostle, also known as Didymus (Greek for 'The Twin'), was away and so missed the event when Jesus appeared.

The other was happy to tell him about all that had happened, "We have all seen the Lord!" They told him.

Thomas was not convinced, "No, I am not going to believe," He said, "Except I can see the nail prints in his hands also put my hand into his side." He was adamant about it.

Again the whole company gathered together on the first day of the week; this was now eight days later; this time, Thomas was there; they were inside with the doors locked.

Jesus was suddenly there standing in the middle of them; he greeted them, "Peace! Be to you," He said.

So with this sudden arrival, he now appeared to all the chosen disciples together.

Jesus addressed Thomas, "Reach your finger here, see for yourself my hands, and with your hand, place it in my side. No longer remain unbelieving; instead, just believe." He said, compellingly, reassuring Thomas.

"My Lord and my God," exclaimed Thomas, worshipping him.

"You can believe because you have seen me," Jesus told Him, "Yet those who have not seen and do believe will be blessed."

Of all the many miracles Jesus had performed, witnessed by his disciples. Only a select few are recorded in the volumes of the Gospels (*Good News*). However, the ones that were written were for the purpose that you also would believe that Jesus is the true Messiah, the Son of God. And, through your belief, you will have eternal life in his name.

Later, on another occasion, Jesus again met with some of the disciples; this took place by the sea of Tiberias. (*'Sea of Tiberias,' or the 'Sea of Galilee,' also called the 'Lake of Gennesaret.' Named after Caesar Tiberias and built by Herod, as a resort city, on the western shore of the lake*).

PETER'S APOSTLESHIP IS RE-ESTABLISHED.

The following is another account detailing how Jesus made himself known.

Seven of the disciples were together, back in Galilee, as they had been told to go back there.

These seven were Simon Peter, Nathanael of Cana in Galilee, James and John, the sons of Zebedee and Salome, Thomas (*Didymus the twin,*) and another two of his disciples.

As they were waiting eventually, Simon said, "I am going to go fishing." We are going to join you also." The others joined in.

Quickly leaving the house together, they went to the lake where there was a boat; and went fishing through the night. But after spending the entire night out on the lake, they did not catch any fish.

After dawn in the early morning light, Jesus was standing on the beach. However, the party of fishermen could not recognize that it was Jesus standing there.

Jesus called over to them, "Children, you have not managed to catch any fish to eat, have you?" He asked.

"No." They answered abruptly.

Jesus instructed them, "Throw out the net, over the right side of the boat, and now you will get some." He called out.

Like a gentle reminder of one of the first meetings between Jesus and Peter, the men did just that; they threw the net over the right side of the boat. As they did, it was filled with fishes, to the point where they were having trouble holding the net; it would take too much effort to get the fishes into the boat; it would have to be dragged. Now there was a dawning realization of who was on the beach.

"It is the Lord!" exclaimed John to Peter, knowing that he had witnessed this before at an earlier time.

Peter, who was lightly dressed for fishing work, simply tied up his outer clothes and jumped impatiently into the sea on hearing that it was the Lord.

Although the other disciples remained a little more composed as they were near to the land. So they drew closer to shore with the boat and hauling with it the net full of fish.

Now on the land, the others were not far behind Peter and could see that a fire made of coals was there. And on the fire were already some fish, along with bread.

"Bring over some of those fish that you have just caught," Jesus called over to them.

Simon Peter returned to the little group of fishermen. Jumping into the boat and untying the net, then putting his total weight behind the effort, pulled the net to land. It was full of great fishes, straining yet held; even though they dragged it over the beach's rocks, it did not break.

They counted one hundred fifty-three large fishes.

"Come now, sit and eat some breakfast," Jesus beckoned to them.

Since it was so apparent to all of them that this was Jesus, they now knew that he was not just the former man Jesus, but the Lord God. They did not think it worthwhile asking the redundant question, "Who are you?" even though they were still slowly recovering from the shock of all that was witnessed at the Crucifixion.

This now made the third occasion that Jesus was with a large group of his disciples since he had come back to life from the dead, as no mere man could, this reality had begun to sink in.

Jesus walked over to the fire, taking the bread, then portioned it out among them, along with some fish.

When the breakfast was all finished, Jesus turned his attention to Peter, "Simon, son of Jonah, these others here, do you love me more than they do?" Jesus asked him, no longer the rock that Jesus had been calling him. Peter had boasted that no matter if all others stumbled, that would never be him, so he loved Jesus, the most of the disciples.

"Yes, Lord. I do have a friendly affection for you; you are aware of that." Peter answered, knowing that with his recent past actions, he could not claim the sacrificial love Jesus was asking for, but just friendly affection.

"Then feed my lambs," Jesus told him.

"Simon, son of Jonah, do you indeed love me?" Jesus asked again, changing the emphasis for the others to a more personal focus on him.

"Yes, Lord. I do have a friendly affection for you," Peter answered again, somewhat stronger this time.

"Tend for my sheep," Jesus told him.

"Simon, son of Jonah, do you have a real affection for me?" Jesus asked him a third time now using Simons' own declaration.

Asking this of Peter, a third time, as they sat there by this coal fire, with its distinct and unique pungent smell of the burning coals, it was impossible for Peter to not remember that other moment a few nights before when he said he did not even know Jesus. That night Peter feared that the guards might think that his presence was some kind of a rescue plan, but his best intention went severely wrong. As he remembered, he was deeply wounded over his actions and words; his love for the Lord was so very much, but how to express it? Peter was sad that the Lord asked him this a third time, even profoundly grieved over it.

"Yes, I do have affection for you; you are aware of it, Lord, you know everything," Peter replied with true repentance from the heart.

"Feed my sheep." Jesus said, "I tell you, without doubt, you dressed yourself walking where you wanted to when you were young. However, you will stretch out your hands when you are old; at that time, another will dress you bringing you where you do not want to go."

They walked off together as Jesus said this, prophesying that Peter would stretch out his hands on a cross and be led by others to his death. Nevertheless, it would not be until he was an older man. And as they went off, Jesus gave him a final word. "Follow me," He said, which for Peter would be appropriate in more ways than one.

(Isaiah 1:18 *"I am, the LORD Come now, let us settle this, let us discuss this. Even though your sins are dark, even as scarlet, I will make them pure, as white as wool"*).

Peter, for a moment, lost focus and turned back to see John walking some way behind; he thought he would ask Jesus. "Lord, and this man, what will happen to him?" Peter said, showing that he was back to his old self.

"What does it matter to you if I should desire that he continue until I return?" Jesus asked him, "You follow me!"

As a result, among all the brothers, there was a saying that spread. Namely, this disciple Peter referred to would not die. However, that was clearly not what Jesus had said.

The disciple John is the disciple who wrote these things and testifies about these things. We know that this witness of his is faithful.

Many of the other things from the life of Jesus that he did are not written here. Should they all be written, I would suppose even the world itself would scarcely have enough space to contain the books that would be written!

Sometime later, the disciples went into Galilee and assembled on the mountain, where Jesus had elected and directed them. There were over five hundred brothers gathered there. Jesus appeared to all of them there; some had passed away when this was written, though most were still alive.

When his followers saw him, they bowed down and worshiped him; some still had doubts.

Jesus approached and spoke to them, "In heaven, all authority has been given to me and also here on earth." He said, confirming his absolute sovereignty.

"Go out into the entire world preaching to all creation, the Good News. And make disciples of people from every nation. They are to be baptized in the name of the Father, The Son, and, of the Holy Spirit, continue constantly following all the commands I have given to you.

The Lord will save the one who believes and is baptized; however, any who disbelieves will be condemned.

Those who believe will have these signs with them: in my name, they will cast out demons, they will speak with new languages, with power over serpents, and poisonous drinks will in no way hurt them.

The sick will recover once they lay their hands on them.

Believe, I am with you consistently; moreover, it will even be to the very end of the age." Amen.

Within a period stretching over forty days, Jesus met all the apostles, proving that he was alive again. After he had been tortured and put to death, there was an early meeting with his brother James, then with all of his followers, when he gave them knowledge of the Kingdom of God.

"This was what I told you, while I was still with you, that all things relating to me written in the Law of Moses, the Prophets, and the Psalms, must be fulfilled," Jesus told them. After that, Jesus opened their minds to allow them to be able to understand the Scriptures.

"So it is written. And therefore, the Messiah needed to suffer and to resurrect from the dead on the third day. So that in his name, repentance and remission of sins could be preached to all the nations, beginning at Jerusalem. You then are witnesses of all these things."

"See, I will send out the promise of my Father on you."

"Stay in Jerusalem! And do not leave. Just wait there in the city until you are clothed through the promise of the Father, from on high. With the power that I have told you about," He commanded them, "Although John did actually baptize in water. However, a few days from now, you will be baptized in the Holy Spirit."

When the disciples were together, they assumed the kingdom would start; they approached Jesus about it. "Lord, are you going to restore to Israel the kingdom starting now?" They asked him.

"It is not your province to know times or seasons which the Father has set within his own authority.

You, however, will receive power when the Holy Spirit has fallen upon you. Then be witnesses to me not only in Jerusalem but also in all Judea, Samaria, and to the uttermost parts of the earth." Jesus told them.

Jesus led the followers out as far as Bethany, and after briefing them of all they needed, he raised his hands and blessed them.

As he was blessing them, and as they were looking, he started to leave them.

He rose from the ground, and as he did, a cloud covered him out of their sight. In this way, he was carried up into heaven.

Because of this, the Lord was received up into heaven. He is sitting down at the right hand of God.

They were all still looking unwaveringly into the sky where he had gone. Then two men in white clothing stood by and addressed them, "You Galilean men, why do you stand persistently looking into the sky? This Jesus, whom you saw received up into heaven from you, he will return in the same way!" They declared to the amazed disciples.

(Psalm 68:18, *you have ascended on high...*).

EPILOGUE

THE NEW ECCLESIA TAKES SHAPE.

As a result, they broke into the worship of Jesus before returning to Jerusalem extremely joyful, traveling back from the mountain called Olivet, which is a brief journey from the city.

On entering the city, they return to the upper room, where they were staying. The members of those disciples were Peter, John, James, Andrew, Philip, Thomas, Bartholomew, Matthew, James the son of Alphaeus, Simon the Zealot, and Judas, or Jude, brother of James.

They remained united as one unit praying continually and faithfully, joined by the women, including Mary, the mother of Jesus, and his brothers.

A short time after, when Jesus' disciples and followers were meeting together, about one hundred twenty people, sitting comfortably in the large upper room.

Peter got up to speak to everyone there, 'Brothers,' he said, addressing them, 'the complete fulfillment of the Scriptures, spoken through King David, inspired by the Holy Spirit. Relating to Judas has occurred, been the one who led the people to arrest Jesus.

Yes, he was counted as one of the twelve and took part in his share of this ministry.

However, he was a man who had bought a property from the reward obtained from his sin. He nevertheless fell headfirst, breaking his body open, pouring out his intestines.'

(*Details of this became well known among the people who reside in Jerusalem. The field is called 'Akeldama,' Aramaic for 'the field of blood.'*)

'In the book of Psalms, the scriptures say, *Allow his dwelling to be deserted*,' (Psalm 69:25), 'and in another place, *allow another man take over his position*.' (Psalm 109:8).

'As a result, we need to find a man, to be a witness with us of his resurrection, out of all the men who were with us during all the time that the Lord Jesus was with us. Starting from the time he was baptized by John to the day he was carried into heaven.'

The names of two suitable men were suggested. One was Matthias (*Mattityahu, gift of Yahweh*), and the other was Justus, called Barsabbas (*Son of Sabba*).

All the people prayed. "Lord, you know all men's hearts, show us of these two which one is your choice to replace Judas who have now fallen away so he could go off to his own place. Taking his place in this ministry and apostleship," They asked?

Then they used the drawing of lots as the simplest way of deciding. Because they were both equally worthy, Matthias was chosen. They then gave him the position of apostle alongside the other eleven.

Then finally, ten days after the Lord ascended to heaven, and now fifty days after he had risen from the dead.

(This is the second major Feast of Israel and is called Shavuot, or the Feast of Latter First-fruits. Having the Greek name 'pentekoste,' 'Pentecost' FIFTY also the 'Feast of Weeks', the 'Feast of Harvest'

Celebrated the fiftieth day after Passover, Shavuot traditionally is a joyous time of thanksgiving, also the presenting of offerings for the new grain from the summer wheat harvest in Israel.

"Feast of Weeks" was the name given because God commanded Israel in Leviticus 23:15-16. That they were to count seven full weeks (or 49 days), beginning on the second day of Passover, then present offerings of new grain to the Lord as an enduring decree.

These Jewish feasts and celebrations were a shadow of the things to come through Jesus the Messiah).

So this was when this day of Pentecost arrived, completing all the promises in the spring feasts. The followers of Jesus that he had instructed to wait in Jerusalem were praying and praising God early in the morning, all together in total unity (*They were sitting in reflective rest*).

Unexpectedly there was a sudden sound like the rushing of a mighty wind. That came from the sky above, and the roaring sound filled the entire house where everyone sat praying.

Above their heads appeared 'Tongues' that looked 'like fire' and then dispersed to them all, and each of them had one of these Tongues resting upon them. (Isaiah 4:4, the Spirit of burning).

Immediately each of them was filled to overflowing with the Holy Spirit. Then they started speaking with strange languages; this was a gift from the Holy Spirit, as He gave them the ability to speak.

(Isaiah 29:6 **you will be visited, from the LORD of hosts with thunder, and with earthquake, and great noise, with storm and uproar, and the flame of devouring fire**).

There in Jerusalem were religious men, Jews, who made the pilgrimage from every nation, where they were dispersed.

Masses of people gathered around the house when the loud, confusing sound was heard. This caused amazement because everyone heard everything they spoke; in his own language intelligibly.

Isaiah 28:11-12 **since with stammering lips and another tongue will he speak to this people**.

The crowds were all shocked and wondered about it, "Look, all these people who are speaking, are they not Galileans?"

"How are they speaking this way, and we are hearing, each in our own native language?" They were asking each other.

(*This was a profound and wonderful miracle and gift, giving to the people of God the promise of the baptism of the Spirit of Jesus. The promise of which He had said, He would send from the Father as another helper and had been spoken of, by John the Prophet and Priest, out in the Jordanian wilderness. This astounding miracle affected both the receivers of the Spirit who were talking and the hearers.*

Whatever the receivers spoke; was heard clearly by the hearers as their own speech, by each person from various nations).

The numbers were vast among the pilgrims of devoted Israelites from foreign nations.

(These devout worshippers expected the dawning of the new age and the kingdom of God, spoken about starting with the preaching of John the Baptizer.

Because of the extraordinary strange and ominous recent events, it drew all to Jerusalem, including earthquakes, Noonday darkness, resurrections of saints who had appeared to some, and the tearing of the incredibly thick veil in the Temple. At the same time, the enormous 30 foot long stone lintel in the Temple was broken, splintered, and fell.

The very place where the Sanhedrin had assembled to pronounce judgment against Jesus, within the Chamber of Hewn Stones, this place was so severely damaged that the High Court had to leave this grand assembly room and take up residence instead, within the relatively inconsequential, 'Trading Place.' The Chamber of Hewn Stones was never again used).

These people were, returning from all over the Roman Empire to reside in Jerusalem. Both Jews and convert's, Parthians, Medes, Elamites, Judea, Cappadocia, Pontus, Asia, Phrygia, Pamphylia, Egypt, the parts of Libya around Cyrene, Cretans, and Arabians, along with people from Mesopotamia.

"We can hear them speaking about the mighty works of God in our languages!" They said as they were all stunned and baffled.

"What does all of this mean?" They continued to ask each other, intently curious about the spiritual truth of what was happening.

"They are drunk, filled, so to speak with new wine." Some said, mocking them.

THE POWER OF THE NEW ECCLESIA IS CONFIRMED BY PETERS EFFECTIVE SERMON.

Peter, however, moving into the crowds with the other eleven, loudly addressed the people. "You men who are Judean's," he said, first addressing the mockers, "Also, all of you who are dwelling in Jerusalem, listen carefully to my words and appreciate this.

Since these signs are not through drunkenness, as you have assumed, considering it is now only nine in the morning.

This, however, is what had been prophesied through Joel the Prophet. 'And it shall come to pass in the last days, says God.

*I will pour from My Spirit on all flesh: then will your sons and
your young woman prophesy.
Your young men see visions.
Your old men will dream dreams:
My servants and my handmaidens, I will also pour out my Spirit
in those days, and they will prophesy:
And I will show miracles from heaven above, and signs in the
earth beneath; blood, and fire, and vapor of smoke:
I will turn the sun into darkness, the moon to blood before the
great and notable day of the Lord comes:
And it will happen; that any who will call on the Lord's name will
be saved.'* (Joel 2:28-32)

"You men of Israel, pay attention to these words," Peter exclaimed as he explained the imminent judgment they needed to escape.

"Jesus of Nazareth, a man who was approved among you by God, confirmed through all the mighty works, wonders, and miracles. Which God did through him in your presence. Just as you yourselves know. Being handed over by God's exact prearranged guidance, he was betrayed and taken by lawless men and killed by Crucifixion.

Then raised up from death by God, freeing him from death's agony because it could not be possible for him to be held by death.

And of him this what King David said, "***I have set the Lord always
before me; because he is at my right hand, I shall not be shaken.
Therefore my heart is glad, and my whole being rejoices; my
flesh also dwells secure.
For you will not abandon my soul to Sheol, or let your holy one
see corruption.
You make known to me the path of life; in your presence there
is fullness of joy; at your right hand are pleasures forevermore'***
(Quoting from Psalm 16:8-11 ESV.)

"My brother Israelites, I can tell you for sure about our ancestor, the patriarch David.

Having died, they buried him in a tomb, which is still here with us today.

David, as a prophet, knew what God had said. The promise from God that he made to David with a solemn oath that one of his descendants from his own family would sit on the throne of David as King.

He prophesied the resurrection of Messiah and spoke of it, *"His soul was not left in Hades, nor did his flesh see decay."* (Psalm 16:10)

God has risen up this Jesus, and we are all witnesses.

As a result of him having ascended gloriously, up to the right hand of God, and having received the Holy Spirit, the promise of the Father, he has sent him onward. The result you now see and hear because David himself did not ascend into the heavens. However, he said, *'The Lord said to my Lord; Sit you down on my right hand until I make your enemy your footstool'* (Psalm 110.)

So then all the house of Israel should know without a doubt that God has made Jesus whom you crucified, both Lord and Messiah."

Then having heard this, it convicted the people in their hearts; they earnestly enquired from Peter and the other apostles, "Brothers, what must we do to be saved?" They were asking.

"Every one of you needs to repent and then be baptized, in the name of the Lord Jesus the Messiah, so that you will be forgiven of all sins, and you will receive the Holy Spirit as a gift.

Since that promise was for you, your children, and even to everyone in distant places. Just as many as the Lord, our God will call to himself." Peter replied to them.

Peter preached and gave evidence, encouraging them, "Get out from this twisted generation, and be saved!" He told them with power and passion.

At that same time, they baptized all the people who accepted his words joyfully.

The number of people that came to believe in and have faith in Jesus grew from that point. With about three thousand additional people that day.

They faithfully continued in the teaching of the apostles. In prayers, and joined in the breaking of bread.

Each person was filled with awe, and through the apostles, performed many wonders and miracles.

The believers were united and often all together, and in general, shared all their possessions.

Selling their property and goods and distributing them among all the people, according to the needs of anyone.

Each day, they praised and blessed God in the Temple, continuing devotedly and united in harmony. The new believers were breaking bread at home, joyfully praising God with one heart; all the people exalted them.

More were saved each day as The Lord increased the numbers of the assembly.

With the power of the Lord working with them, the believers boldly went and preached everywhere, verifying the word by the miracles that accompanied them. Amen and Amen.

A CONCLUDING WORD
FROM THE AUTHOR.

The remarkable and astonishing life story of Jesus for those having read through this book and may not know or are familiar with Christian theology; presents to us an account of two kingdoms.

Both are governed from unseen Realms; both are immensely powerful and directly impact our lives, affecting us all the time.

One of these Realms we are familiar with, yet we still know little of this kingdom, much in the same way that we experience gravity. Yet, we are unable to define precisely what is taking place from moment to moment.

Just the same, we have received a great deal of data and theories from science about gravity.

Obviously, the laws and operation of gravity have always been with us. Still, it was not until men such as Sir Isaac Newton that a defining understanding of some of the principles became clearly understood.

That work continued into modern times, with discoveries by Einstein, Doppler, and Steven Hawking, among many others. Yet, with all the advances, we still know relatively little, at least not enough, to create a device that could manipulate the phenomenon beyond using brute force to lift a rocket or an airplane.

So why is this significant to our understanding of these two kingdoms? Well, just like our increasing knowledge of gravity, we are also now beginning to acquire a fuller understanding of these unseeing Realms.

Of course, some may insist that these Realms do not exist, however for the sake of this discussion, permit me to proceed as if they are an established fact. Then at the end, form your own conclusion on the matter.

Going back to the life of Jesus, this was the first time in history that we were exposed to the hitherto mysterious workings of the two opposing kingdoms.

As I said before, we are intimately familiar with one of those kingdoms, so much so that we assume that to live and operate in the one kingdom is quite natural, when in fact, as Jesus revealed, we are under enemy occupation.

What's more, we are, in most cases, willing collaborators not knowing any better but to side with our enemy.

Jesus's life and work exposed the workings of this enemy kingdom and declared that the domain he came from is far superior and more desirable.

His entering into our space and time initiated a vicious battle with the enemy forces; this battle continued all of his life, and in fact, was an invisible war raging unnoticed by the people of the time, including his disciples.

Jesus repeatedly demonstrated the power he had over the enemy and even over nature. This was one of the principal reasons his disciples found it so hard to hear and conceive of the idea that it was vital for him to go to Jerusalem to be put to death!

They just could not perceive how someone with so much power could simply die at the hands of much lesser men. (In this, they had a point, but the plan was flawless.)

Yet this takes us to the heart of the two kingdoms and how they operate. One kingdom, the one we are used to but have no idea even exists, is ruled by a mighty fallen Angel.

He is powerful, but his power is without authority, meaning that he cannot just command humans to do his will or deeds. He has no authority to do that, so he must use stealth, deception, cunning, and ultimately violence.

It comes down to this, this mighty fallen Angel can use men to threaten death, pain, and misery but can offer nothing to do with life; he can neither create life nor give life.

And there is the rub of our dilemma; we are all endowed with an innate sense of self-preservation, making us naturally afraid of losing our life; therefore, we can be controlled through this fear.

The other kingdom, the one that Jesus exhibited, does not use force or threats, does not use fear, but is able to offer life and create life.

It was quite natural for the people around Jesus (including his disciples) to expect even desire for him to use force and violence against the oppressors, particularly the Roman conquerors, i.e., fight fire with fire as it were.

They did not perceive till much later that the moment you do that, you automatically come under the rulership of the enemy and his forces.

In our physical world, we are used to Kings being crowned and ascending to the throne, to leaders being elected to the position, then inaugurated, then taking the leadership position.

However, the Spiritual Realm does not work like that; the rules are very different.

By agreeing to something or someone in the Spiritual Realm, even if we are tricked into it, we automatically tie our allegiance to whoever we agree with. (That is hardly fair, you might say, and you would be right.)

The enemy's camp does not care if it is fair; they have zero love for humans.

And will equally use and discard (even destroy) anyone regardless if we are a child or a professor of some great discipline, a renowned superstar, or a politician.

So if we look at the temptation of Jesus, the enemy was trying to tempt him to do something that he could do fairly easily without the enemy's help. Then what is the nature of the temptation?

Accordingly, the bait was not about Jesus' power or even about food; it was about (giving in and agreeing with me.)

The moment that would have happened, Jesus would fall under the rulership of a fallen Angel.

We know he did not, and the war intensified; let us look at some examples from Jesus's life.

There was a time when he chose and ordained some followers and sent them out on a mission, giving them authority over the enemy's Kingdom to cast out demons, heal the sick, and preach the kingdom of God. Immediately, King Herod beheaded John the Baptizer in his prison. (That was the counterstroke from the enemy.)

Here is another: Jesus told his disciples, 'come let us cross the lake' he is obviously going there for a purpose; at first, we do not know the reason, but the enemy is very aware of what is on the other side.

Over there is a man with a legion of Demons (that is many thousands). So as they were in the boat, a vicious storm suddenly struck them, so terrifying was this tempest that seasoned fishermen were deadly afraid; the enemy wanted to 'take them out' why?

Through this one man, the enemy Kingdom was ruling over and controlling the whole of that region. (They did not want to see him set free from their control.)

In another case, Jesus healed a man born blind. The enemy stirred the leaders to attempt to stone him; he left the area for a time, so the kingdom of darkness struck Lazarus, killing him. *See John 11.*

Jesus then raised him back to life; this initiated a frantic plan to kill Jesus as well as Lazarus. (Moves and countermoves.)

Every move in Jesus' life bought a countermove from the Kingdom that rules over this earth, but here is the real issue, it is not theirs to rule over; they took it by deception.

Jesus made a plan with His Father before time began; to reverse this situation, if and when it arose, and that is why he came. God's way of doing things is much different from the enemies.

When God wants a mighty Oak tree, it starts with a tiny seed and takes time to grow; the process is vital, during which there are storms and challenges, which serve to make the tree stronger. He, of course, could just create a full-grown tree, but it is not his way. Every living thing in our world comes from a seed, and in most cases, that seed needs to die first before it grows and produces.

The enemy has no power or control over these processes; he can only kill or threaten death; if he has a mighty tree, he has seized it from somewhere or someone.

Jesus' death was not the tragedy that some think or even being depicted in some films. Instead, it was a carefully maneuvered, wielded, and executed plan that spanned the whole of human history until the day that he arrived on the scene; he himself became the seed that dies then is reborn to give new life to those who want it.

Jesus demonstrated that he had much more power than anything the enemy could muster. The Spiritual Realm, however, does not primarily function on power but on agreement and authority.

(*What is the difference? Once he puts on his uniform, a Police Officer has vested or bestowed authority to pull you over for offenses as you drive on the road. An Elephant may have the power to crush your car, but you are under no obligation to stop and allow it to do so*).

Let us just for a moment imagine that a powerful Spirit being who presides over anger and anger is the core of his power. No matter how powerful this Spirit Being is, he has no control over you, cannot touch you or do anything to you in any way, no matter how he tries.

That is until the moment that you become angry (and that is for any reason), suddenly you, through the power of agreement, which is paramount in the Spiritual Realm: can now be targeted and influenced by this Being. However, you were not even aware that it happened.

Jesus showed us that once we agree with God's plan, He doesn't just fix us; He creates a whole new life, which is higher than the Realm of the kingdom that the enemy operates and exists in.

He then supplies the tools and ability to begin to experience something of His Realm.

Then as the tree that is the kingdom is growing, the complete blossom and its fruit will become apparent, tangible, and palpable at some point in a specific time that has been pre-chosen for the purpose by God.

('You shall know the truth,' that is knowing Jesus, it is not about knowing facts) 'And the TRUTH will make you free,' you are made a new creation. This is possible because human rulership over the previous creation having existed from Adam to Jesus was taken into the grave with Jesus upon His death. That was what the enemy had his ultimate controlling power over.

That is why Jesus on the cross cried with a loud voice IT IS FINISHED! That chapter of the history of the world that had been under subjection to the total control of the enemy ended at that moment. (*Though the victory over death and the enemy's ability to exert coercion over the people of the world; still requires us to use our given authority prosecuting the gain made with vigor.*)

Now the new creation begins, and we are invited to be part of it, reuniting at last with our creator, who is also our Father, the one who awaits us with loving longing arms, yearning for our return to him.

Final thoughts, scientists have now identified that our universe has potentially eleven dimensions, we are used to three, and time is said to be the fourth. However, the properties and operation of time are hard to grasp. Yet, in our physical world, if we are able to determine another seven dimensions, we should realize just how limited living in just three would be.

(I implore the reader to search on the internet for explanations on Eleven Dimensions, or Higher Dimensions, or lectures on tesseract's, also 5th and 6th dimensions, etc.)

Then I want you to do a few simple thought experiments, such as imagining that there is a flat world, a two-dimensional world populated with flat people; if we use a piece of plain paper to symbolize this, that will be adequate.

Now the people in the flat world do not conceive of height, that is another dimension that they do not perceive or understand, but we in three dimensions can see above and below the paper, now imagine taking a pencil and passing It slowly through the paper making a hole the size of the pencil, what would the people of the flat world see?

They would see a mysterious dot appear and get larger making a hole. Remember, they cannot see anything above or below the flat dimension, so the hole that the pencil makes would be apparent, but what is causing it would be unknown.

So now imagine a six-dimensional craft or person appearing in our three-dimensional space. What would we see? What about an Angel or a Demon? What would we see?

What if that creature moves at or near or even faster than the speed of light? What would we see then?

What if the things that we are discussing exist and operate outside of time and space? The Kingdom that Jesus taught about certainly does.

There are many examples in his life of an intersecting of our world with the other kingdom trans-dimensionally.

Here are a few, Jesus walked over the water to get to his struggling disciples, who were being battered by a raging storm. But what is often missed is the moment that Peter, who had stepped out of the boat along with Jesus, returned to the boat, two additional miracles happened.

First, the storm instantly stopped, and the other is they were at the seashore immediately on the other side of the lake, boat and all (that is trans-dimensional travel, going outside the natural laws of space and time) we can say they translated there. *See John 6:21.*

There was the occasion when Jesus preached in his local synagogue in Nazareth, they attempted to throw him off of the cliff there because they were upset with the message he brought, but he calmly walked through them. (Again, that is trans-dimensional travel), there are other examples if you are willing to look, then there are also the miracles themselves. *See Luke 4:29.*

When Jesus fed the five thousand (omitting the count of women and children), *See John 6:15.* After eating the meal, the people were determined to seize Jesus and make him king by force if necessary; why, what is in their thinking?

After that, Jesus told them point-blank that they were only chasing after him because of the food they had eaten; why, what was so special about the food?

Well, the bread in question was barley loaves, the lowest and least expensive kind of bread, only eaten by the very poorest of the poor.

To make such bread, it would be full of various imperfections, from microbes and spores to husks and trash milled in with the barley: that goes without saying.

Now ask yourself a question, when Jesus multiplied the bread, did he also multiply the imperfections? The obvious answer is no!

This then was the very best bread that they had ever tasted or eaten (this is trans-dimensional reality, bringing that other kingdom to intersect ours).

Jesus' life and actions showed us the reality of two kingdoms and urges us to make a decision, choosing which one we want to live and operate in.

The reality is we are co-opted into one from birth; the only actual decision then; is whether or not we want to escape that Kingdom supplanted by the deceiver, and in doing so, re-join with our God and father, who is the creator of all things.

CPSIA information can be obtained
at www.ICGtesting.com
Printed in the USA
LVHW050034290122
709249LV00002B/3